Finding Grace

Finding Grace

Regaining My Vision and Soul

Anne R. Davidson

To Pat and Tom
Thanks for your
support and your
friendship.

Anne

Telling My Truth Publishing
Lady Lake, Florida

ISBN-13: 978-1492767541 / ISBN-10: 1492767549

Telling My Truth Publishing
Lady Lake, Florida

Cover Photograph: Reggie Hayes
Cover Design: Jerry Hicks, Ultrex Printing
www.ultrexprinting.com

ACKNOWLEDGEMENTS

I am indebted to the following people for helping me bring this project to publication: first of all to my readers, in chronological order, Beth Stenger, Betsy Lerner, my husband Stan, Keith Alstedter, Pauline Brereton, Rita DeCoursey, Ronni Rabin, and the judges of the 2011 Royal Palm Literary Awards of the Florida Writers Association (FWA) who awarded me second place in the Unpublished Memoir category. Thank you for your time, your encouragement, and your invaluable feedback.

Next, thanks go to my developmental editors, Nini Munro-Chmura, Shamai Currim, Lisa Dale Norton, Mary Lois Sanders, and Janell Agyeman, all of whom gave time and guidance way beyond the compensation they received. I am indebted to my proof editor, Virginia Monseau, for her careful checking of my manuscript. True to the premise of my book, I never could have completed my project without the help of others, and that includes Kay Kudlinski, my first creative writing teacher, as well as all of the inspiring writers hired by the International Women Writers Guild for workshops over the years.

Thanks go to my own Creative Writing Group for its excellent feedback and to the Florida Writers Association, at whose conference I had the good fortune to meet Janell Agyeman who worked with me for two years on the development of *Finding Grace.*

I am indebted to the alumni career officer at my university, who gave me the idea for this project twenty years ago, and to my family as well as all of my friends who have been supportive and generous with their time concerning the practical details of publishing as well as with promoting my book. I never could have completed this project without my computer guru, Richard McClintock, who followed me from New England to Florida via LogMeIn, holding my hand sometimes from across the world if he was traveling, as he told my recalcitrant computer to let me do what I wanted to do.

I am grateful to Mary Lois Sanders who stepped away from her busy life as writer and head of a publishing company to help me start running mine. Her judgment and skill in guiding me has been impeccable. It never occurred to me in 1994, at fifty- eight, that I was beginning two careers, not only as a writer but also as a publisher.

I want to thank my husband for his love and constant support as well as the fine editorial guidance and great chef abilities he has demonstrated during these years, while sharing our "retirement" time with *Finding Grace*.

My thanks and appreciation go to the photographer Reggie Hayes and cover designer Jerry Hicks for their endless patience, understanding of what I wanted, and skill. I am grateful to my models, who answered my search to appear one morning and walk among greenery, as if they were Grace and me back in the forties.

To those who have helped me find the strength and courage for this project, many of whom are mentioned in my memoir, I express gratitude for your skill and care that went beyond the obligations of your professions.

DEDICATION

For all children whose voices need to be heard.

CONTENTS

Remembrance of Things Past...i

Introduction iii

Preface.. 1

Prologue 9

Part One – Love.. 17

Chapter 1 – College 19

Chapter 2 – Austen Riggs Center 33

Chapter 3 – Living Again 51

Chapter 4 – The Netherlands 67

Chapter 5 – Flashbacks 81

Part Two – Grace.. 91

Chapter 6 – Mummy... 93

Chapter 7 – Two Nannies 95

Chapter 8 – Louise...101

Chapter 9 – Joe...105

Chapter 10 – Susie...111

Chapter 11 – Jessie..115

Chapter 12 – Daddy..119

Chapter 13 – Reading 123

Chapter 14 – Joe Saves Me 135

Chapter 15 – Sunshine...141

Chapter 16 – Dreaming...145

Chapter 17 – Saying Goodbye 151

Part Three – Truth..*165*

   Chapter 18 – PTSD and Tranquilizers 167

   Chapter 19 – Saving My Marriage.................................... 179

   Chapter 20 – Losing My Parents 189

   Chapter 21 – Home 201

   Chapter 22 – Keith 207

   Chapter 23 – Phyllis 215

   Chapter 24 – Transition.. 223

   Chapter 25 – Learning to Write....................................... 229

Part Four – Black Roots *235*

   Chapter 26 – Saving Grace.. 237

   Chapter 27 – Psychosynthesis and Feeling Black 251

   Chapter 28 – Analyzing my Mother and Dance as Healer.. 263

   Chapter 29 – Understanding Those I Loved 275

Epilogue *283*

Appendix *287*

Bibliography *289*

Remembrance of Things Past

And once again I had recognized the taste of the crumb of madeleine soaked in her decoction of lime-flowers which my aunt used to give me ... immediately the old grey house upon the street, where her room was, rose up like the scenery of a theatre to attach itself to the little pavilion, opening on to the garden, which had been built out behind it for my parents; ... and with the house the town, from morning to night and in all weathers, the Square where I was sent before luncheon, the streets along which I used to run errands, the country roads we took when it was fine. And ... little dwellings and the parish church and the whole of Combray and of its surroundings, taking their proper shapes and growing solid, sprang into being, town and gardens alike, from my cup of tea.

From *Remembrance of Things Past*
Volume I: *Swann's Way*
(pp. 58, 59)

Marcel Proust

i

Introduction
by Shamai Currim, Ph.D., Psychotherapist

Children learn, sometimes not the lessons we had hoped to impart. While the supple mind of a child takes in experiences from its surroundings, it is the body that first understands what the world is all about, and it is from that basis that our thoughts and feelings are formed.

Who a child becomes can be looked at as both nature and nurture, and yet, children have an innate goodness that can help them cope with the extremes of life. Making sense of the world may sometimes mean hiding experiences, hiding thoughts, hiding emotions deep within the core of their being. Sometimes even the core of a human must hide in order to survive.

With this understanding of life, *Finding Grace* takes us on a journey of recovery, of lost self, and of the goodness that brings us back to conscious reality. It is the hope that helps us through the trauma to recovery, and to the eventual wisdom that can be shared and mirrored for others.

How do you support people who have lived through such ghastly abuse that they have lost their memories? You allow them to tell you their stories.

Preface

We do not need to hear from a counselor of psychosynthesis or a dance therapist—two of the professionals who helped me put my life together—about our inner conflicting parts. We can learn about them every day as we live with the puzzling decisions we make.

The requirement for understanding who we genuinely are, and what lies in our true heart's soul, is to be conscious and aware of the different voices that call to us. We are drawn, like Oedipus, to deal with unresolved issues, through the paths we take in our careers, marriages, travels, or recreation as adults. The trick is to look at our choices with open eyes and ask ourselves, "Hmm, why did I do that, go there, choose that teacher, marry that kind of guy, go into that field? And what does that mean about my decisions now? Am I really thinking clearly, or am I being influenced too much by something from the past?"

I chose for my first husband a man who became verbally abusive, and over time I experienced the hurt as a trigger to my mother's abuse. By being forced to recall how devastated and angry I had been as a child, I was able to tap into feelings strong enough to move me into action and create changes in my marriage. This was a deeply healing experience because I found myself able to control and handle something as an adult that I had been powerless to deal with as a child.

Our past and present are in constant conversation with each other like this, though much of the time we are not aware of it. I was drawn to stay removed from my family at age twenty-three

1

and immerse myself in a world of mythic violence as a young writer, a path that led eventually to my remembering those who had given me support in my New England childhood's threatening household. Writing brought me closer to the truth about my life. My supportive relationship with a Black dance teacher in The Netherlands triggered deep feelings of despair when he left, showing me how it had felt as a child to lose the support of Joe, my Black nanny's boyfriend, whom I loved. Paying attention to my body's pain led me to my first memory of abuse. I received my second flashback after whirling through space in my studio, a dance I felt compelled to do; remembering a childhood injury to my eyes enabled me to begin my journey toward visual healing.

Good as well as bad memories can be suppressed and then plumbed later by adult decisions and experiences. Assagioli, the great Italian psychiatrist who founded psychosynthesis in the middle of the last century, believed that just as we suppress our angers and jealousies, tendencies toward kindness and generosity can be stamped out in our childhood and yearn to be tapped by current experiences. My college friendship with Jenny and a trip to her home in Mexico began my unconscious quest to uncover the truth about my love and trust of brown-skinned people—as I thought of the African-Americans who worked for my family—and the sense that I had lived among them. Likewise, my relationship with my teacher in The Netherlands, Felix White, and friendship with his Black students, took me back to my childhood world of fun times with people of color. These early years had given me excitement and joy in living, and I felt rejuvenated with their return to my conscious memory.

By immersing myself in the songs and rhythms of Black culture, at first with the African music of Olatunji, then by hearing Haitian drums in my Graham dance class, and finally with the syncopation and soul of Motown and gospel music of Felix's classes, I opened myself up to remembering my nanny's singing and the excitement of Joe's rhythmic stomping in my childhood kitchen. I was making an unconscious connection between past and present, between my deepest roots and current life, stimulating my journey into feeling whole and genuine.

The maple-wood jewelry box I created with loving care in my twenties, on which I put a gold clasp so I could keep things "locked up" as my teacher suggested, symbolized my mental container of good memories. When I lifted the lid I could almost see two little girls dancing their hearts out to the sounds of clapping in a yellow-walled kitchen, but these blessed memories needed to stay vague until I felt safe enough, years later, to look back at a time that included trauma and terror. Moving fast in Felix's classes amidst the exuberance of my sweating Dutch peers, brought recollections of the joy I had felt dancing with Joe during the most thrilling moments of my young childhood.

It was not only through the world of dance and music that my Dutch life tempted my good memories out of their lair. Arriving in that small, slower-moving, and comparatively serene land from my large, impersonal, and work-oriented country was a metaphor for how I had felt as a small child, fleeing the huge, complicated, and unforgiving parental section of our house for the comfortable brown world of my childhood's fun-filled kitchen. I enjoyed observing Dutch parents use practical measures and games while disciplining their children rather than punitive measures, and I was reminded of lessons I'd learned from the sensible and loving servants in my childhood, who had tried to teach my sister and me in wise and persuasive ways how to be fair with one another.

This simpler pace of life that I found in my new country reminded me of the pleasant tempo I'd once known with my young nanny Grace who had come fresh from her southern rural

3

home. I appreciated the sense of homespun family and national fun on holidays in The Netherlands, compared to the frenetic pace back in America's northeast, with its emphasis on free time as an opportunity to shop holiday sales and catch important "Deals." I joined in neighborhood activities and local parades with surprise and delight, activities similar perhaps to small-town living back in the States.

This sense of connection to community contributed to the feeling of safety that permitted my mind to download its memories. Not the least important of triggers, the fragrance of the small bakeries I visited daily in my Dutch town, took me back to memories of my early aromatic home and its golden spot in my heart.

We can begin this journey of self-knowledge by ourselves, but my experience has shown that for a deeper and safer trip we need help if the story has been a complicated one. As Richard and Bonny Gulino Schaub point out in *Dante's Path*, the Pilgrim needed many guides to shepherd him safely through his darkness. The brilliant psychiatrist Carl Jung's solo journey into his self-analysis through work with the creative imagination was highly unusual. The amount of consciousness needed to observe triggers we have created for ourselves in order to remember and resolve earlier crises, as well as find our soul's truth while we do this, is enormous.

The overexposure I experienced in my dance studio to unexpected and troubling realities from my past, which had shown up in my choreography, became overwhelming because I did not have the benefit of someone trained to assist me in understanding them. But, later, with this help, I found the chance for creating a changed, more aware, and more empowering way to live.

There are signs that American society is accepting the truth that we can sometimes need help in sorting out emotional difficulties. For many years we have seen how counselors are sent to help the victims of disasters. Recently, goal-oriented and short-term therapy called coaching has lifted participants to new levels of ability, leadership, and independence.

Psychosynthesis, with its efficient and fun tool of role-playing between different parts of the personality, has shortened the length of psychotherapeutic treatment and therefore made it more affordable. If patients are led to believe—as Assagioli taught—that an enlightened and well-intentioned self lies deep inside them, they will trust themselves and the therapist sooner. Difficult revelations they felt ashamed about but are driven to discuss will be easier to share, cutting months if not years from the psychotherapeutic process.

A course I took with Barbara Max Hubbard on the Emergence of the Essential Self began with her asking students to hold a hand over the area of the heart while breathing deeply and saying self-directed loving words. Within minutes we gained a sense of being loved and safe, allowing us to go deeper sooner. Craig Hamilton, in his Internet course on the development of Evolutionary Consciousness, cut through the stagnation and despair of depression with his hope-filled reminder to us that the universe is constantly evolving, and if we become conscious of that evolution within ourselves, we can accelerate the goodness of change.

The growing popularity of these psychological and spiritual forms of guidance demonstrates the public's recent appreciation that medication—the panacea of the past—cannot do the whole job of eradicating emotional malaise. Likewise, it may be that society will begin to recognize that in cases involving child or adult trauma, short-term counseling may not be enough. Insurance companies and many people suffering from depression have chosen medication rather than talk therapy for the treatment plan because of the expense. Yet I believe that cost is not the reason for a dismissive attitude toward verbal counseling. My insurance company paid $30,000 during a six-month period—100% of my late husband's cancer treatments—as opposed to $300—or 50% of my psychotherapy bill—for a similar amount of time.

The stigma placed against going to a professional for assistance about feelings of unhappiness or confusion has, I believe, to do with two American values that are very important to us: first, the desire to achieve mastery of the mind over emotions, even if it means suppressing them; and, second, a great respect for personal independence—the sense that we should be able to handle our problems ourselves. I myself suffered from this stiff-upper-lip attitude after receiving my flashbacks in The Netherlands.

Yet my eventual recovery taught me the opposite truths: richness of living depends on being able to feel strongly, and my survival was possible because I asked for assistance from others. If I'd been unable to receive help, I could have negotiated neither my childhood nor my adult life. It feels far safer to pretend that we can manage alone, but the truth for me was that I was lucky to have been taught by the Black people who nourished me as a small child in my New England home, that all of us need one another; I was prepared to accept help later on.

It is possible that the cultural ethos of this country will change when we recognize our interconnectedness as part of the global community. Then the day will come when we pioneer-spirited Americans can admit our interdependence and occasional need of others outside of our families—even if that means long-term conversations with a well-trained professional. Then we will demand that insurance companies cover the cost of extended talk therapy—and I will not have to hear again from the mother of a teenage daughter who attempted to end her life, this answer to my concerned query: "Oh, yes, my daughter saw a psychologist a year ago, and the counselor helped her so much we felt we could stop when the insurance ran out. Sadly, we found that she needed more time."

Likewise, I hope to see stronger connections made between emotional and physical disorders. Doctors are amazed that I, in my seventies, am on no prescription medicines. I attribute this largely to the vitamin and mineral supplements I take, fresh foods, and exercise. But I am convinced that it is also due to my ability over the years to listen to my body and, with the help of psychologists, as well as my intuitive naturopath, Dr. Sherry Stemper, to learn how my emotions have affected it. Catching physical problems early in this way has contributed greatly to the prevention of sickness and to maintaining my physical health.

I believe that those suffering from chronic sickness can also be helped toward good health by talk therapy. Adult Type-II diabetes is encouraged by the eating of refined carbohydrates and sugar, exactly the foods sought after by depressed people. Liver disease can be a sign of alcohol consumption, which may be a crutch for someone who could benefit from psychological help if it were available and accepted by society as a smart thing to do. It is well recognized that cancer can be triggered by stress. The urgent need to say things to a professional therapist that no friend or spouse wants to hear is one possible cause for inner unrest. Even Alzheimer's is considered by some an illness that can be triggered by inflammation due to bad dietary choices and alcohol, a common reaction to memories that are too difficult to face.

As we grow older it is what we remember of our childhood that appears clearest in our minds. If traumatic problems have occurred that were not dealt with, they can be difficult to handle at this late stage in life. Howard Reich, author of *Prisoner of Her Past: A Son's Memoir* was forced to acknowledge these truths when he watched his Jewish mother, who had fled the Nazis as a young and orphaned girl, hoard loaves of bread in her assisted living residence because she sensed imminent danger and the need to flee.

Psychotherapy at an appropriate time in our lives can give those of us who have experienced trauma and confusion comfort and self-understanding. We learn to recognize the unwanted influence of past experiences on us and receive guidance as to how to reject that interference. A shrewd psychologist can point out in a timely manner where we are being pushed into puzzling situations by earlier events that are begging by their influence to be looked at.

Perhaps increased awareness of the stress our current veterans have sustained from multiple deployments in Iraq and Afghanistan, with not enough chance to get counseling and recovery in between, will help to lead the way. It is a puzzle to me that it has taken so long to recognize the diagnosis of posttraumatic stress disorder, or PTSD, as an aspect of war. Soldiers returning from Vietnam did not receive the understanding or access to counseling that veterans are offered today.

Yet the syndrome of past trauma causing flashbacks and difficulties in current time is not such a far cry from Freud's ideas that troubling childhood issues can create mental problems in an adult—or the wisdom of a famous old English proverb stating that "the child is father of the man."

Prologue

It seemed to me at four-and-a-half as if everyone felt upset during the weeks before Christmas after something terrible called Pearl Harbor, but my mother most of all. One night, I ran away from her, not knowing what I had done to make her angry, but she caught me in the pantry, shaking me by the shoulders and swiping the back of her hand across my face. Her sharp small-diamond ring scraped my nose.

Twisting free, I dashed screaming to Grace in the kitchen. My *brown mother*, as I thought of the woman who had taken care of me all of my life, lifted me up onto the sink to wash off the blood that had begun to crawl down my upper lip. But the scary lady came after us, yelling and hitting Grace on her back for blocking the way to me.

Grace pushed me along the wooden surface of the counter to the corner where the shelving pieces met. Then she grasped their metal edges and held on with her strong fingers. She leaned with her plump stomach against my knees so that the bottom half of my legs hung down next to the wooden cabinets and I couldn't move.

I was horrified at being held back from running away! Grace knew that's what I did to protect myself from "that crazy lady," as I had heard Jessie, our cook, say one night before she left. The wide dark figure in front of me uttered no words of comfort, at least that I could hear above my mother's and my screams. Grace's silence and the tightness of her muscles turned her normally soft stomach into stone. Her bodily defiance of my parent, so unlike the obsequious behavior I had become used to, made her seem weird and scary to me. I became doubly terrified. My brown mother had turned against me! She wanted me to be hurt!

Forced to look at my mother's horrifying face without access to flight, I became hysterical, my eyes switching wildly from side to side while glaring at Grace's tight hands clamped to the counter. My throat uttered piercing screeches that quieted only for the seconds it took for my lungs to catch some breath. I began to pound on Grace's arms and chest, yelling my first word in six months, "Nooooooooooooooooo!"

Suddenly I heard Joe's voice, but it came from my brown mother's mouth!

"Anne!"—Grace never called me anything but Honey or Lamb—"you stay right on where you are." The growled sound, like her boyfriend's bad-mood voice, folded itself out of her mouth in good English, the kind of language Jessie had scolded Grace into trying to use. Her low tones shocked me into silence and calm. I leaned my head on Grace's bosom and closed my eyes, feeling her cheek rest on the top of my head as I dropped into a deep sleep.

I didn't know what caused my brown mother to let go, but when I looked up, I saw a knife in my mother's left hand, and with the right she grabbed my wrist! She started to pull me off the counter but Grace took hold of my arm with both hands. The two of them fought over me until my mother pressed the knife's point into Grace's wrist and she let go. Then the strong lady raised me high in the air, the knife in her other hand directed at my chest! Grace whipped around and grabbed her arm.

"Now, Misus Davidson," the words panted their way out of her mouth, "you don' want to be holdin' no knife with a child in yo' hand. Now you jes gonna drop it."

My mother loved Grace.

She dropped the knife but kept holding me high as if I were

a Christmas ball she planned to hang on the tree. While Grace kept up her talking, my limbs and insides hanging loose made me lose control over my *trickle*. In surprise and disgust at the liquid that drenched her leg, my mother let me down in the puddle I had caused.

"Take your panties off," Grace said. I leaned over and pulled them off, and then I saw the knife. I picked it up and held it so that it pointed at my mother's belly, but Grace was quick. She caught my wrist.

"Go on to the pantry," she said throwing the knife in an angle at the floor so it scurried under the stove. Her voice sounded as dark and controlled as it had before.

I moved away, my chest beating like a drum at thinking about what I'd tried to do. I knew that people who hurt people with knives went to prison. Joe had said that to my mother the spring before when he'd saved my life the second time.

"You go make yo'sef a cup a tea, Misus Davidson," Grace was saying, back in her normal voice. "An' aftah that you go on an' set yo'sef down. Then you gonna go upstairs an' get yo'sef ready for yo' husband."

Grace came to me and took my hand. We walked down the long hall toward my father's study.

She hesitated at the foot of the stairs. I reached up and shook my head, pointing to the outside. We tried the study porch door but it was locked, so we walked back to the dining room and opened the door to that porch.

"WHAT ARE YOU DOING?" My mother's voice slivered the air.

"The roses!" I whispered up into Grace's ear. She curled me up into her side with one arm and dashed through the porch out into the black backyard.

The large and strong woman ran with me on her hip across the dark lawn to my sister Susie's and my hiding place, a tunnel under cascading thorny roses. The protective flowers, though now gone, had climbed their way over a high fence from the neighbors' garden and created a hollow space with their solid wall of decades-old overhanging and long prickly stems. The entrances to this long passage were big enough for a small child to creep through and at the far end for an adult who was willing to crawl.

We entered this safe haven and moved to a spot where Grace could sit up. She took her shoe off and used it to pull down some of the sharp branches so that they became a closed door—in time before my mother stood at the entrance yelling in to us.

"You come out of there, Grace, this minute!" We didn't move.

"I'll go get the gun and shoot you both." I tried to squirm free of the powerful arms that held me. I didn't want to be shot. Susie had explained to me what was inside that great, big, scary, dark brown case—fat at the bottom and thin at the top—sticking up from the floor at the back of our coat closet. But I was held tight though no words came from Grace's panting throat.

Then I heard her whisper, "Yo' daddy gonna hep us…"

We waited, our hearts beating their drums into each other's chests and creating a furnace against the New England cold.

After a short time, we could hear my father's voice through the branches. "Grace? Are you there? Mrs. Davidson said you were out here."

My daddy helped my brown mother push the thorny twigs away from the entrance with his leather-gloved hands.

"What happened, Grace?" he asked as we climbed out.

She tried to brush the twigs and leaves off her uniform.

"Why was Mrs. Davidson angry with Anne?" he persisted.

Grace couldn't seem to get her uniform clean enough. Finally, she straightened up and stood looking at him.

"Mistuh Davidson, Ah don' rightly know why Misus Davidson do' what she do'. All's I know, Sir, she done scared yo' little girl half out of huh mind."

My daddy picked me up and carried me back to his study. He sat down in his big chair and wrapped his jacket around me as he rocked. After a while, he mentioned my mother.

I interrupted, "She's bad," talking to him for the first time in six months.

He pushed me hard off his lap. "Don't you say that about your mother!"

I scrambled to my feet and went to the door. Then I turned around to face him, standing where Joe had stopped the day he'd carried me on his shoulders into my father's study to show him a bloody gash on my head. The heroism and courage I'd seen that day, and in our cook Jessie who had tried to help me too before she was fired, and now in the rescue by Grace, burst into my mind and woke up my verbal and articulate self as it came to help me verbalize my feelings of passionate love and gratitude.

Standing up for the person I loved most in the world, vehemence and righteousness filled my chest.

"SHE HURT GRACE!!" My words came out as loud as my screams in the kitchen, but now I spoke in clear phrases, my mouth and face screwed up with my effort to say each syllable as well as my out-of-practice tongue could make it. "SHE HURT MY GRACE! SHE HURT MY ... MOTHER!" The last word was blurted out with love and truth, but accompanied by a sense of warning.

"WHAT DID YOU SAY?" My father leapt from his chair.

I ran down the hall toward the kitchen.

Grace was standing in the dining room waiting. She grabbed me and swung us both through the doorway into the pantry. Letting the door close by kicking its metal pin off the locked position, she hurried with me through the second swinging door to safety. She held me on her lap as she sat at the kitchen table and shook. Then she tried to get me to eat, but I squiggled off her legs and slid down to the floor, lying on my back and beating the yellow linoleum as well as the air with my feet and hands, my screaming tantrum the only answer for the disaster and confusion that had descended on me once again.

"Why doesn't he stop her?" I managed to ask before falling asleep.

When I woke up, Grace had cleaned up. Feeling bad about it, but needing food, I went over to my brown mother as she stood at the sink.

Speaking in sentences that must have surprised her, I explained, "I'm sorry Grace. I'm hungry now." The young woman sighed but went to our *icebox,* as we called it back then, taking something out and warming it up on the stove.

Strengthened by the food I'd eaten and feeling the comfort of Grace's lap, I mumbled, "Why don't mah daddy make mah mother be good?"

"Honey, yo' daddy don' know what to do 'bout yo' mother."

"But you say he a smart man!" I jumped off her lap and stood up to face her with this important question.

"Ah don' know, chil'." Grace took my dishes to the sink.

I lay down on the floor, this time shaking my hands in the air without sound or force as I rested on my back and thought about these adults who didn't know what to do about my mother hurting me. Then I got up and walked through the swinging doors into the dining room, going out through the porch into the dark night. I went to the middle of our huge back yard and yelled as loud as I could up into the black sky, "HELLO! ... HELLO!"

"WHAT ARE YOU DOING?" My father came running from his study as Grace dashed from the opposite direction.

14

"I'm calling up to Grace's God." I told him. "She says He knows everything." I looked up at the deep dark blue sky. "He's up there and I'm asking him what to do about my mother."

My father and Grace looked at each other for a long time. In the blackness, I couldn't see their faces, but apparently they could read each other's. What were they saying to each other? I couldn't hear a thing, nor could I see their expressions. I moved from one to the other, touching them to make them notice me and tell me what was going on.

Finally, Grace offered up this idea.

"Mistuh Davidson, Misus Davidson might like to go on down south an' see her sister, Gloria. She like her so much, an' you know all this war talk an all, I think it too much for her 'round here right now. Gloria, she off in those mountains. Misus Davidson, she kin get herse'f some res' down there with her."

"You mean for Christmas?"

"No, Sir, jes fo' a week so's she can have a little talk with her sister. They gets along so good."

"Well, I'll think about it, Grace. Thank you." My father stretched out his arm and laid his hand on her shoulder. They appeared to be two dark-skinned people in the black night. "I'm sorry, Grace, that you got hurt. I know you were doing what you thought was right."

"That's one thing fo' sho', Mistuh Davidson." She touched her wrist with her other hand and bent her head forward, the top of it touching my father's chest as she burst out crying. Grace loved my father. We three girls heard almost every day how wonderful our daddy was.

I'd never seen Grace weep. I went back to moving around the two dark figures, trying to get rid of the pain in my stomach from seeing my brown mother so sad. Finally she stopped and we, all of us, started walking toward the porch outside my father's study.

"Grace is good!" I said to my father.

"Yes, Grace is a good person."

"Now Chil,' you knows I loves you." Grace put her arm around my shoulder, so she could pull me away and stop my tongue, but I finished what I'd planned to say.

"And my mother is bad!" I looked up at my father.

"She's not bad … she's just sick."

"She should go to a hospital where the doctors can get her well," I repeated Jessie's phrase that had explained my mother to Susie and me before she left.

"Well, aren't you the know-it-all now?"

"Jessie said, Jessie said!" I defended myself as we moved into the screened porch.

"I don't want to hear anything about what that drunk told you!" My father opened the living room door for us and then disappeared through a second door to his study.

"Grace, what do drunk mean?"

"Oh, Honey, yo' daddy is jes' upset."

The next morning, very early, Mrs. Strong, a neighbor and my mother's best friend, came to our house. My mother walked in with her. I guessed she must have gone there for the night. They packed one of my mother's suitcases. Then my father drove her to the railroad station on his way to work.

Peace came to visit us, as if it were fresh air breathed deeply. A sense of space and spirit of gentleness filled our house. Those of us left behind after my mother's departure felt our freedom, including my sisters, who returned jubilant from their holiday visit at our cousins' house, and we—Grace, most of all—began to concentrate on preparations for Christmas. Our kitchen, with its warmth and delicious fragrances, became again a beacon of safety, the meaning it had lost the night I felt that my mother had brought the world's wars into the warm yellow glow of the small room I had considered home.

Part One – Love

Chapter 1 – College

I spent most of my freshman year at college sitting in cafés after my classes drinking black coffee and pretending to do homework, watching people rather than my books, and experiencing the universe of male and female energies I'd landed in. After living a cloistered life at my all-girl boarding school, I found the opportunity, in the middle of my bustling new world, to absorb what I considered real life.

I didn't make friends. I had no idea what I wanted or who I was, other than an upper-middle-class eighteen-year-old who needed to be where I was—plunked down in this place where I felt safe and free. My drive to relax in my new surroundings became stronger than the desire to join a club or get good grades.

I had always liked the company of strangers. Surrounded by throngs of interesting people with whom I'd never had a connection, I felt I had a chance, as if in their strangeness, to find a clue to myself. Perhaps I chose cafés because on some unconscious level they reminded me of the kitchen home I had once known and where, at an early age, I had enjoyed fun and safety.

My parents had no idea that I was spending my time at college dawdling it away in cafés. I managed to complete all of my homework assignments and check into the dorm at night on time, giving the impression that life was normal. My need to go through a time of self-discovery was at such a deep level that I had no explanation when the dean asked me halfway through sophomore year why my grades were sliding. I agreed with her that a leave of absence might be a good idea and I went home.

My mother had been seeing a Jungian therapist whom she liked. I didn't know what Jungian meant but was willing to talk to this psychotherapist about my inability to study. I went to meet with him at his country house on a Sunday. The tall, elderly man, dressed in brown informal slacks and a thick tan sweater, his luxuriant, wavy white hair falling around his large friendly face, attracted my interest with his warm manner. So I began weekly trips by train to his city office.

Dr. Bennett had to work hard to establish communication with me. One day, he pulled his chair closer so that our knees were touching. With his kindly eyes peering at me from under bushy eyebrows, the therapist leaned forward and placed his hands on the outside of my thighs about two inches above my knees. I was shocked. My legs shook and my brain struggled with trying to balance the good and the bad: *This therapist is also my mother's; she recommended him—is that going to make what he's doing okay?*

The doctor's large, weathered-looking hands, which had not moved an inch farther up my legs, sent waves of warmth into my body, just as I had seen small flames catching onto a pile of autumn leaves at the roadside.

"Why are you doing this?" I stammered.

"Because I want to make a connection with you," he answered.

I looked into his eyes, warm and golden brown, like those of a charming cocker spaniel. I decided to believe him. Suddenly I felt myself warm and alive.

A strong and vibrant person named *Anne* came back into my lonely ghost-like form, returning to me not as a girl in her late teens, but as a young woman. A demanding voice inside told me to toss out the boy's name *Sonny* that my mother had given me at five-and-a-half.

My therapist never had to touch me again to make contact.

He instructed me to put a notebook by my bed so I could write down dreams or any fragment of one the minute I woke up. My ramblings didn't have to make sense.

To every visit I brought in my notes with great eagerness. I learned that my dreams were teaching me, through symbolic objects and people, how to manage my life, though if a character I dreamt about was someone I recognized, then the image probably represented that actual person.

One of my dramatic dreams indicated that I had struggled with a great deal of anger at an early age.

> Three young female pigs, with the flesh color of human children and completely naked, sat in a circle. The smallest of the three stood up and said to the medium-sized one, *"Et tu, Brute?"* Then the little one drove a large knife through the middle-sized one's chest.

Neither the therapist nor I knew why I had dreamt this. The violence shook me, but the doctor said, "Don't worry about it. All dreams are tools that teach us about our feelings. They are not telling us what we will do or have done."

Joanna Field's record of self-discovery, *A Life of One's Own*, accompanied me as I commuted on the train from home to my therapist's office. I marked passages in every paragraph of the small volume that leaked pages as I grabbed my belongings to get off the train in time. On return trips, the setting sun reflected its warm light on my open book and me through the churning vehicle's western window, while I settled back to connect the words I read with ones I'd heard in the therapist's office. Both kinds of light, physical and mental, encouraged me to discover who this person, Anne, was.

I learned that if I dreamt about a car or a vehicle of

transportation, I was dealing with myself as a social being, as opposed to thinking of myself as a sexual or spiritual one. If I raced downhill in my dream's car, heading for a crash, this meant that something was going wrong in my relationship to the world.

I must have changed from a swerving car to a train in one of my nightly adventures, because my motivation about returning to college switched onto a strong and steady track. I returned to my studies, taking two summer courses called *Twentieth Century World Wars* and *Government* instead of classes from the English major that had become boring to me. I also attracted the boy who lived one flight down in my summer apartment house. Weekly rides to country haunts on the back of his motorcycle complemented my summer life.

Carl, a dark haired Jewish boy, reminded me of my two friendly cousins, Jewish by marriage, with whom I'd hung around the summer I was fifteen. This friendship with Carl led to a three-hour trip to meet his family. It was an enlightening experience because his household was so different from mine. Money was ostentatiously and unashamedly used to full enjoyment.

My friend seemed to treasure our breakfasts out on his weathered balcony, even after he'd failed in several attempts to awaken my interest in sex. The summer closed down, and I did, too. I had reached a point in my life with which I no longer felt comfortable, either expressed or caused by my inability to respond physically to the boy I had spent the summer with.

Picking up on my depressed state when college began again, my parents offered to send me to a regular psychotherapist, that is, not a Jungian. Dr. Smith helped his patients change their lives through talking and reasoning, rather than through the language of dreams. My trips ran shorter than they had the spring before, this time just a bus ride to the next town. The visits to Dr. Smith, with their easy sessions, brought me back out of my black and empty state.

Though less sensational than Dr. Bennett in his ideas, my new therapist was right on the mark.

"Well, Anne, tell me," Dr. Smith asked, "are you happy?"

The stocky, forty-something doctor, dressed in a tweed jacket and brown trousers, sat back in his leather chair. From there, he gazed out his window at the woods or swiveled the seat back to face me, just as I could do while figuring out what to say.

"Oh, is that what people are supposed to be? I thought you were supposed to do what you had to do," I answered finally.

"Well, I think most people want to be happy and try to arrange their lives so they can be."

Why had I never considered it important to be happy? Even the question made me struggle with effort at the idea that someone should bother to ask it.

Dr. Smith worked with me in a subtle and steady manner. He increased my confidence and sense of identity, but without the dramatic leaps and insights that had occurred during my dream-work the spring before.

The biggest change in my life came from getting to know Jenny, a freshman who had grown up in Mexico. Though an American, she had lived most of her life in a culture different from anything I had yet run into during my school years.

I met her as I walked along the upstairs hallway of my dorm one late afternoon, a few weeks into my fall term as a second semester sophomore. She was dancing the Meringue to music in front of a mirror, her hips moving up and down and side to side at the same time. As sunlight streamed through the hallway's large window and struck the mirror, I felt dazzled by the reflected image of Jenny's sensual body and mesmerized by the real one. I was also terrified by the sensations her dancing

23

evoked in my stiff woman's pelvic area.

Dr. Smith praised me in a later therapy session for the courage it had taken for me to stay watching. My willingness to experience something new served me well, compliments to Jenny on her dancing and a request for some instruction beginning the strongest friendship of my college life.

My new friend was homesick for the land she loved, for its warmth and beauty, its sensuality and romance. We spent every evening in one of our rooms, usually hers, because she had pictures of her adopted country on every bit of wall space, and she would tell me about her home and friend, Manuel. She described the sea at sunset, the Mariachi bands that came to help the boy with his courting, as well as the flowers—some wild and some planted in beautiful arrangements along the streets leading into the city.

When I visited Jenny during our summer vacation and felt the luminous air while stepping out of my plane near Mexico City, I rejoiced, as if returning to a country I had once known. I grew to love Manuel through Jenny's eyes, a dark-eyed young man, thrilling in his dashing black suit as we watched him from the upstairs window walk to our front door, though I was scared of the blind date he'd brought with him. I had dressed with pleasure in the close fitting and chic black dress my friend had helped me pick out in the city's boutique section, and we took our time putting flowers in our hair, knowing that the boys would arrive the customary two hours late.

A small waterfall greeted us as we entered our dinner nightclub, and a brook gurgled behind heavy-leafed palms along the path we followed to our table. A fountain danced in the water behind it. As we ate and chatted, the mural next to us depicting a bridge and lagoon took us away to a magical place.

After another day for Jenny to go out with Manuel alone, we left for Acapulco, which she had explained would charm me as much as the city had. Leaving our beach-side hotel early in the morning, we found a café where we sat outside and watched the passersby. I remember my amazement that the entire breakfast Jenny recommended consisted of a large plate of fresh and ripe fruit, sliced and colorful in its glistening juices. We munched in the partial shade and loved the idea that we were far away from studying or serious thinking. Later we cooled ourselves from walking in the blinding sunlight by swimming and resting under palms, where cold pineapple drinks were sold at tented stands.

We drove to Tasco, up in the mountains, where we bought bracelets on which miniature charms hung, tiny cups, pitchers, and hats, made from silver that had not been processed. The nearly white delicate paper-like quality of the jewelry delighted me, as did the orange roofs of houses I gazed down onto from the balcony of our hillside hotel.

On the way home before catching our train across the country back to college, we stopped at a tiny village halfway to the Texas border, where Jenny's parents were building a motel. While riding horseback through the flat sage-filled desert, a sudden and scary storm brought us to a café, where I learned from laughing Mexican men not to drink water to quench the fire in my throat from our spicy snack, but to sop up the burning juices with bread.

Every day we strolled along hot, sandy village streets to the bakery for steaming loaves passed to us through a half-door that opened into the street. I hadn't noticed anything that looked like a store, only the front wall of a low adobe building. But once the thick upper door was pushed outwards, I could see into the courtyard of the baker's home and smell the delicious aromas.

I stood in shock as my wash-and-wears hung wrinkled from the lines hung across Mrs. Donaldson's courtyard, having been heavily centrifuged along with the other clothes.

"The girls will be happy to iron them up along with everything else," Jenny's mother told me, laughing at my surprise.

Standing in the grassy dirt yard, watching two servants talking and giggling as they reached into their baskets for clothes in spots of leafy shade, I caught a hint of something I had once known. The warm southern land Jenny had introduced me to with its strange language, joking men, the fragrance of fresh baking, and the sight of tawny-skinned people everywhere, became another step in my long unconscious labor to remember my young childhood and the people I had loved.

After the summer, Jenny surprised me by signing up to live in a different dormitory. Once I no longer saw my friend, I didn't feel able to visit her, as if my memory couldn't hold her image or that of our wonderful trip. Instead of giving into my passion about this southern land where I had felt at home, either by going to the International Club that I had often visited with Jenny, or even by changing my major to Latin American Studies, I returned to a state of loneliness and depression, confused and made helpless by an overwhelming and debilitating sense of loss.

Dr. Smith tried to help, and he probably did, but the stimulus for my mood change came through the brilliant sermons I heard in the university's nonsectarian chapel, as well as from a few courses I loved. Music appreciation charged my soul with energy as I listened to thunderous orchestral symphonies or received a strong sense of discipline and safety through the dynamic organization of Baroque fugues. During a semester of studying the heroic poem, *Beowulf*, Old English rang out at eight o'clock two mornings a week via the sonorous voice of our excited professor. He seemed so in love with and so capable in this ancient language, that he stirred our sleepy souls in spite of the early hour. We filed into his lecture hall and settled down to listen, our faces glistening from the warmth of our professor's own brand of morning sunshine.

The artwork of this medieval time, full of reds and golds, jeweled knives and raging animals, yelled at me with meaning, helping me strengthen the message of the pig dream, that somewhere deep down under my emotionless personality I was familiar with feelings of passion and anger, even violent rage. These same colors were reflected in the gorgeous pictures that appeared in my geology book and in the specimens we studied. The beauty of the earth stared up at me as if saying *this is what's real, this is yours*, perhaps reminding me unconsciously of how, as a five-year-old, I had hugged the dark brown earth under a huge oak tree at the back of our yard after my nanny Grace had left our house for good.

At the Christmas break, the last four weeks of my eighth semester, I didn't go home, but stayed in the university town at a graduate dorm for students who didn't have anywhere to go. Dr. Smith had helped me find the independence enough to say "No" when my family expected a visit. I told them that I had a lot of work to do, but instead I began writing, telling stories one after the other, and only taking breaks for meals and sleep.

My tales were mythic adventures involving animals that charged through caverns that turned out to be, after many versions, the hallways of my childhood home. I sensed the danger for little girls amid fires, blood, and screaming, partially stimulated by what I'd learned about female child sacrifice among the Indian tribes of Mexican history.

These harsh and wild stories were counterbalanced by the relative peace of my half-empty dorm. Foreign students, mainly from China and India, made a convivial vacation home for themselves, chattering in their different languages as they cooked up aromatic meals in the small kitchens located on each floor. They lounged downstairs for casual get-togethers in the comfortably furnished living room, or bustled through the front door with packages from snowy trips to the stores.

These students hardly noticed me, but their presence was essential for my success. Though I didn't interact with them because they rarely spoke English, I loved hearing their voices and knowing that they were there. I felt accompanied and safe while spending every hour I could with my papers and pens, scribbling perhaps fifty nightmarish adventures about my mythical creatures. My doctor was away on vacation, but I was glad, as the excursions to his office would have interrupted my work.

I should say, my "play." Work is what I had been doing at the university, plugging and plodding my way through hours of studying, writing papers on professors' questions, cramming my brain for exams, and extending every fiber of enforced mental energy in order to be allowed to stay in this place where I was starting to be me. No, this activity I had begun was play. These were *my* questions that I was answering, *my* time I was giving freely, and *my* deadlines.

I loved what I was doing. The more emotions I poured out into this strange verbiage, the more I became aware of feelings I apparently had about everything in my life. *I don't need Jenny to show me in a vicarious way how to live!* I shouted to myself. Through my writing, I dared to experience anger, terror, and the stirring of sexual desire. For the first time I thought of myself as an independent woman who knew what she wanted and who could make decisions on her own.

A month later I walked out of my last exam. That unfinished test and one incomplete paper meant that I would receive no diploma, the recognition for my four years of hard work, but this did not bother me. I'd gotten out of the eight semesters what I'd wanted. I had found out who I was, a young woman who *could feel!*

I left the university and its all-girl residential dorm behind me. A coed rooming house appealed to me, full of young men, dark-looking and attractive in the dimly lit corridors. The house had one vacant room left, a small and sunny attic loft with space for not much more than the large double mattress on the floor that lay in front of a wide window. I loved my new, cozy bedroom, with its low, peaked ceiling, assured that here I would find the home I was looking for. I signed the lease, figuring that my parents' allowance could be used for rent, and my other expenses would be paid for with a job. I was convinced that I would find in this residential house all I had been searching for.

Was my father a player in those mythic stories I had created? The truth had been unclear to me when I wrote them down, but it was as sharp to me now as the ring of the doorbell downstairs, that he had taken a role. Why, he was the Knight in Shining Armor, dashing to my university town at sixty-miles-an-hour to save his daughter from the fateful adventure she had created for herself! Whether he was right and I was wrong, I didn't know, but I chose not to fight him—though at the age of twenty-three I was within my legal rights to do so.

It appealed to me that he had been so affected by Dr. Smith's evening telephone call telling him about my change in plans that he had risen at dawn to call his secretary and tell her to cancel his day. Then he'd hurried away to practice his legal expertise and financial power on the manager of my new residence in order to get me out of the lease I had signed.

I packed the suitcase I'd barely opened, and allowed myself to be bundled into the cold wintry car for our drive home. As I walked out of the building, I glanced soulfully at the handsome dark-haired young manager, whose office/bedroom my father had visited in the bowels of the building, and wished I could have gotten to know him better. Yet I didn't mind the idea of going home, knowing that I could continue my agenda since our house was near in an equally interesting university city.

To my surprise, however, at home my mother started acting in weird ways, doing things like pushing me away from a sunny spot on the red and blue Oriental rug in my father's study.

"That's my place," she said. Nor did she respond to my request to massage the front of my legs when I asked her to, my shinbones feeling as if they had been broken in half, an unconscious reaction to an injury she had indirectly caused in my childhood that I would remember eighteen years later.

I didn't have to put up with her unwelcoming and uncooperative behavior for long. My father came to tell me that he had consulted with his most trusted colleagues at work and had been told that, if I were their daughter, they would put me in a place called Austen Riggs Center, located in the Berkshire Hills of Massachusetts. They all swore that this long-term residence for troubled young people, where the patients develop independence and responsibility for their therapy because of the open setting, was the best place around and not to consider any other idea.

Yet there was something cold about my father's announcement, which surprised me, for it didn't fit with my picture of the rescuing knight, whose caring actions I had enjoyed. But I forgot about this because I appreciated that he was the one to take me for our initial visit to the center. Otherwise I might not have remembered Grace. As if triggered by the feeling that I was about to get the help and support I needed, the memory of how much the brown-skinned woman had loved me flowed into my conscious brain. In the weeks while waiting to be admitted, I sank deep into the sorrow I had experienced as a child at her departure.

I arrived at Austen Riggs Center with a small suitcase and dressed in a thick brown wool three-quarter-length coat with a hood. I'd made a drawing of myself for the interviewing doctor, using a purple crayon to draw the figure that stood in the hooded jacket in front of a pasture fence, with her back to the viewer. A few days later, at a conference with all of the staff present and looking me over, this doctor said he thought the significance of the drawing was that I was gazing at life from behind a fence.

For me, the greatest significance about the picture was that the figure in the woolen coat was female, whether a child or a woman it was not clear. For most of my school life I had been undecided about which gender I thought I was. My weeks of writing and finding my soul had freed me to accept my real identity, part little girl whose emotional life had been stopped in its tracks at five, and part grown woman.

But I didn't voice my opinion to the psychiatrist, for fear that he wouldn't like to be argued with and send me home. I liked the place. Soon I grew to love it. I had had to wait eighteen years, but at last I'd found the help I had needed as a child who had found herself abandoned like an orphan in a house with light-skinned parents whom she didn't trust.

Chapter 2 – Austen Riggs Center

I asked my interviewing doctor for a halt on communications from my mother. For the first time since my early childhood, I realized how angry I felt towards her, though I didn't know why. The center, respecting what they called a *moratorium*, a period of hiatus within troubling relationships, held to their promise for the two and a half years it took me to be able to see her again. I said my father could visit anytime.

"My story is very simple," I told my therapist. "I've remembered the Negro woman who I felt was my real mother and who left me at the age of five. I forgot how much I loved her until just before coming here." I then went on to assure him how easy it was going to be to get me straightened out because it was clear that I was just suffering from unexpressed grief, and all I needed to do was to release it.

"I never was able to mourn as a child because of my mother's jealousy," I explained. "When my brown mother Grace left me, I stopped feeling anything. After that, everything in my life seems unimportant, and therefore is a complete blank. But I can feel things now, so I'm basically fine." I used the mental color code I'd developed as a child to explain the difference between the period before Grace's departure and after she left.

"Before five my life was brown," I told him, "which means that it was filled with love." I had blocked all memory of my mother's violence from my conscious mind. "After that, my life was the color of light gray-blue, meaning emptiness and hating. Before Grace left, I was a real person, who loved life."

A few days after entering the treatment center, I received two letters from Grace, who had been told by my mother where I was. These were the first she'd ever written me. They were each a short page-and-a-half, but they said several times how much she loved me and always had. She could have used brown ink for all the power those letters had to feel like love treasures for me. Wrapped up in them was a little child's silver ring I had never seen before. I clutched my treasures and hid them away, keeping out in view only the can of oatmeal-raisin cookies Grace had baked for me.

But I took the letters to show the therapist. They were proof of my story about who I truly felt myself to be. During my months of vigorously recording stories, my handwriting had switched from the vertically aligned and often disconnected vowels and consonants I had used to do my homework and take notes, to a forward-leaning and flowing hand.

During my writing, I'd remembered the mood of my earliest days and in doing so had re-identified with Grace. It was from these pages that my brown mother's handwriting stared up at me, graceful and flowing, giving time for the fullness of each letter, and rich in clarity, as if each word had been loved. Perhaps as a grieving child I had stared at Grace's script looking up at me from polite letters to my mother after she left.

The doctors must have found it easy to believe my story, for I hardly spoke about my White parents during the first year I was at this supportive institution. I spoke only of Grace, who had left me feeling like a prisoner in an empty house. I had gotten back to my roots, my sorrow at the departure of my soul mother, the one who'd called me "Mah Baby," who'd been there all my life, until the day she wasn't.

Yet, in my behavior when I first arrived, I must have appeared excited rather than mournful. I could not stop talking. The knowledge of having discovered who I was, and who I felt my mother had been, thrilled me. I felt released from years of frustration and effort to keep up the level of pretense my life had required. My mood was one of relief—even happiness—as well as confusion about how my discoveries would fit into the trajectory of my current life's path.

After a few weeks, having responded to a small amount of calming medicine that ended my excited talking, there was nothing left in my mind to help me pretend to others or to myself that I was able to return and function as a normal twenty-three-year-old in *the outside world*, as we patients called it. I gave in to my relaxed state, accepting my sense of vulnerability, and allowing myself to linger inside the Inn, the largest part of the treatment center, the main house of a country estate now used as residence for the patients. Beautiful with its glistening white wooden exterior and dotted by green shutters, the rambling building included a large, comfortable if somewhat shabbily furnished living room with high ceilings; a pleasant and sunny dining room; wide airy hallways; and about twenty-five bedrooms.

Later, I had a dream that described my feelings about my first months at the center. I saw a huge and deep crater-like trench in the street at the end of the medical building's driveway, separating the institution's grounds from the town and the rest of the world. Two narrow and flimsy looking wooden boards crossed the ten-foot-wide and twenty-foot deep ditch, connecting the center's land and the public road. The meaning of the dream was that once having entered Riggs and having faced the crater in my soul, I was neither willing nor able to cross back into the life I had led, with its extreme effort to pretend to be someone I wasn't. The problem was I didn't know how to replace this rote way of living. I remember that accompanying other patients on Saturday night outings to the movies felt threatening because I feared being out on the streets without a unified voice inside me giving me a sense of *self* or any way to make decisions.

I became aware of another reason I was afraid to go out in the evenings, and that was the blackness of the world outside, as seen through windows from inside the Inn. I know now that the color represented the horrible feelings I'd pushed away to let myself feel safe. I feared being aware of the darkness in my mind at an hour when the world itself looked black. I couldn't sleep for the first half year and would stay up chatting with the night nurses, Allen and Shirley, each one a source of stories or attempts to answer my questions on a cheerful and casual level.

I remember Kathy—whose name and caring face evoked love and trust in me, though I didn't realize until later, that she reminded me of Cathy, the college girl who had been concerned about me and my unhappiness as a five-year-old. Kathy took turns helping me brave the night, lounging as I did in the overstuffed chairs placed along the sides of the downstairs hall, dressed in her regular clothes rather than a uniform, as was all of the staff at Riggs.

Then my companion would drift off to the nurses' lounge, and I'd stay curled up in my comfy chair, trying to doze. If I woke up, the warm dim hallway light assured me I would be safe until dawn, minimizing the fact that I was, indeed, falling into the syndrome of day-and-night reversal, experienced by many mental patients.

A place I loved, but where I couldn't stay long, was the library, a small room with wall-to-wall books, except where the records were stacked. There, I learned to listen to opera. This was a scary discovery. The music, with its expressions of love and terror, grief and torture, anger and joy, seemed appropriate for the rich emotional life I was coming to know and which I felt I'd once known well. But I could only listen for a few minutes at a time, the depth of emotion terrifying to me.

I'd found a warm welcome to the Inn on my first evening—a cold, snowy January night. Some of the bedrooms in this large country house had fireplaces, and my mentor, a fellow patient, invited me to her own corner in the Inn where a fire burned brightly and friends stood around drinking wine. In those days, the center allowed its patients to have alcohol in their rooms. This young woman's neat and cozy though large bedroom was filled with interesting animal figures and pictures, the overall colors being brown and deep reds or orange, my favorite shades.

I remember nearly dying inside from the amount of relief at the welcome and acceptance I felt that night. At boarding school, I'd never sensed that I was in the right place and thought others agreed with me. Here, I received the impression that everyone felt this was the place where they wanted to be and enjoyed sharing this reassurance with me.

My mentor left Riggs soon after my arrival, finished with her long-term travel through her own darkness, a journey of several years, like mine was to be. Uncanny, I'd think back at the end of my stay, how the doctors could have known she would be the right guide for me. But I didn't miss her when she left. Attachments to other patients were beyond me at this time.

When I was able to get close to people other than my therapist, it was with the maintenance staff and gardeners. I learned from Ernie, a sixty-five-year-old gentleman who managed the green house, that we had to wash out clay pots with soap before reusing them.

"Oh, yes," he said to my surprised inquiry, his kind eyes with just a bit of twinkle in them, "plants get sick just the way people do."

He didn't know that his kindly remark was hard for me. I didn't think of myself as sick. I knew that I was dealing with sadness in my heart's core, but I didn't consider that grieving should be called sick.

In some ways, I was right. With my emotions no longer suppressed because of all my work with Dr. Bennett and Dr. Smith, as well as my own creative writing, and aware of having deeply loved and been loved by Grace, I had broken down the impenetrable fence that mentally sick people can erect between their therapists and themselves. I was open and ready to find the love available within this psychotherapeutic setting. The white buildings and beautiful snow-laden fir trees on crisp winter days became brown in my mind, proving to me that this was a place I could count on to give me love.

My next attachments were to the teachers in the wooden building in town called the Shop. This barn-like structure, which I adopted by the end of my first year as my new home, contained areas for making crafts and carpentry downstairs and painting in a studio upstairs. Under the guidance of teachers who were artists, not therapists, I moved from carpentry to craft, and finally to painting.

Joan Erikson, the wife of the German American psychologist Erik Erikson and head of the Recreation Program before I came, had believed that patients should, in their off hours, mingle with non-medical people. So sculptors, painters, and architects had been hired, not occupational therapists trained to work in the arts as requirements of their professions. We were immensely fortunate in this decision, the architect and master of all crafts, as well as of the Shop itself, David Loveless, being a wonderful teacher and over time becoming a good friend.

My first creation at the Shop was a simple footrest that David helped me make. It consisted of two pieces of wood with interesting grains, stained and oiled into red and gold browns as if it were the color of dark autumn leaves. The two pieces intersected about one foot from the ground. The longer piece, once it was fastened with strong wood glue, supported the lower legs, and the top half of the shorter piece gave support to the bottom of the feet.

I gave this simple but comfortable footrest, satin smooth from fine sandpaper, to my father for a Christmas present. The piece was remarkably useful and felt good to my legs when I tried it, but my father didn't like it very much, and I never saw him use it. The second year, he joined my mother in being on my no-call list. I didn't know why. I just knew that every letter or attempt by either of my parents to get me on the phone drove me into waves of anxiety and rage.

I remember the joy with which I allowed myself to stay at the center and not go home for Christmas my second year. I enjoyed the camaraderie among those who chose to stay, our celebration a kind of closeness under fire, others having also been badgered to come home. The large roast beef cooked by one of the older patients was the most delicious I had ever tasted.

At the Shop, I went on to ceramics, making small cups on the wheel, an activity that gave me the emotions of peace and control. I began to make jewelry, gazing into the flame of the Bunsen burner as it melted sticks of brass into dark brown joints, a metaphor for the melting that parts of my heart were doing. Shaping a pair of copper earrings like baby carriages, I tucked into each a green stone, as if the glass gems were babies. Apparently, my unconscious mind was responding to my biological clock!

I carved a young pregnant woman out of wood, the curving grains of blond and auburn tones having called out for such a being. For my sister's eighteen-month-old daughter, I sewed a large duck, covering it with heavy cotton printed with orange and yellow flowers and strong enough for a toddler to sit on.

But my most serious work was with oil paints, encouraged by the famous cartoonist and artist Leo Garrel. I painted the face, neck, and shoulders of a pretty, wide-cheeked, dark-brown girl, about five years old.

Our superb teacher said to me, his curly dark hair waving about as he gesticulated to enforce his message, "A painting is not a painting until it is finished."

"But it is finished," I said, staring at the white canvas around the little girl. I didn't say to my teacher *I was a brown child left in a White world*. Even if I had, Leo would have said he didn't want the white canvas to speak for me. I thought a bit and then filled in the background with more brown. But I didn't stop there. I painted my arms, too, and my face.

Leo laughed. He would enjoy telling me the story when I visited him thirty-five years later. The cruel message that I'd been forced to learn from my skilled teacher, who had not been trained in psychology, but who was a master in expressing truth, was that brown children, who are not pretending to be brown, live in brown people's houses and in a brown world.

I painted the same child in the earth, and all that could be seen of her was the surface of her face, covered loosely with leaves and dirt. I felt nauseous at the time. I didn't know that this was a portrayal of what I had done as a child after Grace left, when I'd buried my little brown-girl self under an oak tree next to the tunnel of rambling roses where Grace had taken me to hide.

My teacher had made me sense a misunderstanding I had had of myself. Soon after this, I noticed that my eyes were hazel and green. All my life I had seen brown eyes in the mirror.

Learning to deal with my grief and difficulty with loss turned out to be a longer process than I'd planned. I was helped along by having to deal with the pain of a current abandonment. My beloved first therapist, Dr. Deikman, wanted to go into private practice, which meant he could no long see patients at Riggs.

In a perfect example of how traditional psychotherapy

works, the impending separation from him triggered the hurt I'd felt at Grace's departure. Overwhelmed by the devastating memory of how I'd suspected she left because she didn't like me, I *projected*, as it is called in the world of therapy, the same thoughts toward my doctor.

Dr. Deikman told me his decision one month before the last time I saw him. My final four weeks with this wise, comical, kind, intuitive, and dynamic therapist were spent in stony silence, as opposed to the hours of vibrant and intense give-and-take we had shared about life and the traumatic changes I was going through. Convinced that he had never been fond of me during our close work together, I reverted to my withdrawn and emotionless self, incapable of articulating to him, and therefore being comforted by him, that I looked at his leaving as a betrayal of my trust.

It took months of work with my new therapist before I could verbalize any feelings to him. "Dr. Deikman must have really hated me," I said one day. On another, I added, "He lied to me to let me think I could count on him." Inside I confided to myself that this meant the new therapist, Dr. Trunell, *will go any minute, too, so I won't let myself get close to him!*

One Friday, my new doctor took one of his pens, a beautiful silver one, and asked if I would like to keep it on the weekend. "So you can be sure I will be back here on Monday," he added.

I couldn't believe what I'd heard. This doctor had seen into my mind and realized that I did not have the capacity for holding his image in my brain in a way that would give me belief in his return. This was my first glimpse into the fact that my ability to remember people had not developed properly in my childhood. At that time I didn't make the connection to what had happened to me in college with my friend, Jenny, but I do now. When we returned from Mexico, she had gone to a different dorm with friends of her own age because she had outgrown our relationship, but I hadn't had the ability to trust and remember her enough to create a changed and sustainable form of our close friendship.

Dr. Trunell didn't go to another job for two more years, and within the security of this dependable relationship, the lesson began to circulate in my brain: *When someone says he'll stay around, he means it, unless an accident of some kind interferes.*

My skillful doctor perceived my growing strength and interjected one day, "After all, by the way, Grace's leaving had nothing to do with you, you realize. Her boyfriend went to work for the Navy and she needed to go with him."

I sat there, speechless, a file in my brain turning over, a severe and life-hurting event from the past partially released. I had the proof of what Dr. Trunell said in a drawer in my room. In both of Grace's letters she had written, "Don't ever think I don't love you. I've always loved you." Yet I'd needed the long, therapeutic experience to feel it. A dependable ability to trust, considered in psychology as the most basic prerequisite for a grounded life, had reentered my emotional make up at twenty-five.

About this time, I painted a picture of a brawny tan-skinned young man, standing as strong as the tree he leaned against, an intense look coming from his boney sharp face and sparkling eyes that stared out of the canvas at the viewer. Anticipating my art teacher's recurring complaint to me concerning my bits of unfinished pictures on white canvasses, I dashed off a tennis court around the smart-looking fellow like the one down behind the treatment center, and put a racket in his firm hand.

Suddenly I took a second look. The man was Dr. Deikman, my first doctor, the one who had betrayed me by leaving. He was saying, loudly and clearly, as he looked out at me, the same silent message I'd received from him in that one year of working together: "I am a strong man and an honest one. Life is fun and

I'll help you to learn that, too, if you engage with me just as intently as I do with you in this thing called therapy."

Wow! I thought. *I love this man who had left me! I don't hate him after all, as I've been pretending because I thought he hated me!* This change meant that my former doctor's departure had become separate in my mind from the therapist himself, and that I had developed the ability to go on loving someone, even if that person left me.

"This doesn't mean you'll never have to say goodbye to anyone," Dr. Trunell said, when I told him the change in my thinking, "but you'll be able to survive the loss if it happens."

Besides confusion about my racial identity and difficulty with remembering people, the emotion of anger had been a problem for me. I had been reprimanded as a child for showing even annoyance at what was happening around me.

"Anger is not bad," my therapist told me. "It can be a good emotion when it's channeled into actions for a good cause."

Once I heard this, gates inside me flew open. I began to experience outbursts that I found difficult to control. One night I had a dream about a spot in my childhood backyard. Someone was saying, "There's a bomb buried there set to go off twenty years later." I didn't know what the dream meant because I didn't remember that I'd tried to bury the White part of myself at that spot when I was five. However, I did find a bomb's worth of rage in me when I finally allowed myself to engage with other patients.

At first I would flee to my bedroom whenever anyone angered me, but even in this safe place, I did not feel comfortable. I paced the wooden floor, walking along the edge of a large round braided rug, gazing into the corner of my left eye finally able to face my anger, as if my emotions had been located along the neural pathways of the suppressed eye.

Over time, I became comfortable with these feelings.

Through experiencing minor explosions without being punished for them, I learned that it was safe to feel rage and that it would not kill anyone. I had taken another step in my ability to stay connected with the world around me, even beginning to feel affection toward some of the other patients, capsules of misery and charm like me.

An overweight car salesman, who handled his unhappiness with joking, was a buddy of mine. I became close to a dark-haired slender girl from Philadelphia, whom I missed when she left after six months. There was a Jewish boy who built a beautiful and bountiful *sukkah* for us on the back lawn. Enjoying the oranges and reds of fall leaves and vegetables, Rob used to decorate the small structure many of us loved to go sit in, I began at this time to sense a strange emotion called joy.

In the Shop, I built a small wooden box of maple, staining it with care and putting on a gold lock for a small key. I kept this box and used it later to keep important cards, but back at Riggs, the box seemed to be a symbol for a time I'd once known that had been fun and engaging. It had to do with a kitchen, as if I could open up that lid and find a play going on in a small yellow-walled room that I found fascinating, like dramatic action on a stage. I could almost see two little girls dancing in a warm, tender, light.

Yet I didn't connect the glimpse of that cozy room with my deep love for Grace or remember the charming man, her boyfriend, for whom the little girls were dancing. At this point in my life, while building a psychological center inside me, the significance of this box meant only that there had been a time when living had been meaningful and good.

With this recognition of pleasure and satisfaction in my past came the fear that I would be considered well enough to leave Riggs, an ironic result of the Puritanical way I had been raised. I had absorbed the lesson of my parents' own childhoods, that having fun was not only suspect but financially dangerous. Riggs was expensive.

There was an annual conference, in which it was decided whether a patient had progressed enough to be discharged. At the end of my second year, I trembled before hearing the doctors' recommendation, but was relieved to hear that I needed "more time." I was extremely fortunate that the center gave me a scholarship so that I could stay on.

I am indebted to the teacher of an exercise class, Jayne Mooney, for my discovery of African dance. One day, she played music from Olatunji's *Drums of Passion*, and encouraged us to move in whatever ways we wanted. As we sensed the excitement of the rhythmic drumming, we stamped our feet, bent our knees out to the side, and assumed bodily positions that felt earthy and inelegant, giggling in our mock embarrassment. This bodily openness, somewhat like the plié of ballet, except directed into the ground rather than upward, felt freeing to me probably because I had grown up with the scolding mantra of "close your legs, close your knees, sit ladylike!"

In the town, I became a frequent visitor at the dress shops, buying several skirts of different colors for the different moods or parts of my personality. Away from the center, I went skiing with groups of patients, for the first time in my life able to love cold weather, its brightness and exhilarating air a delight instead of making me shiver with the fear that I might freeze to death. Every Sunday in off-season, we visited a ski lodge that offered chili and Dixieland jazz, and I realized that traveling for a distance away from the center was no longer a problem. I bought a car, bright red, like my spirit, which took me home for a weekend now and then. I joined a sewing class, learning from a great teacher not to be fussy with the small things like an uneven seam.

"Get on with it!" our teacher would say, "so you can see

45

right away what you can do!" I found that I could wear the beautiful skirt with its small orange flowers soon after I had cut the cloth, experiencing the joy of watching my dream become reality! In this way, our teacher brought her beginners to love sewing—even me, with the serious visual problem I developed while doing the close work that the class demanded.

As I looked at the needle coming out of the machine, my left eye began to hurt, and by the time I had succeeded in pushing my thread through the tiny hole, the pain had become unbearable. As with many physical responses I had to deal with for the first time during these catch-up years, I could hardly describe the situation to my therapist, but he suggested that I visit an optometrist in Pittsfield, who was working with children experiencing difficulties reading.

I don't remember wearing red and yellow tinted glasses for the exercises, but it is likely that the ball moving in a circular motion on a large wooden wheel was white. I realized years later by reporting that I saw the image of a yellow ball and a red one above it as well as to the side of it, I was showing the optometrist that my eyes were seeing two different images. But the optometrist did not explain to me what was going on with my eyes, probably because he was used to working with children. It is also likely that he did not realize, as I did not, that the emotional relaxation at Riggs had allowed an eye that had been repressed to start working again.

All I knew about this whole experience was the joy I felt from playing this circular visual game twice a week. My left eye clung to the yellow ball as if it were small golden sun symbolizing something long lost and very meaningful. I sensed that great changes were being made in my life, an increase in certainty, decision making, independence, and intelligence.

Several weeks into treatment I was able to start reading again for the first time since college, and I relished choosing my

46

books rather than following a reading list. Managing every bit of the small print in a paperback of Dr. Spock's book on childhood, I gained the confidence that I might someday have children and do well by them. At a nursery school run by the treatment center for its employees, I offered to help out a few mornings a week and loved it.

During a course on Erik Erikson's *Childhood and Society*, the brilliant study of how children's basic ideas are formed and affect the adult personality, given by a member of the staff at Riggs, I devoured its stimulating theories on the stages of childhood and adult life. Joyfully, I crossed off the levels I thought I'd finally passed through, not in my childhood, but during my therapy. Trust having been the most developed, I was pleased to sense that my stage of Industry was also strong. The ability to act with Autonomy and Independence needed the most work. I began to realize that my years of learning about life at Riggs, crowned now with the new joy of reading material connected to my life, was the college experience I had not been available to receive.

In spite of these great gains with reading, my parents stopped the visual work after two months. They claimed that my difficulty with details like threading needles or adding up numbers had not improved, and I could not disagree. Reading fast went fine, but focusing on small static objects was impossible for me without great discomfort. When driving and trying to read road signs, my eyes would handle the task with rapid alternation and become exhausted, ending up with the pain that had sent me into treatment.

Perhaps my frustration over my parents' decision, made for financial reasons, led me to get a part-time job. I worked as a receptionist in the Shop, my teacher and good friend, David, becoming my employer. This was a liberating experience. The building, where I'd passed the darkest and most depressed days of my young adulthood, became the bright light of my current life, with David as a business partner instead of as a teacher.

The check I received every week, showing the signature of the treatment center's office manager, Dalton, on it, gave me a satisfaction unlike anything I had felt before. The positive impression on me was so strong that the word "Dalton" became my mental reminder thirteen years later to rouse myself out of the all-engrossing, but sometimes boring, world of motherhood into the teaching of dance.

It was about this time that I received a surprising message from the assistant director of the center, a doctor whom my mother had once consulted as a therapist. He said that she had written a letter to him before undergoing an operation that she wanted to read to me, and that she preferred to do it at a place where we both felt removed from any aspects of our earlier relationship. Dr. Howard advised me to accept.

I took the drive to a country inn in a village halfway between Riggs and my mother's home. After lunch, she took me up to her bedroom and read me what she had written. At sixty, in anxiety from the fear that she might die in surgery, she had looked back over her life and seen that she had been a difficult mother. She apologized for being cross and unapproachable during times when my sisters and I had needed her for support.

I accepted her apology without understanding the importance of it. I had no memories of the physical harm she had caused me in my early childhood, even when I'd glanced at my father's five-year diaries from those years in the middle of the night when visiting my parents' home. The abbreviation *dep.* for depression, with my mother's initials above it, in the upper right hand corner of numerous four-line daily entries was the most interesting thing I discovered about my early years, except for the mention of a month when my mother had been in a mental hospital when I was two. I decided that the apology meant she would be less touchy and easier to get along with. I was right. She even became fun.

My first romantic attachment since my friendship with Carl at summer school years before helped increase my sense of change and delight during my last six months at Riggs. A patient named Ron, also struggling with learning how to handle feelings of love and attachment, was the first person I dated without feeling a need to keep myself at a physical distance. Though my romantic fling didn't last very long, it laid the groundwork for the dating I would start after leaving the center.

In the fall of 1963, my boyfriend ran across a wide leaf-strewn lawn to tell me that our president had been shot. I had become a Democrat, believing that people can sometimes need assistance from a source outside their own families and religious institutions. My resulting grief over President Kennedy's death made me realize that I was back in the *outside world*. I remember attending meetings of The National Committee for a Sane Nuclear Policy (SANE) in the town, pleased that I felt myself to be a responsible citizen just as much as the therapists who strode into our town hall alongside me.

During my last conference at the Medical Building, the doctors decided that I was ready to leave the center as soon as I could make plans. I felt delighted at finding a summer job as a counselor at a nearby camp that specialized in the dramatic arts.

Yet I cried from homesickness during a speech when I came back to the center at lunchtime one day, saying to those sitting in the dining room what a "wonderful place" Riggs was. The droopy faces of new patients looked up at me as if I had lost it, and in a sense they were right. Coming back to a place I had outgrown, when the excitement of a new one was calling me, seemed a little strange and showed the vestiges of my difficulties with separation and independence. But it was my way of acknowledging the debt I owed to this skillful institution for giving me a second chance at life.

I should have decided to work in the Dance Department at my summer camp as part of the commitment to campers' lives required of counselors beyond regular tent duties. I had chosen Theater, but sorting through props and costumes for dramatic productions did not interest me. I hung around the dance classes that were offered in an open-air studio as often I could manage. My one intriguing semester of study in the creative exercise class at Riggs had not been sufficient to help me state with confidence a preference for dance to the interviewing camp administrators.

This was one of my pitfalls as a late developer. Others in the *outside* world expected me to have established my main interests by the age of twenty-seven, yet I was just beginning to do so. It took me another year before I could formulate my intention to study and then teach dance, but I had a good time finding that out.

Chapter 3 – Living Again

After summer camp, I walked out of the Berkshire Hills, ready for the fun of play, the discipline of work, and the warmth of relationships. The change in me was tremendous. I don't think I could have achieved this level of transformation without being at Riggs, although, if I could have found a safe and supportive place to live while getting bi-weekly therapy for at least twice the number of years, perhaps I could have.

I had entered the center an empty and confused young woman. I knew intellectually that I had stopped feeling any emotion at five, yet I did not know how to use this knowledge to get my adult life going. I had spent my years at Riggs filling in that gap and developing a personality that felt genuine and whole. In short, I had received the chance to grow up.

I was fine now, according to the doctors at my final conference, no longer showing any signs of the emotional and psychological disarray they had seen on my arrival. Maybe I would need some serious therapy again after I had children, but for now, I was essentially finished.

Follow-up supportive therapy was recommended to ease my transition, and I did try one appointment. The excitement and tension of going back into the world had stopped my menstrual flow. My new doctor warned me that I was jeopardizing my chance to have children if I didn't deal with this psychosomatic disorder. Nevertheless, I left his office before the hour was over and skipped out into the sunshine, glad not to waste another minute with talking.

I found that underneath the part of me that had been a

serious and hard-working mental patient was a carefree and sensual self, bursting to be manifest. I found an outlet for this latent part of me in the large and comparatively relaxed city of middle-sixties Boston.

My parents helped me get set up in an apartment, my ability to receive their warmth and support being evidence of the therapeutic work accomplished at Riggs, as well as proof of changes in my parents themselves. I got a job in one of the department stores and took dance lessons in Broadway jazz two evenings a week. Losing the sales position because I was considered "too well educated"—by which the manager meant I asked too many questions—I decided to go to a simple form of secretarial school, where they taught an easy kind of short hand as well as typing. My parents offered to pay for it.

Unfortunately, we had forgotten about my eye's inability to focus on small objects. I spent many painful minutes each hour in the bathroom trying to rub the spasms out of my left eye. Running helped me relax, and I ran to and from class as if I had been the city's first jogger.

My most fun time was going square dancing. Some of us made mistakes and tried desperately to catch up to the caller and to others who had not slipped up. In this nearly impossible effort, we were hobbled by our laughter, which we couldn't control. I didn't remember ever having laughed like this, doubling over with spasms of shaking that made my belly ache, causing great relief, joy, and wonderful deep breathing afterward. Fortunately, for my developing sense of balance in life, this lightness and sense of fun became a new ingredient of my life.

Later on, in Europe, my son would join me in the fun of making mistakes, as I struggled with my Dutch and he with his English. At seven, he walked into the house and said he'd left his bike in the vegetable instead of vestibule. We giggled together, often referring afterwards to this fun moment with language. At another time in my Dutch town, an American friend and I, exhausted in the middle of a day's preparation for that evening's Thanksgiving dinner for eighty people, turned ourselves upside down with feet in the air for our break. Later we roared at ourselves for how we must have looked.

In Boston, I lived in a comfortable residence, a modern YWCA building, where dinner was provided. Joining the Unitarian church, famous for its Sunday suppers and trips, I met Nick, a good-looking man of thirty-six and a wonderful dancer.

I temporarily set aside my evening study of dance, as it hadn't been what I was looking for. Training with seventeen-year-olds for spot parts we hoped to get in musical shows was neither what suited me, nor what my twenty-seven-year-old, untrained body felt like doing. I didn't take my failure to heart, however. My evening hours were filled with the thrill of dancing in nightclubs with my new friend. The music of a current hit, "Downtown," ran through my mind all day while at my secretarial school.

Nick was unemployed, living on money from his mother, but I didn't pay attention to that. I was swept up in the joy of my relationship. He introduced me to sex, his version being the kind for a man who doesn't want complications. We didn't have intercourse. The first time he did his oral technique on me, I came many times, as if I were relieving a lifetime of sexual frustration. We were both amazed at the electricity he was able to create in my body, and we counted my orgasms with pride.

Nick introduced me to nudist camps, an exciting idea but boring in reality because of the unattractive bodies we had to look at. The sensation of the sun tanning all of our skin was a delight, however, and the relaxation of living "as nature intended" became addictive. The owners of the camp were friendly, with a kind of missionary zeal.

After five months, I realized that I was in love and edgy with the idea that my companion hadn't mentioned anything about the future. One day he bought a cheap engagement ring for me. I was delighted, though disappointed that he'd not spent more and skeptical about his level of commitment. In anticipation of problems, Nick took me to a favorite counselor of his, a Mr. Dearborn.

The kind, soft-spoken elderly man told me in a German accent that I was about thirty on Nick's list of interested women, one at a time, he assured me. He said that because my friend was still strongly attached to his mother, he would never allow himself to get involved in a serious and committed relationship. However, it would be a good idea if I went for a diaphragm fitting just in case our sexual relationship changed. So I did.

A knowledgeable woman pressed me gently every week to stretch the hymen and then joyfully inserted the custom-sized diaphragm into my pristine vagina. And it would stay pristine. Nick would have no changes. It began to occur to me that maybe Mr. Dearborn was right about Nick's inability to have a serious relationship.

Appointments between my parents and Mr. Dearborn to try to figure out what was going on with me may have helped them as much as my sessions with him. They both seemed delighted afterwards. Mr. Dearborn taught all of his counselees that masturbation was the answer to mental problems. If I had pleasured myself as a teenager, my parents never would have had to pay thousands of dollars for treatment at Riggs. Rather than rubbing my eye in the secretarial school bathroom, I should have been rubbing my clitoris and getting better relief. "How great it is to have this simple answer to everything," I thought, and I would use Mr. Dearborn's magic for any problem that came up.

But the time had come for a change, not the least reason

being that I'd been kicked out of the residence because of my messy room. I told Nick and Mr. Dearborn goodbye and went home to my parents' house. It was hard to do this and give up fantasies about my fiancé, as I had thought he would be, but I had no choice.

My parents were very helpful, calling on their friends for advice. Knowing of my interest in dance, one neighbor suggested the study of Labanotation, the small diagrams and stylized figures with which a choreographer notates her dance. He didn't know about my eyes.

I signed up with the Arthur Murray dance program for teachers, or rather, I brought the registration papers home, but my lawyer-father told me "No." There was something in those papers that said I wouldn't be able to teach dance in my own studio later. I followed the advice of another parental friend to do summer volunteer work in the *developments*, which meant the poor section of town.

This amounted to helping two ten-year-olds with math. They were shy, blond-haired, brown-skinned identical twin boys whose mother had just died. Each had a runny nose every day that summer. "Oh, just an allergy," I was told by the staff, but I knew that the constant sniffling was from hidden grief, and I tried to be gentle with them.

In the afternoons, I assisted a group of African-American girls with their work on a dance program, which meant that I unlocked a classroom door, turned the lights on, helped move chairs away, and plugged in the phonograph. Then I sat and watched as the thirteen-year-olds scrambled, argued, cavorted and shimmied through the next six weeks. When they were finished, they had created an exciting group of dances for our end-of-summer show, entirely without my input.

By that time, I knew exactly what I wanted to do with my life. I wanted to learn to dance just like those girls and then to teach it to others like me who had grown up stiff and unfeeling. The freedom with which these girls moved, the ease they had with their bodies, and their joyful spirit reminded me of the class at Riggs that I had loved and where I had first heard the sound of African rhythms.

But I couldn't find the kind of dance teacher from whom I would learn to relax and dance in the sensual ways I had seen. No one I knew moved this way. I didn't realize for another thirty years that there was a school in my hometown attended by mostly Black students, in which I would have found many of the African moves and rhythms I had loved at Riggs. At fifty-eight I discovered the school, having been attracted by a recital notice. While attending the students' annual performance, as one out of four White people in an audience of four hundred, I wondered why all my dance-lover friends had missed such a fabulous show.

At twenty-eight, I settled for a modern class in the Martha Graham style, taught by a Haitian woman who used the sound of Bongo drums for her musical accompaniment. Two dark brown Caribbean men at the head of the room produced the syncopated sound that satisfied me.

My teacher made it very clear that I didn't work hard enough. Her sharp comments were a rough way for me to begin my path toward dancing like those relaxed and vivacious girls whom I'd watched in the summer, but I stayed with the class. Even though the technique required great self-discipline, I found excitement and passion in learning to dance in this strict modern dance style.

Martha Graham had wanted to separate her technique from earlier forms of American and European dance in order to create more viscerally intense choreography. I was told by my Haitian teacher that Graham took the static positions of Yoga and added the dynamism of transitional movements between postures to create a warm-up technique that would build the strength needed for her choreography. These exercises to work the abdominal muscles, practiced while seated on the ground in what is called the *tailor* position in modern dance, had become the basis for her work.

My torso felt drawn inwards to my backbone as I sat with my legs crossed, my back curved and head slightly bent, my lungs emptied of air and my lower abdomen pulled into a tight contraction. The core muscles then worked to straighten the curve of my back like a grinding wave upwards, reaching from my abdomen to chest, spine, shoulders, until my back was perfectly straight, my neck and upper spine stretching up and then slightly backward. The enormous amount of air that entered my lungs during this progression, allowed me to hold the final open position with arms stretched to the side an amazing length of time. Then, at the crack of the drum, or my teacher's voice, tightness in my abdomen would start the pull of the torso back downwards to the original contracted curve.

The strength in my core, developed by weekly repetitions of this exercise, allowed me the power to straighten a leg and extend it from a sitting position into a forward diagonal up into the air and hold it suspended, while, in breaking with the harmonious balance of ballet, my opposing arm reached backwards in extension. This move demanded a grueling twist in my torso before a return to the tailor position, the muscles gearing themselves for a rise toward the other diagonal. We repeated these moves to the drum rhythms at an increasingly fast pace until we felt we would fly off the ground.

The tightening of the core muscles necessary for this powerful move came to be called the Martha Graham *contraction* and the torso's twist was labeled her *spiral*. I didn't care what the movements were called. I cared that they gave me power, they allowed me to express the oppositions within me, and they allowed for the dynamic and passionate moves, both slow and fast, that Graham's choreography demanded of me, once we danced out on the floor.

The technique also created relief for my eyes, which had been stressed by my increased need to focus on the small details of print in job applications, newspapers, and announcements about city life. The Graham classes, especially the warm up technique, seemed to take away the pain in my left eye. I came to depend on dance for creating in me physical, emotional, artistic, and now visual relief.

At this point, I began attending the International Center in our town where foreign students gathered. Instead of a man from another country, however, the person who attracted me was an American, a Black resident of my city.

I loved dancing with Jason and spent one of the best evenings in my life at a club where a dancer entertained us, twisting and turning while striking his flashing tambourine. I found the beauty and speed with which the tall, dark, and coordinated man twirled and tossed his instrument dazzling. Just for those evenings, I wanted to continue the relationship with my new friend, but I didn't because I felt it had no future.

My parents helped me get a job as a receptionist. I went to live in a summer house with a great view, sharing it for the winter with other working girls. This residence had a large empty and gleaming wooden floor for a living room, which we were not supposed to use. I dreamt for years about dancing on this floor until the day I bought a house that contained a similar gem.

For now, I would just look and yearn, as I took myself off to my job at the insurance company. Again, I had forgotten my eye problem, and the pain from doing detailed paperwork, assigned to me as a receptionist with plenty of free time, sent me to the cellar during coffee breaks to dance out my agony.

One day, in October of 1965, while walking past a record store, I heard music similar to what the girls in the summer program had played. Glancing at the *Help Wanted* sign in the window, I went inside, and once hearing the sounds, I knew this was where I wanted to work, getting to know the kinds of songs I would use for my classes. The music was early Motown, something that didn't seem to be played on my radio stations or by the girls I lived with or by anyone I knew. I was certain that if I didn't work in that store, I wouldn't be able to find out about the music for the teaching I wanted to do.

However, I'd made an appointment for job counseling with Dr. Stein, a psychologist from Riggs who was practicing nearby, having told him that I didn't seem to know what I was doing, or where I was going. I almost canceled the appointment, feeling so joyful at seeing the serendipitous Help Wanted sign still hanging in the window the day of the appointment. But in the end I went, only to make sure he agreed with my decision. To my great disappointment, his help turned out to be advice that I should go back to college and finish up my work for the Bachelor of Arts in English Literature I had walked away from.

"But the job," I said. "The music is so perfect for me, as a preparation for teaching dance." I knew he would discard my ideas if I claimed, at my age, to be preparing for a career in *performing* dance. But even my idea about learning what music I'd need for teaching seemed silly to him.

My counselor continued. "In this world you need papers for whatever you do, and, anyway, a college campus is a great place to find a husband."

He won.

A month later, I found myself accepted at a state university starting in January. I still had my doubts, standing in line with my registration papers, since I'd spent the last few weeks looking through lists in library manuals of colleges that offered dance majors. Almost walking away from the registration line while thinking about the Department of Performing Arts at Washington University in St. Louis, I remembered that my parents had already spent that kind of money. My unusual choice of that school may have come from a skewed understanding of my Haitian teacher's information that a Black dancer, Katherine Dunham, from New York City, was making efforts to open a dance school in East St. Louis.

At the university I hunkered down to *Psychology 1, Modern American Literature* and various other courses, all of which I grew to love. However, the only way I managed the reading of my textbooks without pain, was standing up and resting my book on the top of a bookcase while shifting my weight in a kind of treading motion. The habit I developed of standing on my right leg and rubbing its shin with the left foot caused such an irritation to the bone that it chipped and had to be repaired after college by minor surgery. Every morning I sat on the floor of my dorm room and went through the warm up I had learned in the Graham class. These practices, I now believe, were an unconscious effort to stimulate and therefore strengthen my left eye through activating the left side of my body. Whatever the reason, I had no eye pain for this entire semester at college.

Restlessness with this life of study took me to the gym in the evenings where dance classes were offered, though I don't remember them very well, because I became distracted by meeting Zach, the man I would marry six months later.

The first time I saw my future husband, the dark-haired assistant professor was sitting in the town's Greek restaurant looking with eagerness at a large birthday cake that his companions had placed before him. My girlfriend and I were standing at the cashier waiting to pay after enjoying our thin-crust pizza. I stopped to watch as Zach took a big breath to blow out the candles.

I saw a rosy-cheeked fellow, his wide face flushed and glistening in the light of the flames, someone engaged in life and loved by his friends. Intrigued by the brainy-looking man before me, his high forehead gleaming under the restaurant lighting, and attracted by the casual manner in which he sat with his winter jacket open and showing a stocky chest—as well as the passion with which he attacked his piece of cake—I asked my friend Sophie about him.

She'd been watching the trim-looking student sitting next to Zach and said, in surprise and disapproval, "Oh, Zach, he's their professor and almost ten years older than you." Amazed that she hadn't agreed with me, I made a note to watch out for the interesting fellow myself.

Zach stood out in the crowd at a discussion following the university's weekly showing of art films. I was impressed with him because he asked questions that challenged the opinion of the evening's organizer. I asked the girlfriend I was with, a different and older one, to introduce me.

On our first date, Zach brought flowers from the woods around campus, aware that he had bucked the customary practice of buying flowers and sharing with me the thought that he had not quite done the right thing. This was typical of the volatile man, I would find out, someone who could alternate between daring and adventurous behavior and insecurity as to whether his differences would let him fit in. I only knew that I was attracted to someone who did things his own way. I was also impressed that as a scientist he had studied botany and could give the Latin name for each flower he had picked.

Zach's most important characteristic for me was his honesty. I had the sense that he was real. Having lived my life with a father who hid his feelings, I was impressed by anyone who spoke his own mind without hesitation. In some ways Zach appeared to represent the very opposite of the culture in which I had been raised.

He was a Democrat and a strong one, only recently switched from connections to the Socialist Party. My father was a strict Republican. Zach's preference for spicy foods contrasted to the bland diet I had grown up with, and his Jewish outspoken nature, sometimes verging on rudeness in social settings, made a contrast to my father's over-attention to correctness and polite behavior when with his peers.

These differences gave me a sense of freedom and adventure. I suspect also that deep down the love I'd felt for my brown mother and her boyfriend Joe influenced me to choose a mate outside of the Anglo-Saxon gene pool of my birth parents.

Zach combined many of the characteristics of the doctors I had loved. His older age made me feel safe, as I had with Dr. Bennett. I found his strong and chunky body comforting in a huggable way, as Dr. Smith's had been. He was Jewish and dynamic like Dr. Deikman and felt stable to me in terms of loyalty like Dr. Trunnell.

Having been in therapy for five years after a divorce, Zach had become insightful and supportive to others who had emotional issues, and this sensitivity reminded me of Ron, the young man I'd loved at Riggs. Highly educated in his scientific field and self-taught in the arts, Zach stimulated me intellectually and artistically. He had a good job, which meant that I felt financially secure thinking about him as a future mate—the need for safety a driving force for me.

Even with all of my positive feelings, I found it difficult to accept Zach's proposal of marriage three months later. Something inside warned me against setting up a household paralleling the one I'd lived in as a child.

"I'll *engage* you, rather than marry you," I told him, and soon I became more eager than he to start living together. We drove all the way to New York City, where we looked at rings in a Greenwich Village jewelry shop. I didn't want a diamond like the one my mother wore. I loved color and picked out a turquoise blue beauty called a black opal, an iridescent stone laid on top of a black base. I stood transfixed by the ring's similarity to the color of my sister Susan's eyes. In many ways Zach reminded me of her.

My fiancé had a conservative side to his liberal personality. He made me wait until after our wedding in the fall to live together, even though I spent every weekend with him. I was thrilled to have finally found someone who was ready for a full expression of sexual loving.

Dance fought back for my attention that summer. I attended the American Dance Festival at Connecticut College, studying the Graham technique again as well as the more relaxed style of José Limón, based on the work of Doris Humphrey. On several Saturdays, Zach drove all the way to the campus and sneaked into the dorm so that he could spend the night with me in my single bed, leaving me blurry eyed for the next day of classes.

In September, my mother and I went shopping together and found a sleeveless lime-green dress with a coat to match for my simple wedding, which was to be in my parents' house. She and I drove into the country to a farmhouse to pick up the wedding cake I had ordered, made with fresh ingredients and layered with the fruit of strawberries mixed with real whipped cream, stabilized with a small amount of gelatin to hold the shape.

We invited Grace, who lived in the next town. My sister, Susan, came from Florida and took a beautiful and tender picture of me looking into Grace's eyes, which she later made into a 5" x 7" photo. My mother gave me a triple frame of wedding pictures, including this one of Grace and me, but she had cut the brown woman out of the picture, the person for whom my intense and caring look was now gazing out of the frame. I didn't complain, confused about how truthful I wanted to be with her about Grace's meaning for me.

Married life didn't diminish my need to dance, and in spite of the long distance I would have to drive, I joined a class taught by a former member of José Limón's dance company, Dorothea Buchholz. Like her teacher, she based her technique on the Doris Humphrey method of fall and recovery to achieve the excitement and flow in dance movement. As a student who had come to dance at the late age of twenty-eight, I benefited from this method, with its large and flowing movements that were gentler on my body than the Graham technique had been.

But I found that I missed the syncopation of the Haitian drums. The sound of even beats, simple melodies, and props such as scarves were used as the inspiration for the students' dancing. I bought rhythmic records to take with me for my volunteer work teaching dance at Head Start.

My baby, who emerged from this period of continual exposure to movement and rhythmic sounds, was a beautiful little girl we named Sarah, so eager for every moment of life that afternoon naps were quick affairs. She would become a dancer also, and political, as her mother and father were. Walking from door to door in my precinct while pregnant, and speaking out against the Vietnam War, I had watched and experienced the change in my neighbors from rejection to acceptance of my message that we needed to have a president who would end the fighting.

Our side lost, however, and one of the first things the new president did was cut university research grants for science. Zach lost his job, exactly three years after our marriage. This was my first experience at witnessing the black moods that could descend on my new husband. Hurt that the professor he had worked closely with for a long time was not able to rectify his financial situation, Zach moped. Then, at a party in Washington, he met a Dutch professor who offered him a job doing research at one of the large state universities in The Netherlands. We were thrilled at the choice of our new country, as we had heard it was a wonderful place to raise children.

I stood on the deck of the Holland America Line's *SS Statendam* on a clear September morning, holding my small daughter tight but high in my arms so that she could wave goodbye to her grandparents. I was glad to be leaving the United States. I had not been happy to see our president continue the war I had marched against. I was sad to be leaving my dance teacher, but I had been assured by one of her former students who happened to be Dutch that I would enjoy the same kinds of classes in her country, as long as I first studied the language.

Living felt good to me. I'd been out of Riggs for five years and most of it had gone well. Zach and I had surmounted many of our differences, some of them having to do with food. He hadn't liked my cooking, but a month-long camping trip across the country, in which he'd shared the shopping and preparation of each meal on the National Park system's stoves, had brought him around.

The only downside of my life had been that the eye pain had increased to the bothersome level I had known at Riggs. Now, not only small signs or figures in my check book gave me problems, but also reading in general.

I should have looked for a practitioner who did the fun and satisfying wheel-and-ball games that had improved my vision in Pittsfield, but I hardly remembered my eight-week training and didn't know what such a practitioner was called. None of the eye doctors I consulted directed me into the area of visual training, the rift between traditional and new branches of optometry as wide as the one I was finding at this time between ballet and modern in the dance world.

Perhaps I was influenced in my lack of effort to find a solution by the conversation I had with an optometrist whom my parents had found for me when I left Boston. "What's a little pain?" this optometrist, whose son had just been killed in Vietnam, asked me?

Sure, I had thought. *What's a little pain?*

Yet it could become huge. And it could be worsened by disappointment, my left eye blocking its use if I felt hurt—the rigidity in its muscles causing the pain to grow. On one of my honeymoon days while traveling on Cape Cod, when Zach wanted to spend the afternoon at the beach reading in the September sun instead of returning to our motel after lunch, I felt surprised and disappointed. I tried to join him with a book, but this caused my left eye to act up. Once started, the lacerating ache did not leave, only mitigated hours later by a return to the room where we napped and followed our rest with the love-making I had wanted and felt cheated of.

I didn't mention my eye problem to my husband, thrilled as I was with everything else in my life. I just stopped reading, and if I had to check a train schedule or sew a hem, I ignored the pain in the same way that I dashed over any unexpected reminder of my time at Riggs.

I had rarely needed to refer to my time at the center to anyone, and I had tucked my memories safely away, not only because of society's stigma about mental illness, but also because I didn't want to think about those years—or the painful ones that had preceded them

My life was basically wonderful, including my certainty that getting away from the country of my birth was going to bring me even more joy, which it did.

Chapter 4 – The Netherlands

I fell in love with our new country, delighting at seeing my favorite color, orange, everywhere. It shouted at me with cheer from the clay ceramic roof tiles, stunning against an occasional blue sky, and from wet cobblestones shining in the sun, or among bunches of flowers bursting with fresh colors from the ubiquitous street-vendor stalls.

My husband and I took pleasure in discovering our new lives together, taking excursions both within the country and out into the rest of Europe. On Zach's trips to scientific meetings, I often accompanied him. We enjoyed a particularly nice trip to Zürich, where his boss treated forty of us to a splendid dinner following a beautiful boat ride. Afterwards, Zach and I roamed through Paris for a week, never taking a cab or tram and eating in whatever small restaurant attracted us.

Back in The Netherlands we sat side by side in language classes, learning about the surprising differences between Dutch culture and our own. We were told to use last names and the formal *U* when meeting a Dutch person, until given permission to switch to the informal *jij or je.*

I remember the first time I felt comfortable with this social custom. I stood at a cocktail party, given by my husband's department, and munched on pieces of my favorite cheese, the slightly aged Gouda, while enjoying the red wine served with it—hard liquor was not usually served at these get-togethers—and chatting. In the middle of a fast and fascinating conversation in Dutch, I felt the urge to drop the formal *U.*

"May I use *jij*?" I slipped the necessary request into the

next point I was making.

"Oh, naturally." The Dutchman waved away my hesitation without losing a beat in our conversation. I felt pleased with myself and well on my way to becoming Dutch, my dream of emigrating from America beginning to take a strong hold on my mind.

Zach and I fought sand storms in the village by the North Sea, near our first rental house, and enjoyed a year of Sundays without cars, the government having declared that one day a week should be free of gasoline use. We walked the beaches near our home, took trams around Amsterdam with our three-year-old Sarah in tow, or I explored the city by myself. The train ride took less than thirty minutes to switch my windowed landscape from endless pastureland and grazing cows to a bustling city. As I stepped from the huge station's interior, I was greeted by crowds of travelers mingling among colorful kiosks of fresh flowers, including my favorites—sweet-smelling freesias, as yellow as sunlight.

I loved wandering along the narrow canals and varied streets, crossing over stone bridges and seeing parked bikes everywhere. In spring or summer, trees heavy with green made shimmering reflections in the water. In the winter, I'd step into a café on a quiet side street to warm up. Because Amsterdam is a city of low buildings, whatever sunshine and light emerged from an often-gray sky would find its way to accompany me.

I relished the Dutch emphasis on family life, tradition, and community rituals, amazed to walk down the street of my small town and know what month it was according to the kinds of freshly baked cookies I saw in the bakery windows. Halfway through a cold and rain-filled November, I noticed the appearance of *Speculaas*, a body-warming, thin, brown spice cookie. Then in December, large chocolate letters appeared, one for the beginning of every child's name, to be given as presents for *Sinterklaas*, a holiday of gift-giving and clever rhyme-making.

Apple *taartjes* were the exception to this rotation, these one-crust pies appearing year round. The Dutch cooking-apple, with its rich, sour/sweet taste and dense texture, was the fruit of choice, except for a few months in the late spring when strawberries competed with it on bakery shelves. In the summer I could find—if I were lucky—raspberry, cherry, blueberry, peach, pear, even bright red current pastries in small neighborhood bakeries, freshly baked that morning, along with the many different shapes, sizes, and mixtures of white and whole wheat breads. I'd bask in line with the other customers, mesmerized by the shop's tantalizing aromas and hardly able to choose which delectable items to take home.

Our second child, Kenny, was born in The Netherlands, a wonderful and easy experience for me, though it was more difficult for him. I had read a book the night before that was too exciting for the period of pre-labor; I remember the minute when I caught my breath at a scary incident and lost my waters. My baby was two weeks early and extremely sleepy, as if he could have used longer time *in utero*. But he slipped easily out of me an hour after we arrived at the hospital. Because I had developed anemia after my first baby, my Dutch insurance covered ten days of inpatient care. Kenny was brought to me on a schedule that my breast milk responded to lavishly. The free assistance of a part-time home helper when I left the hospital ensured I would conclude that Holland was indeed the place to have children!

I enjoyed bringing up my youngsters in a country where a great emphasis was placed on domestic life and good times for families. This was often provided by fun-filled national and local holidays, such as the Queen's Birthday. I liked the country's sensible and caring attitude toward raising children, an example of the common sense I had found and appreciated in other areas in The Netherlands. I was delighted when, at the North Sea beach near us, I saw toddlers run around completely bare, their limbs and bodies brushed by the wind and sun and easily washed off at the end of the day by a dunk in the sea.

The public schools my children attended were excellent, and within walking distance from our semi-suburban home. I watched our youngsters develop independence as they went off by themselves every morning, traipsing along our neighborhood's small and safe sidewalks.

The government's position that economic success depended on its citizens' feelings of well-being and trust in social fairness made sense to me. The Dutch are a good business people, the country noted for running one of the most successful economies in Europe at the beginning of the European Economic Community's formation. The Dutch economic system, often called socialist by Americans, is, on the contrary, capitalism, but capitalism with a heart.

The country is modern, at least in its heavily-populated Randstad, the name for the crescent shaped chain of many cities and towns including Amsterdam, The Hague, Rotterdam, and Utrecht. Yet, being an agricultural country, The Netherlands still retained the slower rhythms of country living when I arrived. It was being said at the time we left America that whatever happens in the world comes twenty-five years later to The Netherlands.

"You're lucky," our friends joked when they heard that description of our new country before we left in September 1969. "That means the bomb will get to you later!"

In the Dutch culture, where the domestic work of women has traditionally been treated with honor and respect, the Women's Liberation Movement, in the sense of encouragement for wives and mothers to have a career outside the home and family-run store, had not arrived when I settled into my Dutch life. I was relieved. I was happy to go backwards in time, having felt pressured in the States by the hype of other women to begin a career.

I had recognized that I couldn't go further in academia or business, not only because of my visual handicap that had developed in my twenties, but also because I did not want to. I preferred being at home for a while with my two young children. I enjoyed seeing my toddler-son playing with other preschoolers along the sidewalks of my Dutch suburb, while his sister attended *Kleuterskool,* or in the living rooms of women like me, who were not away at work and able to meet for coffee and friendship.

After a few years, however, a part of me felt restless with the emphasis on domestic life and tradition in my new country. I decided that I didn't want to have a third child as my mother had. She'd never seemed a happy woman until she began to paint at age fifty. I was determined to avoid her depressions and start my own artistic endeavors sooner. I had put off my dream of studying dance because of my second pregnancy and the remarks of a Dutch acquaintance I met before leaving the States who said that I should learn the language first. After a year of studying Dutch and seeing that our toddler, Kenny, seemed happy and well adjusted, I felt it was time to get back to studying and working in the field I had chosen in America.

I read about a class called *Soul Dance* in the university paper. Though I felt nervous, never having heard the expression, I went to check it out, but my surprise became even greater at hearing my instructor's greeting: "Good evening, ladies and gentlemen." Realizing that I'd missed a year of studying with this tall, good looking Black dancer from America, I regretted that I hadn't trusted my instinct to go ahead and find a class, Dutch language or not.

On the other hand, I recognized my luck at finding Felix White. It is strange that I'd needed to travel to Europe in order to find a class that used the drum and jazz-based rhythms and movements I'd been looking for. When I'd searched the yellow pages in the States, I'd found listings for ballet and modern, whereas, in The Netherlands, comparable entries included ballet and jazz. Just as Black jazz musicians had come to Europe in the twenties to be appreciated, Black dancers followed Katherine Dunham's successful journeys across the ocean to find eager audiences and students in London, Paris, and Amsterdam. Felix, a long time student of Dunham in New York City, was one of these.

"Feel!" he shouted out to us during my first class in the large second floor loft of the university's recreation hall.

The students stopped wondering if they had locked their bikes well enough against the ubiquitous bike thieves. I tried to control my own thoughts—would my husband remember to warm up the children's dinner slowly, and would he read to them with expression, in spite of having come home exhausted?

"Feel your bodies!" Felix's tenor voice carried out over the music of Barry White, as we began his opening section with movements not unlike yoga's *Salutation to the Sun* put to tempo. My limbs lengthened and my lungs spread themselves wide from the stretching and reaching. My mind quieted and became a tool of awareness and attention to sensation. The rhythmic flow and speed of our simple warm-up combination, based on the Lindy steps of Swing, charged my muscles and swung me into action.

"Can I call your class jazz?" I asked Felix one day. I'd found that the ballet *barre* routine reminded me of my modern classes in America, yet his choreography provided the flare, syncopation, and surprise of a jazz class.

"No," he answered. "Jazz classes prepare people for

Broadway numbers and emphasize the legs and feet. I work the chest and shoulder area."

And work that part of us he did! The force of deep contractions between my shoulders and pelvis made it possible for me to do double turns that stunned me as I whipped around to the syncopated beat that had stimulated them.

Later, when I knew Felix better, I said, "Those contractions are like Graham."

"You're wrong," he said. "They're African."

Yet, soon after this conversation, a teacher from the Martha Graham studio, visiting from America, came to give us a master class. I would learn the reason for Felix's answers to me. Just as his teacher Katherine Dunham, in New York, had done before him, my teacher wove African moves into his modern classes so skillfully that to name his style, you had to either mention four techniques—modern, African, jazz, and soul—or just say "Dunham."

However my classes with Felix should be called, they were perfect for my development as a dancer and as a human being. I'd spent much of my life pursuing intellectual goals and putting more emphasis on my mind than on my body. Now, as I watched Felix demonstrate his choreography to music, rather than describe it in words, as many dance teachers do in a silent studio, I learned to relax and *feel* rather than figure out his choreography. The dynamism of African movements, involving the contrasting directions of arms and legs, twists of the torso, and sudden changes in the diagonal line of the choreography requiring changes in the direction of the dancer's gaze, reminded me of the excitement I'd found in the Graham technique I had studied back in America, and had the same beneficial effect on my vision.

One day, Felix used the song "Natural High" from the movie *Superfly* in one of his classes. During the end-of-class choreography, as I whirled by my teacher's friends who had shown up to watch, and saw the delight of visceral excitement on their faces, I thought to myself, *Yes, this is my natural high!*

I felt massaged and toned after class. Later I tried to do the same thing in my own teaching, beginning my classes in the same gradual manner and ending them with a flourish. My American friend, Ellen, who had attended modern classes with me in the States, and then gone on to do massage for her life work, asked me when I visited her, "Why don't you let me give a massage? You'll never feel anything so good."

"Come to one of my classes and you'll feel the same thing," I answered her back.

A warm bond developed between my teacher and me, sparked by references to the United States when I walked into class, and jokes about our country no one else could understand. The forty-year-old, sitting on a stool to wait and welcome his students, would slap his thighs and put his head back, his teeth shining as he laughed if I'd made an insight that worked for him. We would clap our palms together or hug and I'd go change for class. Sometimes, in an afternoon session, my six-year-old daughter Sarah would come with me and be entertained upstairs by Felix's kind and gentle White partner.

My teacher taught all ages. The children who came in the afternoon to his studio didn't talk in class. They had to concentrate on their mentor's strange combination of Dutch and English, as he praised or corrected them with his hands-on reshaping of their limbs. Those boys and girls knew that the long brown fingers on their white arms or ankles would transform them from gangling lumps into strong and controlled bodies of intention and purpose.

The mothers attended classes in the evening, relieved to leave the dinner dishes for their husbands. I joined them during my second year of study, giving myself another class each week at Felix's studio near Amsterdam. With delighted eyes, we watched ourselves transformed in the mirrors, the heavy bone structure of my Dutch friends made graceful, and, in the combinations, sexy. We fought for technique and steps, moved by the beauty of our teacher as he demonstrated the choreography tens of times for his struggling adult students.

"You have to feel that every movement you make is a dance," Felix reminded us, explaining why he taught his combinations to music rather than through words or silent demonstration. A path was well worn back to the phonograph, as our perspiring teacher reset the needle to coordinate with the piece of choreography that needed work. Then he would start the music from the beginning, so that by the time the sticky place came, an abundance of dramatic energy had built up that would push us through our cautious over-thinking into moments of glorious flow.

Over time, my body became one of strength and balance, transformed by my teacher's disciplined training. After three years, I turned my struggle with his fast combinations in the last third of class into skillful moves and exhilarated liberation.

On Saturday afternoons Felix taught classes for his advanced students, most of them in their twenties, many dark and agile, from the Dutch islands of Curaçao and Aruba. These young men and women were getting ready for performances. In my fourth year, while taking four classes a week, including one from a small French woman who taught classical ballet, I reached this high point. The level was too difficult for me, however; the speed of the turns, leaps, and "falls" to the floor, as well as the lack of time for me to memorize the steps, were too much of a challenge. I would return home to my family exhausted and glad for another part of my life that was not so demanding.

In December of 1974, Zach and I found the perfect house. It was not only near his laboratory so that he could walk to his job, but it also contained a long wooden-floored room for a living room, a shining gem similar to the one I'd dreamt about ever since staying at the shoreline summer house back in America while working for the insurance company.

"This can be my studio!" I declared, transformed from the uninterested person I had been in the real estate office. We stood side by side at the southwestern window, both intrigued by this thought—we had spent months looking for a house that could include a studio—and struck a compromise to make the long expanse half studio and half living room.

The three-story dark-red brick building, covered with green vines and attached on either side to our neighbors' dwellings, stood at a convenient ten minutes by bike from downtown and on a busy road. Yet the long back garden exuded peace, protected from noise by the great height of our house and made private by its tall wooden fences on either side, one of them covered with dark red rambling roses.

Each morning Zach's walk to work took him through pastureland, where he could have conversed with the cows if he'd wanted to. But this would have interfered with his listening, through large earphones my parents had sent him, to news and music received on three BBC radio stations. Zach adored all programs from England, including those on television, and when I was not at my dance classes, I joined him in the evening to share the pleasure of several excellent year-long series—hour-long dramas without commercials—that held our interest week after week. Zach never missed an episode of *The Brothers*, or, in Dutch, *De Gebroeders Hammond. Are You Being Served?* delighted us at an early hour on Saturday evenings.

Once we were settled and I began to use my new studio, I

realized how much I'd longed for it. At any time, day or night, I could go into the large first floor room with its high ceiling, and use my dance technique for a work out, playing either jazz or classical music. The bookcase that separated my practice area from our living room served as my ballet *barre*. I learned to listen to my body in order to know if I was doing the technique organically, as Felix had taught us; that is, if my legs, hips, arms, and ribs were comfortable with every movement at each stage of the increasing level of demand I was asking from them.

From someone who had neglected her body for much of her life, I became a person who attended to it. I used Felix's Dunham-style *barre* series for lengthening my muscles through a continuous flow from one position to another, my arms and legs stretched kinetically instead of statically. I grew strong with this daily practice, my body-shape changing. One day I looked in the mirror and saw a broadening in my formerly skinny hips, a stage my body hadn't seemed to have gone through in puberty.

"My body has grown up," I said to myself.

Occasionally I branched out into movements other than *barre* work, my limbs feeling beautiful as I pretended to be the ballerina in *Coppelia*, or expressed dramatic tension when I became one of the characters in *Slaughter on Tenth Avenue*. No matter how I had been feeling at the moment I entered my studio, I came out refreshed and clear. This experience, making dance my own instead of a skill my teacher had given me, caused a break-through in my artistic as well as psychological development. As if responding to the book I had loved in my twenties, *A Life of One's Own*, I was experimenting with developing a life of my own, one that didn't have to do with my role as wife or mother or housewife, but totally mine, from my heart and soul and inborn creative energies.

Three evenings a week I left home for my classes in town or at Felix's studio near Amsterdam an hour's drive away.

Sometimes I would take the train instead, having found that the combination of exhilaration and fatigue after class turned to stupor on the way home. I had to stop for coffee to keep myself awake and would arrive home jittery, jarring Zach's quiet mood with my talking and unable to sleep. I was left to putter around as my husband took himself off to bed.

Instead, I rode my bike to the station at 6:30 in the evening and carefully locked it to make sure it would be there at 11:30 that night. Then I wound my way through the hundreds of other bikes left early that morning by their owners, and climbed the stairs to enter the state-run Dutch railway system that would help wean me from my tendency to be late. One minute of distraction, I found, from glancing at a magazine counter or watching a loud bunch of laughing teenagers as they passed by, and my train would have come and gone by the time I reached the platform upstairs.

After class I waited to change trains in a small station on the outskirts of Amsterdam, often alone upstairs above the dark tracks, but never afraid. Semi-urban Holland felt much safer to me than the same situation would have seemed in America, and I was convinced that nothing could hurt me. I grew stronger every week, not only as a dancer, but in all ways. I had reached my self-proclaimed pinnacle of adulthood—the age of thirty-eight—which, as a thirteen-year-old, I had decided was the most perfect of all. I had met an adult male cousin of that age whom I'd admired. Jaunty and self-assured, though kind enough to notice me, cousin Bob had convinced me that the world was his, and I had waited to feel the same thing.

Like a red-winged black bird showing color in flight, I winged my way toward artistic freedom, learning the tools I needed to dance out my modern, jazz, African, and soul choreography that I planned to use someday for students in my studio.

But life interfered and pushed this fantasized future of mine farther away in time and place than I could ever have imagined.

Chapter 5 – Flashbacks

My occasional eye pain had made me irritable at times throughout my marriage, but I'd tried to keep annoyances to myself, knowing that my dance classes or a nap would get rid of it. Zach, on the other hand, expressed his irritations in a more verbal fashion. Early in our marriage I had gone through a short period of thinking that my marriage had been a mistake because of his outspoken negativity.

"He needs something exciting and new every couple of years, or else an innate gloominess settles in," Zach's closest friend mentioned to me one day, and he may have been right. Eighteen months after meeting each other, we enjoyed the birth of our beautiful baby girl. Another two years brought our exciting trip by boat to Europe, and twenty months later Kenny, a peaceful little boy, slipped into this world, creating a calming influence on all of us.

Five months after our son's birth, Zach signed a contract of tenure with the university. He had never shown any doubts to me about accepting this good offer, and I thought our relief and joy at achieving financial security was mutual. During the following year, however, my husband became gloomy and irritable.

One spring evening, on a family outing, Zach embarrassed the children and me with his loud criticisms at a restaurant. Afterward, at home, I tried to get him to understand our discomfort, especially because the Dutch society is a private one and patrons had stared at us in shock. I wanted an apology, but instead Zach broke the fireplace grate in his fury and slammed out the door.

I tried to figure out what my husband's problem was. Knowing that during most of our marriage Zach had been a social and verbal person, I thought that if I could help him with his study of Dutch, an improved ability to speak the language would make him happier. But even with my help, he gave up and dropped out of the new class we had started together.

Excitement from looking for and buying a house rescued our situation, but a year later, my husband's grumpiness reemerged, and when his irritability turned on the children, I fought back. Our talks turned into yelling matches that could be heard throughout the house. They accomplished nothing except to tell my son and daughter that we were not getting along. I felt helpless and attempted to block out the unpleasantness that had entered my life.

The summer of 1976 my family took a three-week trip to the United States. I spent five days of our vacation at a creative dance workshop in New England near where my parents lived now, staying with my father and mother while Zach and the children visited friends in another town. Toward the end of the course, my teacher asked a student to critique the choreography I'd just performed, a running and twisting among rocks and trees in our hilly outdoor classroom.

"Frenetic," my classmate said. I was surprised at his description, but it's clear to me now that my choreography had expressed my panic as I mentally twisted and turned from facing my marital situation.

Deep inside, I knew that I should walk out of the relationship because it had become intolerable. Yet I didn't dare face this truth, overcome by terror at the poverty I feared I would suffer if I left my husband. I knew that I should be teaching classes instead of taking them, and I was frantic in my efforts to become skilled enough to do so.

I approached my last evening with my parents in a vulnerable state. Just before retiring, my seventy-four-year-old mother walked toward me in the kitchen with a flinty look in her gray-blue eyes, her arms held out towards me with hands curled in the shape of my shoulders. I felt sure that she was going to shake me.

"You haven't paid any attention to us this whole week!" she said.

I had shared both morning and evening meals with my parents, but my mouth froze from defending myself at the sight of her. Her crazed face was more forceful than her words, and I carried that look back across the ocean in a dazed shock.

Toward the end of our flight home, I watched Hasidic men standing in the aisle of our airplane as they faced the East to pray. I lifted my window shade and felt glad to glimpse the rising sun. Looking down from high above the Atlantic Ocean, with strident symphonic music from my earphones heightening my mood, I recognized my tremendous relief and joy at coming back to our Dutch home.

After returning, a persistent pain at the back of my head bothered me in the midst of my daily life. I tried to massage it away any chance I could, sometimes using Myotherapy, a theory for pain reduction developed by Bonnie Prudden that my American friend Ellen had written me about. Marathon runners were using it to get them through their races. By putting hard pressure on a painful part of the body and stopping circulation, it is possible to cause muscle fibers to relax. This technique had helped me with muscle spasms after dance classes, and sometimes with my eye pain, but it only benefited me for a few minutes now. The combination of emotional hurt from the harshness between Zach and me, chronic pain at the back of my head, and the haunting memory of my mother's scary face created the triggers for my first flashback.

I learned that Felix had begun to form a professional company with his advanced students. Most of his classes became as hard-working and fast as the one on Saturday afternoon, his criticisms sharp, even when sent in my direction, his good friend. The slow rhythmic warm ups I had loved were run through at a fast pace, the two-hour sessions no longer expressions of exuberance and joy. I couldn't keep up, so I cut down on the number of classes I attended, going only once a week to the one for mothers of his young students, and these lessons were sometimes taught by a substitute teacher.

My consequent malaise from lack of exercise and feelings of loss at missing the frequent contact Felix and I had enjoyed for four years, as well as worry about the lack of dance training now available to me, contributed to my state of confusion and unhappiness.

One day in early spring, seven months after returning from our summer vacation in New England, I sank onto my bed for a morning nap, from which I could not arouse myself in spite of hearing my son open the back door, as he returned home from kindergarten. While lying immobile on my back, I remembered a scene that had happened when I was two years old. My mother had banged the back of my head down on a wooden changing-table in the middle of the night.

That evening I shared this memory with Zack.

"That's unbelievable," he said.

I agreed. Our incredulity kept us from being concerned about the memory's effect on me. My headache disappeared and my normal energetic mood returned, helped by the fact that my husband's irritability had disappeared.

Exactly twenty-four months after getting settled in our new house, friendship with a colleague had pulled my husband up out of his biannual darkness. On an airplane going to a scientific meeting, Zack had met a Canadian Jew named Gary, a new arrival at the university and working in my husband's scientific field. The absence of Jewish companionship, culture, and food in our Dutch life had evidently contributed to my husband's sense of isolation and unhappiness. One of the first things Gary did was to tell Zach where he could buy Hebrew National hotdogs.

"I've met a very nice person," my husband said, looking at me intently to make sure I'd heard him. "His wife is a dancer."

Mary Ann, a protestant in a mixed marriage, as I was, became my closest friend and the first teacher to share the use of my dance studio.

Suddenly Zach had an interest in doing things and going on excursions. We went with our new friends for family hikes and picnics on the beach during the weekends. The two men walked ahead of us, rattling off about their work and anything else that mattered to them, while Mary Ann and I waited for our children.

An acquaintance had heard about my disappointment with Felix's classes and mentioned that I might want to visit a teacher of creative dance, a graduate of an American university's dance department, who ran a school in Switzerland. In March, my nine-year-old daughter and I took a trip to the snowy mountains where Adrienne lived to meet her.

During our friendly dinner at the hotel, it was thrilling for me to hear Adrienne describe to my daughter and me how much encouragement she gave to her young students for their choreographic work. While studying with Felix and pleased with a dance I'd created to George Benson's version of "A Change is Gonna Come," I'd been disappointed at my teacher's lack of interest in it. I invited this cheerful and confident woman to come for a week during the summer and give a workshop in my town. Her style reminded me a bit of work I'd done in New England as an assistant to my Limon-style dance teacher, Dorothea, in her classes for children. I was pleased with myself for having found another form of dance with which to continue my training.

When I returned home, the only remnant of unease that lingered from remembering the difficult scene from my early childhood was frequent pain in my left eye, a symptom I had learned could be caused by emotional distress. I remember the day and the moment when I made a decision to do something about the annoying pain.

On the way to one of my classes, while stopped at a red light, I allowed myself to feel the pounding in my left eye instead of ignoring it. When the traffic started up again, I felt jaunty as I declared to myself, *I will look inside that eye and find out what's going on!* I sensed that another memory was about to emerge and felt adventurous about it, believing that I could handle whatever I might find. I made a plan to make time for this introspection as soon as the summer workshop was over, sensing that looking at what lay under the pain would stop the hurt, just as I had caused my headache to disappear.

Childless evenings out with our convivial new friends restarted a touch of romance in my marriage. It seemed that, as long as my eye was not bothering me, I was the strongest and happiest I had ever been. My children, at five and nine, likewise appeared more grown up and confident in their phases of life. I felt that it was time to stretch myself, and this attitude fit well with my satisfaction as I began preparation for the creative dance workshop I'd scheduled for July. I assembled a group of dancers from different parts of The Netherlands, confirmed arrangements for our teacher's living quarters, and negotiated with the university about renting its dance hall. Mary Ann helped with printing up materials.

Adrienne's class was a success, although we almost lost two students halfway through the first day. Two girls from the Dutch island of Curaçao hadn't understood our advertisement.

They had expected dances choreographed to jazz or popular tunes of the day. The dark-skinned girls had been astounded that Adrienne attempted to stimulate our creative moves using props such as scarves or verbal suggestions to vary the speed and shapes our bodies made, or the intensity of our physical relationships to each other. In the cadre of American-taught creative dance at this time, rhythmic music wasn't being used as the primary stimulus.

"We don't want a class without dance music," the students said at lunchtime, and they demanded their money back.

Adrienne told them to bring in the songs they loved and use them to spark their creative experience. The girls agreed and brought fast, syncopated Motown pieces. Over the next ten days they created choreography that launched one of them into her career as a teacher of jazz dance.

To my great confusion, a part of me had agreed with the girls. Their predicament had given me the embarrassment of momentarily questioning what I was doing. I had organized my workshop as a substitute for Felix's style, yet like these girls, I would have preferred working creatively with the music of jazz or Motown as the stimulus. Diplomatically, I pushed these thoughts down and went ahead working on a piece with Mary Ann, our choreography stimulated by props and ideas rather than music.

Each evening she and I drove back home together, chatting about how the day's session had gone, our friendship cemented by this mutual project. We decided to use the different parts of our bodies as stimulus for the dance, working ourselves from head and neck to toes in separate, disjointed, and striking ways, as if we were early hip-hop dancers. We were proud of our technique, strength, and agility with isolations—as the use of different parts of the body is called in jazz—while doing choreography that would have sent many people our age to the

87

nearest hospital.

I don't remember if I communicated to my partner my preference for working with drum rhythms or jazz, but in the end we chose the gospel song "Dry Bones" to go with our dancing. To my delight, the song's syncopation turned our choreography into a stunning piece of funky jazz, as we adjusted the timing of our quirky movements for each set of bones to the music's off rhythms.

I had been able to combine my creative drive with the kind of music and rhythms I preferred, just as those girls from Curaçao had done! I was ecstatic with my success.

Proud of the workshop, including the performance our class put on after only eight days, and confident in my ability to create my own choreography, I felt ready to do the inner exploratory work in my studio that I had decided would bring me relief from my eye pain. I waited until the day my children started school in mid-August and then began my experiment, hoping that creative dancing would relax my left eye.

After an hour of floor and *barre* technique, I danced in any way I wanted, stimulated by the choice of music I had made, pushing myself to my maximum in expression of energy and feeling. Then, after cooling down, I stretched out on the wooden floor that had been warmed by the sun coming in our southwestern window, enjoying the sudden silence as well as my feelings of relaxation and lack of pain under my closed eyelid. Sweaty, but refreshed, I felt myself open to every flashing thought.

One day, while resting after a session in which I'd whirled through my spacious half-room studio, a second incident of physical harm from my early childhood flowed like water from my memory into my conscious mind. I remembered that a few months after my second birthday, my mother had thrown me across the living room into the andirons, injuring my left eye.

I discussed my second recall memory with Zach, but again we found my mother's behavior impossible to believe. She had seemed like a calm person to both of us, though I knew that bouts of despondency had encouraged her to consult psychotherapists during her whole life.

My main reaction to the flashback came from relief that my near chronic visual pain had disappeared. Even during difficult moments when doing close work, I found a slight improvement from the fact that I was now able to distinguish and separate my physical pain from the sense of terror, worry, and helplessness that I realized had always been a part of it. So clear was this distinction that I began to consult Dutch optometrists and even opticians for help with my residual pain, though none of them were able to solve the problem. I have since learned that an optometrist in Rotterdam was working with visual dysfunction, but the news had not reached anyone I consulted.

Pushed by curiosity about my childhood, I continued my creative dance work, finding that the slightest pain or sensation from moves I made spoke of something strange that had happened to me as a young child, as if my skin and bones had formed a psychological map back to their childhood history of hurtful and scary experiences. The fact that I lived three thousand miles away from where these events had occurred in a land with a different language had helped to give me the feeling of distance and safety my brain needed in order to relax its inhibitions on memory.

The stories that came to me had lain pristine and sealed in an unused part of my mind, a treasure chest of movie reels about my early years, locked up at the bottom of my mind's sea. When the images emerged into my consciousness, they appeared as if three-dimensional and in full-spectrum color, whole scenes accompanied by intelligible sounds, even complete sentences.

I fought the recall of each event that tumbled into my mind

with a mantra that became well known to my brain: "No, this didn't happen." A few days later, the thought came to me, "Well, maybe this happened, but certainly not that." After another week, I allowed even that unacceptable piece to be part of my life's truth.

I shared all of my stories with Mary Ann and Zach. Every day there were new memories to report. My response was similar to that of my two listeners—that we had watched an exciting movie, come away surprised and stirred, but none of us emotionally thrown off balance. The next day I continued with the tasks of my regular life and more creative dance work. Through unraveling my strange early history with my husband, who enjoyed stories of drama and intrigue, I was able to create threads of communication for a much-needed new connection between us.

By the end of September, I had remembered many more instances of my mother's cruel and dangerous behavior. But I had also recalled the affection, courage, and love of my older sisters, our cook Jessie, my *brown mother* Grace, and her boyfriend Joe, all of whose support gave me the strength I had needed in order to survive.

Part Two – Grace

Chapter 6 – Mummy

"Mummy" was the name my sisters must have used as they peered over my crib, because their excitement about me and the celebration of our family that seeped into my earliest grasp of life was accompanied by the idea that a *mummy* was a wonderful thing, even sublime, I would learn, because of her singing at naptime.

Later on, I learned to use other ways of thinking about my birth mother, until I had a whole alphabet of names in my head based on what other people used. Grace called her Misus Davidson or "yo' mama" when she was talking to me. Jessie, our cook, muttered "that lady" enough times to make an impression, and after two I adopted Jessie's idea, saying "the lady" or even "the scary lady" to myself.

Sometimes I imitated my sisters, who said "our mother." By three I could think of the lady as *my mother*, but this created problems for me. My picture books told me that mothers were kind to their children instead of hurting them, so I was forced to block out my own meaning of the name in order to understand these stories. When I learned, sometime in my fourth year, to place the word *brown* in front of *mother* in my head, a feeling of warmth and support filled the phrase, and I was able to remind myself that, indeed, I had a *mother,* and she was called Grace.

Chapter 7 – Two Nannies

I learned from Grace that living was a fun game. When the young and energetic woman was not bouncing me as a baby and singing her gospel tunes, she brought me peace. The plump but firm and beautiful woman set my carriage outside in the fresh air for hours, and held me tight in stiff sea breezes on a huge boat my family took when making a trip to The Islands off the coast of New England. I felt both excitement and safety in her protective arms, her wide chocolate-colored face framed against the stateroom's white outer wall that glistened from sunlight and the ocean's foam.

Grace's language sounded different from the rest of my family, yet I loved it because every word she uttered assured me that I was adored and that life would bring me nothing but joy. When I was better able to understand specific words, she expanded her teachings to include a wonderful God high up in the sky. "Why he gonna take good care o' you jes like he do ev'ryone in de whole worl'," she reassured me. The twenty-two-year-old had come fresh from the south. Our cook, Jessie, tried to change the way Grace spoke, even though I thought her language was perfect.

Just before my second birthday, my family changed houses, moving out of a tall brown wooden structure with high ceilings and dim lighting that was located at the bottom of a sloping road. Our new house was a "modern" one, according to our father, a rectangular-shaped, flat-roofed brick building painted white that sat on top of a large hill. Though the rooms had low ceilings, they seemed bigger than the ones in our old house, filled with light from their numerous windows. I had loved my first home. I hadn't been bothered, as others seemed to be, by the "dingy" bare light bulb that hung down over my crib, but soon I caught my family's excitement about our change.

Everyone went for a tour of the new house just before the move … everyone, that is, but my mummy, who had gone to a "rest home." She had become "tired while getting ready for the move."

There were happy calls of "Look at that!" and "Here is this!" as my tall and proud father led us through the bright hallways. His voice joined ours with excitement when he pointed out the things that had been his ideas.

"Look at this! Jim thanked me for it!" he beamed as he pointed to a certain kind of doorknob he had suggested to his architect friend. The shape of the shiny white building and its breezy light reminded me of the bright boat that had carried us to The Islands.

Looking backwards out of our car window as we drove down the curved driveway after our visit, Grace exclaimed that the elegant house, settled between the trunks and branches of strong and tall oak trees, was "one beautiful place!" I watched the stone banks on either side of us replaced by beautiful bushes, filled with pink and white blossoms at the bottom of the drive. As we drove slowly along the quiet, dusty country road that rambled in front of our house, Susie tugged on my sleeve, "Maybe we'll see a horse!" and we scrambled to the window to look into a small stable where its owner bustled about. We already loved our new home.

After the move, I benefited from my daddy's good mood when the servants were allowed to sleep at night. He picked me up if I cried and danced with me all the way to the kitchen. After my drink he would hum and bounce me while looking out at the black street through the front windows of his warm study. I loved the golden wood that lined the walls of this room almost as much as the colorful books that filled the shelves. My daddy seemed to like caring for me and sharing his talent for moving in time to his tunes.

During this month when my mummy was away, I came to know Jessie, our gray-haired cook. In her mid-fifties, she had been in the north awhile and didn't talk like Grace, nor was her skin as dark. I didn't like her at first, but I came to love her. In the month after the move, Jessie spent every afternoon with me at naptime, while Grace cared for my older sisters. I found the comfort of her soft breast better than sleep as she rocked me in a chair by the front window of her bedroom, a small room just like Grace's, both of them in the "maids' quarters" right over the kitchen. I remember the sound of a steady click and the shift of my eyes as I tried to keep the light of window and fluttering white curtains in my view at all times.

"This baby don't want to sleep. She miss her mama."

"Tha's a fac,'" Grace answered as she looked in from the hallway outside the bathroom they both shared. She was taking five-year-old Susie out for a walk to meet my oldest sister Louise on her way home from school.

I guess I liked Jessie too much, because I didn't remember the light-skinned woman, whom Grace called "Misus Davidson," when she returned a month later. The lady enticed me to take a nap by starting a song I loved. She had a beautiful, high voice, and suddenly I recognized the *singing mummy* I'd loved.

Louise told me when we were adults that she thought it had been sweet of our mother to take her young child into her bedroom for her nap, but something must have happened because I started screaming, which my sister did not remember.

The vigilant nine-year-old burst through our mother's door

with Susie following, my middle sister's golden ringlets flying. They found me screeching at the scary lady who was shaking me with a terrifying look on her face.

Louise grabbed me up in her arms and ran down the hall to the children's bathroom with Susie running behind us. They locked the door behind them.

The lady said from the hallway, "I'm going to get the key!"

Susie yelled, "Get Jessie, get Jessie!" Grace was on her day off.

"You stay with Annie then!" Louise thrust me, frantic and yelling, into Susie's arms, which made her cross, but she tried to hold me anyway. Louise dashed out of the bathroom, and returned with Jessie just in time. The angry lady had entered the bathroom, but had not reached me!

Jessie grabbed a glass, filled it with water, and threw it in our mother's face. "What you think you're doing, Mrs. Davidson? You get back to your room this minute!" And she did! She did! We three children stared at her. We stared at our disappearing mother. We had never seen her ordered around by anyone.

That night it seemed to me that a friendly stranger was changing me. After being liberated from my diaper, I reached down to touch my cooling skin. Suddenly I saw the stranger's hand come down toward my body from a great height. I jerked my hand away as a stinging slap hit the bone I'd just touched.

"That's something Jessie taught you! I'll fire her!" my dark-haired mother yelled.

"Jaazz!" I screamed the word I used in my attempt to copy Grace's name *Jaassi* for the cook.

This made the lady more irate. "You're *my* child!" She took my shoulders in her hands, and lifted me high above the changing table. Then she cracked my head down on the wooden surface.

I imagined that I had gone far away to a safe place, where I stayed for a while, but the sound of crying brought me back. The lady, a woman the height of Jessie but thinner, was leaning with her elbows on the changing table, her face in her hands. I twisted to see her better, and fell off the table, my head banging on the wooden floor.

When I woke up, my mind must have been jolted into forgetting everything the lady had done. I lifted my head, and saw my mummy bending down to look at me. Expecting her to pick me up, I felt my eyes brim and shine with tears, but instead of reaching out to me, she lay down on her stomach on the floor and began to sob, her low moans sounding as if she were in the greatest pain. I went over to pat her head, but this only made her weep more.

Watching her cry would have been better than the scary ride in her shaking arms right by a dark window open to the June night. I had the sense that she was going to drop me onto the grassy front lawn below. Instead, the wobbly woman placed me in a high-sided crib at the end of the bedroom. I became a screeching child while the door closed gently on the darkness and me.

Later, in the kitchen, Grace divided her love between the lady and me, a pattern that would continue. The brown woman could somehow see and not see at the same time. Grace could support and nurture the woman who continued to hurt me, the child whom she called "Mah Baby."

Chapter 8 – Louise

When my mummy returned from the rest home a week later, though I remembered nothing about what she had done, I was nervous around her and liked running away. This made her angry. One day, when Grace and Jessie were on their day off, the scary lady ran from her bedroom trying to catch me.

I managed to get downstairs first and scampered into my father's study so I could curl up in his chair. When she came after me, I slipped back down to the ground, ducked under her arm and raced as fast as my legs could go along the carpeted hall. Dashing into the spacious and beautiful living room, the couch and chairs still clothed in their winter jackets of cozy pink and red flowers, I ran to hide behind my father's giant-sized armchair. I delighted in my game of moving from side to side, peering out at my mummy from behind its high back.

Once I left my hand too long on the stuffed armrest and she grabbed it. I tried to get away but it was too late.

She pulled me out from my hiding place. Her face looked black with rage, reminding me of the stranger who had cracked my head on the changing table. *It's the same one!* I thought! My mouth flew open. *She did that, too! My singing mummy, the angry lady, and the friendly, scary stranger, they're all one person!*

"I'll teach you to run away from me!" The lady grabbed my arm and zigzagged me five or six times across the floor, making my small legs work hard to keep up with her speed and changes of direction. Then she let me go, a zinging ball whirling toward the fireplace mantel.

Her hand shot up between my temple and the wooden edge, the impact of my hit sending me plummeting into the andirons below. The metal frame bruised my nose and one of the brass sticks caught the outside corner of my left eye.

I woke up in my father's study, where I drank in comfort and safety from his chair. The pillows, in which he relaxed every evening and on Sundays, helped me say to myself, "My daddy is good. He knows things. He helps me. He loves me. I can depend on him."

My left eye couldn't see through the thick dark red color in front of it, but suddenly my right eye noticed the scary form standing in front of me! In terror that she would throw me across this room, too, I screeched for help.

Yelling at me to be quiet, the lady swiped her hand across my face, hitting my still good eye and cracking her knuckles into my nose, imprinting on my brain, for my whole life, the notion that to cry out for help and protection meant I would suffer pain and punishment.

Terrorized, I imagined flying away to the giant oak tree that grew way across our huge back lawn. In my mind, I chose the highest branch and sat, looking back at the scene in my father's study.

Louise, whose bedroom was the nearest to the stairs, heard my cry. She ran down to us and stood watching my stunned expression and closed left eye.

"She fell," our mother said.

Seizing this moment of inattention, I squiggled away from the scary lady's hands, and jumped into Louise's arms, locking my legs around her slender waist. The force of my flying leap drove my sister backwards, out of the reach of her mother. The agile girl whirled around and headed for the living room.

Once there, my sister swung me in a circle as fast as she could, a game she and I both loved, my upper body leaning out and my head flying through the cooling air, my delight distracting me from what had happened.

Suddenly I shrieked as a pain burned its way into the left side of my face. Our mother came running and yelled at my sister for her "stupidity" at making my eye bleed again. I lay on the floor, screaming and twisting my body, whipping my head from side to side to shake off the terrible creature that had taken hold of me where my left eye had been.

Louise, on elbows and knees above me, repeated some words of comfort as her anguished face alternated between glancing up at the shadowy figure next to us and looking at me. Unable to catch my whirling head between the towels her mother had given her, she raised herself from her elbows to her hands and spoke to me in clear loud words, her love and trust of language giving this studious girl the tools she needed.

"STOP... MOVING ... THE ... BLOOD ... WILL ... STOP."

From writhing and snapping my head back and forth, I slowed my pace and looked at my articulate sibling, grabbing at the pleading tone in her voice. My pain diminished with every moment as I stuck myself to her hazel eyes, their color drowned in her teary need for me to stop moving and let her repair the damage she had caused.

I heard my normally shy sister yelling out to the figure standing near: "WHY AREN'T YOU CALLING THE DOCTOR?" She repeated the question several times, her crying voice catching itself between every call, until the hazy form standing beside us left the room to telephone.

This caring love by my oldest sister turned her into a new *young-mummy*. I took anything that bothered me to her receptive ear, until one day I heard our mother berate my sister for trying to figure out "everything that stupid two-year-old tells you." My wonderful new mummy began to shun me, and the rest of the family as well. She told everyone that her new public school gave her a lot of homework, and she withdrew behind a closed bedroom door.

The truth is that—unlike Susie and me—she had been raised by our mother alone, before either Grace or Jessie came into our household, and she was fragile. My sister had needed the private school, where she'd made friends and received attention from the familiar teachers who had sustained her self-esteem.

Thanks to psychoanalysis in her twenties, Louise led an exciting and fulfilling life, just as I did. Yet it was not sufficient to erase all the destructive lessons she'd learned as a young child. I am grateful that I remembered the help she gave me on the day my eye was hurt in time to thank her before the paranoia she developed in her seventies prevented her from receiving any family member's love.

In the months after the andirons incident, I wore a mound of white on top of my left eye that kept it from seeing, starting the habit I acquired of blocking out the vision of that eye. My right eye developed a steady ache from the work it had to do in order to watch out for me, looking in every direction at once, during every minute of every day, checking to make sure that the scary lady was not approaching. Yet when the bandage came off, I continued to let my right eye do all the seeing, my left eye suppressed and unused. I had come to prefer two-dimensional vision in which my surroundings did not feel real.

Chapter 9 – Joe

I clung by Grace's side or sat in the wooden high chair eating the new foods she had found for me, hominy from her home country, which she called the "Souf," and goat's milk at a farm. We walked from my father's car down to a pasture where brown animals, a lot smaller than cows, looked at us in surprise, tiny white flowers hanging from their lips.

"Hea,' Honni," Grace said to me, picking me up so I could see over the fence. "These heah yo new mama's! They gonna give you what you need to git all nice 'n fat agin." I fell in love with the bony, fat-bellied animals and stretched out my hand to touch a long nose reaching toward me. But the animal jerked away from my efforts, as if she were just as scared of White people as I was. When Grace said to her, nice and respectful, "Yo' gonna save mah baby Miss Miss and Ah gonna thanks yo'," the goat let the brown hand touch her.

In the pale-yellow kitchen, I deepened my bond with the big and loving woman, crisp and energetic in her white uniform and frilly apron, who provided me with the only ingredients that my stomach would accept because they didn't remind me of the lady people called my mother.

When meeting people, Grace always referred to me as "Mah Baby," explaining that she had come to our house in the same month that I had. Everyone would laugh when she said that, as if she had made a joke, but after the andirons incident, I began to wonder if it was true. My bonding with Grace became so strong that she must have felt guilty about it. She tried to get me to show some interest in "the unhappy lady," who had secluded herself in her bedroom instead of going back to the rest home.

"Yo' kin make yo'sef a drawin'," Grace said to me one day, as we hesitated outside my bedroom door. "Then you go on and take it to huh!" And she pointed to the closed door at the opposite end of the long hall.

"NO!"

"You don' have to go on in. Yo' kin jes put it under the do'." She bent down and demonstrated how I could slide the paper under the blue-green wood, and back in my bedroom she helped me make a drawing on a piece of paper with bright crayons.

"Come on now." She started down the long upstairs hall holding my hand.

I went slowly and cautiously the rest of the way, putting my drawing under the bedroom door and turning quickly to run back. Before I could get to Grace, the lady ran out of her room, screaming at me for bothering her and waving my picture in the air.

A few minutes later, there was the sound of glass breaking from inside the children's bathroom. I ran to my bedroom.

"Mummy's cut her hands off!" my sister Susie called to me where I stood in the doorway of my room.

"Yo' go on an' git Jassi! An' hurri yo'sef!" I heard Grace's voice and watched my sister spin around towards the maid's quarters so she could dash down to the kitchen by using the narrow tunnel-like backstairs our servants used.

When Susie returned with the cook, the constant reports from my excited sibling made me part of the event, even though I'd climbed up on my bed to escape. Excluded from helping, Susie continued to peek. She ran back to tell me about the "red, red blood" and how the wrists were being wrapped in towels, which "are now red, too!"

Susie reported how Jessie was leading our mother back to her bedroom. She pulled me off my place of refuge and dragged me down the hall so we could look into the light-blue-walled room. The pale, quiet lady was lying on her blue chaise lounge.

"Jessie, I don't want you to tell Mr. Davidson about this. Do you hear me?" Our cook said something, and then came our mother's voice again. "No, I promise I won't ever do it again." She glanced at us.

Jessie turned around and waved her hand. "You children get on out of here right now!"

We found Grace in our bathroom down on her hands and knees, inspecting the floor with her long, rough fingers, muttering loudly, "Don' wan' mah babies gettin' no splinters in they feet."

When Grace had finished, she took us for our afternoon stroll, not down the driveway to the sidewalk as she usually did, but out the backdoor, across a field of soft grasses, as if she wanted to hide us from the rest of the world. She settled herself on a thick pillow of pine needles, inside a grove of towering dark fir trees, and gathered my sister and me onto her lap. Then she uttered the first criticism of our "mama" that we'd ever heard her make.

"She don' nevah should've did that." Grace, in her great agitation, was using her heaviest dialect, the one Jessie criticized so much. Then she added, "She don' never should have done that ...and in the chillen's bathroom!" There was some mention of God, and how He didn't like people to do what our mother had done. This was a spiritual lesson for Susie and me, confirmed by the serenity and beauty of our surroundings, but I had received another warning. I had learned to be suspicious about giving a present to someone because I might get anger hurled back at me instead of love.

I wonder now if Grace picked up on this faulty learning of

mine, because she made a point of teaching the opposite almost thirty years later, during one of the visits I made with my children to my parents' house when my parents had invited her.

"Make sho' you let them give to you," she advised me softly, as the two of us watched Sarah and Kenny play, no reason being added why that sudden wisdom had been slipped into my ear.

For a long time after taking the drawing to my mother, I was cross with Grace. She hadn't listened to me, making me go to that dangerous lady. In the days that followed, if I glimpsed the scary woman in the distance, I blocked out the sight of her, her outline filled in with black in my imagination. When she approached me, spasms of terror cut into my chest and told me to "Run! Run!" If the lady caught me, I tried to disappear from my body so I wouldn't feel her touch.

One day, at the end of summer, Grace found me dashing down the hill in front of our house, running along the sidewalk "as fas' as yo' little legs could carry you!" as she would tell it later, twisting her large body in a frantic way to show me. I suppose I was on my way to Mrs. Strong, my mummy's best friend, whose sweetness was like the garden in her backyard— fragrant and full of pleasant surprises. It was probably my memory of a flat-rocked path, with the sound of a fountain tucked behind dark green leaves that drew me to come and hide.

Grace caught me halfway. She carried me back to the kitchen, where her new boyfriend sat visiting her, as he would continue to do every week—on Jessie's day off. I hid behind the white uniform where I felt safe and took peeks at the dark brown man named Joe, whose face was almost black and lined with wrinkles. He was much older than my smooth-cheeked Grace, and, like Jessie, had lived long enough in the north that his speech had little dialect.

After a time, I ventured from Grace's side to see Joe better, but ran back to her as soon as the swinging doors announced the arrival of the person Joe called "Annie's mother." I clung to Grace, burying my face and the eye that still throbbed into the folds of her uniform. After the lady left, I cowered in a corner.

"Let's see about fixin' this little girl. She one scared child," Joe said, after watching my reaction to these visits week after week.

I watched from behind the safety of Grace's starched uniform as Joe picked up my doll, tossed her in the air, and then caught her. It was hard to follow my *baby's* trajectory from behind the white skirt, and I stepped away for the duration of the throw, my heart beating at the audacity of this boyfriend who had taken something of mine for his plaything.

Each week, Joe repeated his game, and soon I ventured farther away from Grace and nearer to him, until one day, I became the doll, and my tiny baby lay on the ground, watching me catch my breath seconds before Joe caught me. Then the dark brown man called me the name that he'd used for my baby. By swinging his "Pretty Doll," Joe made me feel as if I were a little girl who was loved.

All during a sunny September, Joe's cure for my timidity continued, until the kitchen rang with my screeches of joy and his laughter. Each time he caught me my relief grew stronger. When Grace turned to smile and caution him to "Watch out now!" we didn't listen. Neither of us wanted to be careful anymore. I knew Joe would catch me no matter where he tossed me.

As if sent by Grace's God to heal me, the skillful man took my terrified self and made a living child of me again. This boyfriend, who had understood my situation and changed me into a normal and adventurous two-year-old, was added to my circle of guardian-caregivers. Soon he became my favorite person in the household.

Chapter 10 – Susie

My sister Susie liked Joe, too. We loved dancing and jumping around as he clapped and stamped his feet. We were eager for the laughs and praise he heaped on us when we took our bows, my blond waves and Susie's dark golden curls bobbing up and down.

That winter, we sisters began a fun game with Joe down in the cellar playroom. Susie and I discovered that if we rode on his legs we felt pleasant sensations. Our *good-feeling places*, as we came to call those parts of us, rubbed back and forth against the top of his thighs. All three of us laughed at the wonderful time we were having.

When Joe stopped coming around, my sister and I practiced on our own. Down in the laundry room we found that we could get these same sensations by lying on the cellar floor and twisting our bodies together crossways so that our wiggling hips could make those good-feeling places touch each other.

We could do it "real good!"

Susie was my parents' favorite child. A family photograph shows my mother and father looking fondly down at her as she sits cuddled on my father's lap, her curls for once in place. Louise, at nine, with her straight brown hair held tight by a barrette, and I at two with my light wavy locks bouncing out to the sides, perch on flowery cushions at either side of, but not touched by, either parent. We are leaning forward and staring into the camera as if hoping to get attention from it.

My middle sister had arrived at a good time for my parents.

In contrast to Louise's birth, which had coincided with the Stock Market Crash of 1929, Susie had come into their lives at a prosperous time. Louise has told me that our middle sister's early childhood was smoother than her own because our mother was going through an improvement in her mental state around the time of Susie's birth.

During her third year, however, our mother, pregnant with me, needed to leave home for a three-month stay at the rest home. During that time, Susie adopted Jessie as her substitute mother, just as I did with Grace. She turned to the kitchen where she received delicious treats from the cook for her source of comfort. At my birth, Susie proclaimed that I was *her baby*, as if my mother didn't exist, and she smothered me—quite literally it seemed to both Grace and me—with her love and tight hugs.

The games in the cellar changed our relationship into one between equals and made us instant buddies. From the kitchen, our sustaining place of comfort and identity as the beloved *colored* children we thought we were, we danced through the *White people's* house, alternately pushing and hugging each other, all the time giggling about our secret delights down in the laundry room.

One day, my sister and I were bathing and splashing together in the children's bathroom. We laughed while we tickled each other's good feeling places with our toes and chanted our bathtub song in a loud sing-song way, "We hates White folks. We hates White folks."

Suddenly our mother came through the mirror-covered door.

"WHAT ARE YOU SAYING?"

We looked at her with tight lips.

The scary lady pulled me, dripping and cold, out of the bathtub. Susie giggled nervously. I was taken into the middle of my bedroom and gentled up with a word or two as the towel was fixed around me. Then my mummy bent down and looked me in the eye.

"Now, Anne, tell me what you were singing," I told her.

"What?" she said, slapping my face and making me bend over. She grabbed a hanger from the closet and whipped it down on my bare back repeatedly until I fainted. Then she left.

Susie entered the room. She must have gone to the medicine closet in the hall outside my bedroom, taken out a bandage or two, and put them on my wounds. I began to move, slowly. Susie didn't touch me but stood waiting. My body's efforts to heal itself must have seemed queer to her, progressing incrementally, each tiny curved fluctuation of my backbone slightly bigger than the last. I would remember this inch-by-inch easing of sore vertebrae while resting in my dance studio after a workout, and wonder how Susie had known not to touch the victim of a back injury. When I stretched out and lay still, Susie picked me up and put me in bed, lying down under the blankets and holding my freezing self against her warm body. I lay with my chest pressed against hers for a long time. When I opened my eyes, I saw two beautiful clear blue eyes looking at me. I fell in love with them.

I put up my mouth to Susie to be kissed. She did. My love for my sister became passionate. She changed in my mind from a sibling with whom I had bonded, to a guardian, my newest in the growing list of people taking turns as substitutes for the singing mummy I had lost.

Chapter 11 – Jessie

One day, soon after the hanger incident, with Susie at kindergarten and Grace on her day off, I stood by our cook's rocking chair in her bedroom. I liked being with Jessie because she was smarter about my mother than Grace. She saw the truth. She knew that the scary lady did bad things. The cook was resting in her chair after cleaning up the breakfast dishes.

In an off-hand way, I told her what had been done to me with the hanger. Jessie didn't have much of a reaction until she walked down the stairs into the playroom to check on me in the afternoon. She found my doll's head broken, with its sawdust brains scattered on the floor.

"Annie! What've you been doin'? Why'd you do that with your doll?" She seemed a little cross.

"That's what my mother did to me!"

"What?" She sat down on a stool and took me up on her lap. "Your mother did that?"

"Yes." I enjoyed her focused attention and warm comforting body.

"You must never tell anyone. She could go to jail."

"And she did this, too," I said, squiggling off her lap and picking up the doll. I zigzagged it through the air, letting it fly across to the opposite wall.

By then Jessie was charging her way up the stairs. I would hear later in the kitchen that she'd gone to my father to tell him what I'd said, and he'd told her she should stop drinking her whiskey.

The next day, Jessie took my sister and me downtown on

the bus, all fixed up in our best dresses. We got out at our father's law office, a white two-story wooden building with an elevator. We went out the sliding door to the blond haired woman at the desk. My father came down the hall to see what we wanted.

In front of the lady at the desk, Jessie flicked my dress up in the back so that everyone could see the red marks of the hanger. "You didn't believe me Mr. Davidson, but here's proof of what Mrs. Davidson's been doin' to this child."

My father's hushed voice seemed louder than thunder as he pushed the three of us toward the elevator, quickly stepping in front of the desk lady. "You have no right to come down here. You take these children home this minute!"

And that's how we lost Jessie, who was allowed to stay for a few weeks after being fired, so she could be at Susie's sixth birthday celebration. I listened outside our cook's bedroom door the next day and heard her answer to my father's offer of money.

"Mr. Davidson, I don't want money from you. I just want you to promise that you're going to keep an eye on Mrs. Davidson and what she's doing to that child."

A promise! I knew what promises were! My daddy was promising that my mother was going to be good! I jumped around with joy!

Before she left our house, Jessie took Susie and me down to the playroom and spoke in a low, quiet tone of voice. She held our hands and leaned down to us.

"I want the two of you to listen to me." We watched her face. "You children have to look out for each other now, after I'm gone. You have to promise me to take care of each other, you hear?"

"Oh yes," we each said. "Oh yes, of course, Jessie, of course we will."

The day Susie's substitute mother left, my sister and I took a walk down the quiet road in front of our house. We loved it because we could scruff our shoes in the dust or reach up to pull down one of the gentle pink roses that climbed a neighbor's trellis and inhale its fragrant beauty. We peeked into the small stable-like house at the end of our two-block road where we hoped to see horses. We found out later that the animals lived on a lower level because the house and stable had been built into the side of a steep hill. We had to imagine the horses galloping through pastures below, just as we would do ourselves later on, at a friendly stable farther out in the country.

On our way, Susie told me how much she loved the brown-skinned woman she had gotten to know so well and how much she would miss her.

I said, "Oh, she'll come back."

"No she won't. Never!"

My sister was right.

We were told that Jessie had gone to her family in the south. This lie of my parents worked well, preventing any chance that Susie might try to find her in our own town. As we left the short dusty road to follow sidewalks, we passed a wood frame house nestled among pine trees where a cat sat on the back porch, serenely looking at us. We said how nice it would be to live there, where we could just sit calmly on a back porch and watch everything.

Then we went home and curled up together in my wooden rocking chair. This time I was the one who did the comforting and my sister the one who needed hugging. It made me feel grown up. After all, I was almost three!

Chapter 12 – Daddy

As Grace swung through our house, dynamic in her speed to keep up with the cleaning as well as take care of me and cook our meals, I rushed after her, dusting all the small and shiny wooden tables at the ends of our couches and muttering under my breath the hardly audible grunts and sighs and complaints I heard from her. With her doubled workload there seemed to be no time for the humming that I had loved.

Sharing her kitchen as well as cleaning tasks, I threw away apple peels, peach pits, or anything else she asked and helped to dry the dishes. Making fruit pies was my most fun task. For blueberry, my father's favorite, I made tiny holes in the crust with my fork for the dark purple juices to bubble up through while the fragrant and yummy pie was baking. Grace was a wonderful teacher, praising me as I took the ends of dough strips she had woven across a bed of dark red cherries, *my* favorite kind of pie, and pushed them down on the raw crust around the pie plate's edge with my fork.

In the dining room, I imitated Grace's cheerful voice when she served my family, though not her accent. I knew that while in the White people's part of the house, I shouldn't speak in the southern way I used in the kitchen. I learned how satisfying it was to wait on people and do things for them to make them happy. My enthusiasm for serving people became as boundless as that of Grace. Not knowing that she was paid for her work, I believed her whole purpose was for making "Mistuh and Misus Davidson" pleased with her warmth and joy of living. I copied this attitude towards my mother, who kept herself at a distance, as she had done ever since Jessie's departure. I regarded her as another very much older sister, whom I didn't have to worry about because I could keep her good through doing things to please her.

The mental radar I'd developed when trying to survive my mother's moods the year before helped me in my server's role. I would know what someone wanted and then run to get it, gaining a great deal of praise for this talent. The word "bright" began to be used about me. I didn't know that this meant smart; I thought that there must have been a lot of light in my face.

Because of my success in demonstrating these new talents, as well as my skill with crayons, my daddy began to pay attention to me. My drawings brought great praise from him and his friends, who would come over for a drink or dinner now and then. From a parent who had seemed annoyed by what I had told our cook about my mother, my father changed into one who was joyful and spontaneous when I was around. This daddy reminded me of the one who had danced with me in the middle of the night or come to my bedroom to tuck me in, as he had done when we first moved into the new house. He'd climbed the stairs the minute he got home and kissed my head as he fixed my blankets.

"Yo' daddy never missed a night," Grace told me years later.

"As tight as a bug in a rug," he would say when he closed the door. I had sensed his love back then, but from a distance. Now I felt his warmth and affection close at hand. I didn't know that the Scotch whiskey he drank after coming home from work helped him be like the fun daddy I'd known from earlier. I was allowed to stay up in order to see him, and I would help Grace prepare the bit of food he needed to accompany his drinks as he relaxed in his soft study chair. Sometimes I'd be allowed to bring his crackers to him.

When dinner was ready, I stood in the hall with Grace and my giggling sisters, as we watched daddy delight us—and his smiling self—with his nightly game of stumbling to the table.

At Christmas time, my father called me his "Little Angel," and from that endearment, I felt I held a solid place in the family. It was my assignment to be cute, affectionate, entertaining, and my father's favorite, in a house where the mother's existence was unimportant. I compared myself to angels on the Christmas tree and found them mirrors, with their long, golden, silken hair and sparkling smiles reflecting back my new personality. Because my mother had behaved perfectly since the time of my father's promise, I felt safe and loved. Susie had cheered up enough from losing Jessie to be a playmate, and Louise emerged from her room to join us with preparations for Christmas.

Two months later I remember looking out of the kitchen window at a February snow scene, while Grace and someone else talked about school for me, too, for the "grown-up girl" I'd become. This was a place where I'd do fun things and be with other children! Hearing the adults talking and looking out the window in the direction they were gesturing, I felt big, excited, and ready.

Soon afterward, I went to this nursery school and flourished, coming home ravenous for food and Grace's ear, which I filled with my stories. I basked in her attention as I sat at the yellow wooden kitchen table having lunch with her.

My left eye, which had turned inwards ever since my mother had wounded it, no longer did this. My universe changed back into a vibrant three-dimensional one. I felt glad with my life, happy and calm for the first time since the difficulties with my mother had begun.

Grace noticed. She began, out of the goodness of her heart and respect for the boundaries of her job, to try again to get me to trust and love the lady that was my mother.

Chapter 13 – Reading

One day in April, Grace shared her ideas with me after our lunch together.

"Honey, you go on up to that livin' room an' see yo' mama. She want to read to you, an' she so lonely."

I hung around the bright kitchen, looking through the window at the ugly dark-yellow bushes called forsythia, their sad blossoms drooping and wet. Grace told me it was nice to stay inside on such a wet day.

"You kin be warm an' cozi, all curled up on a couch an' bein' read to." Grace opened the pantry door, giving me a gentle push. "You go on, now."

So I went down the red oriental carpet everybody called a "runner." I wasn't running. Fear walked with me, and my lunch felt like a rock in my stomach, but I was pushed on by my love of being read to, and some feeling of compassion that I'd picked up from Grace for this lonely woman.

"Hi, Mummy, I'm here," I announced, crawling up onto the flowered couch, looking eagerly at the little book held on my mother's lap. She began to read, and I relaxed with the joy of listening to the three little pigs' story.

"The wolf huffed and puffed," my mother read, while lifting my hand from the page she was turning and putting it on her body down to a warm place, forcing my fingers to go up and down there.

She stopped reading. I waited, but she didn't continue. Angry at the disruption in my story, I jumped up, pulling my arm away from her and standing still while my mother glared at me. She grabbed my hand and tried to force it back to her warm body.

"No! I don't want to do that!"

"Yes you're going to, or I won't read anymore."

Struggling with the choice, I let my hand be guided up under my mother's skirt to a silky wet bumpy place. I waited to hear what the wolf did next, but the words never came. Instead, there were the beginnings of another kind of noise.

I yanked my hand back, fury rising from deep inside me.

But the lady's anger was greater. She jumped up and grabbed my book with both hands. Walking to the end of the living room near the porch, she tore *The Three Little Pigs* down the spine, pages spilling everywhere.

"I'll see that you never read this again," she threatened. Her twisted tone, spoken through clenched teeth, made her threat sound like, "I'll see that you never read again."

I scrambled for the precious pages, so intent on getting the pigs' story back together that I didn't realize the angry lady was pulling me toward the white-walled screened-in porch. She closed the solid oak door to shut off the living room and the rest of the house from my screams.

Grace wouldn't have heard them anyway. The lady squashed my sounds with her strong slender fingers around my throat, holding me on my back against the green canvas-covered couch cushions. But my slashing nails saved me, scratching her arms and neck and making the crazed woman let go.

I rolled over and off the couch, squiggling under the low-slung wrought iron fortress and reaching the smooth porch wall where I hugged the couch's back legs for safety. I looked up from the ground at the green canvas-covered cushions held by white slats. I felt comfort from their protection as if they were the good mummy I needed.

The angry lady couldn't get at me and slammed her way

back into the house. It's good that Grace didn't find me for a long time, because I needed the chance to be still so that my throat could relax. Blood poured up into my head and pounded like thunder as my eyes reset themselves. I had only a headache by the time Grace came, but the pressure on my throat would return periodically throughout my life at times of great stress.

When my father came home, Grace tried to hold me to the little brown wooden step stool where I sat in the kitchen.

"No, you don' run to him jes yet. You let yo' po daddy get his drink."

But Grace wasn't strong enough to stop me, and Joe, who had started to appear in our kitchen again, didn't help her. I freed myself and dashed out through the swinging doors down the long hall to my father's study.

"Daddy, Mummy tore my book and—"

"Harry, don't believe her. She's lying." My mother came running.

I flew back to the kitchen for the book that Grace had fixed, but the furious lady got there first. She grabbed the small volume from Grace and thrust it into Joe's hands.

"NO!" I screamed, trying to stop him from taking away what I needed so badly to make my daddy believe me.

"Burn it, burn it, go, go!" she shouted, pushing him out into the night to the small section of yard outside our kitchen where I soon saw orange flames shooting up from the incinerator. Again, I ran back to the study and my father, with the angry lady in pursuit.

"Daddy, Daddy, they burnt it, my book, my—"

"Don't listen, Harry, she's making it up. She's lying!"

"No, SHE'S lying!"

We screamed like an operatic duo, a mother and daughter become equal in their intense need for a man's attention and belief.

But my father heard only my mother.

"Anne, you are being rude!"

I felt my size and insignificance and jumped up on the two-seater corduroy couch across from my father's chair. I picked up one of the pillows, throwing it with all of my strength at his chest, using both hands and aiming perfectly.

The drink spilled on his jacket and tie. He held the glass out to save himself from more of the icy Scotch. "You get out of here this minute!"

While he mopped himself with his handkerchief, I leapt down off the couch. On the way out, I gave two hard whacks with my little-girl shoes to my mother's beautiful slender shins.

My father jumped up and chased after me. I fled to the playroom, down the stairs by the kitchen where Grace and Joe watched. My father took his belt off as he went downstairs, but once in the cellar, he took a minute or two before using it, in order to kick my shins with his big-father shoes.

"Now you can see what that feels like. Don't you ever do that to your mother again! Get down on your hands and knees."

I obeyed, though the tile floor of the darkened playroom was cold and hard. Heavy, stinging, blows whipped down on my bare back, precisely where the marks of the hanger had been one year earlier, until his fury was spent. Then he left me and went upstairs.

I stayed on all fours, rigid with pain. Joe came down to the cellar playroom and found me. Had my father told Grace not to come to me? The dark brown man cuddled and rocked me, while my tears fell on his skin. He told me that the best thing for me would be if I could be adopted by Grace and him and come live with them when they got their own home.

During the peaceful weeks while my mother was away at the rest home, now called *the hospital*, Louise kept her bedroom door open, and she shared with me her love of learning.

In the afternoons, she taught me to draw pictures of the sounds that words made. We laughed over how "SHUSH!" looked on the paper. The sinister reprimand, so constant in our lives, was reduced to funny squiggles before our eyes.

Louise's attention and her admiration of my ability to draw letters made me happy. I took my precious drawings down to a newfound secret place in the playroom, a small closet tucked under the wooden staircase that zig-zagged downwards from the kitchen, where I could hear Grace's radio playing. I felt warm and comforted in this new spot I'd found, safe enough to bring the most forbidden of all objects—the books I loved that I'd heard my mother say no one should read to me anymore.

I didn't like the room that was called the playroom. It was a cold place, its black and shiny hard tile floor edged by high white stucco walls that hurt me if I got bumped into them. The only warm color in this room, other than the brown wooden stairs going up to the kitchen, was the pile of toys way over at the northeast corner … my corner. Though I loved color and wanted everything *colored*, perhaps because that was the word used for Grace, at night the small rectangular windows placed at the top of the stucco walls looked like eyes. Their sills rested on the same level as the cold earth outside and their blackness made my toy corner seem like a scary place. No, the closet was better.

There was one hanging bulb inside that shed its yellow warmth and danced like a companion if I brushed against the long pull-string. I loved the cozy lamp, so different from the long white and cold lights that shown down from the playroom's high ceiling.

One evening, after dinner, I began to use the drawings of sounds I'd learned from Louise to write a letter to Jessie. I took my time. Sheets of paper were strewn around next to my books as I discarded unsatisfactory efforts. I had to be very careful and

127

very clear. Jessie must be told that my father had not kept the promise he'd made to her before she left, to keep my mother good. I wrote:

S H E S B A D A G I N

Suddenly Susie appeared in the doorway of my closet. She was always making marks on my pictures and laughing at them, or she would tear them up. I had become used to her annoying habits, but this time I was on an earnest mission and acted fast. I grabbed up my papers before being chased by my sister out into the wide expanse of the playroom.

"You're not supposed to be reading!" she yelled, grabbing the heaviest one of my books and hurling it down on my head.

As I crumpled to the ground, she must have panicked and run up the stairs to call for our father. My daddy found me picking up my precious sheets.

"I don't want you writing. I want you to wait for school," he said. He went into the little closet where crayons, books, and papers were lying around on the floor and pulled the hanging chain of my little lamp; then he unscrewed the bulb, leaving the socket swinging bare, though I'd been taught that was dangerous.

"I need the light to read," I said.

"You can't read."

"Louise is teaching me."

"No, you wait for school," he said and started to walk away.

"BUT I WANT TO READ MY BOOKS!"

"Someone will read to you."

"No they won't." I knew that Grace and Louise wouldn't have time, and Susie wouldn't want to. "My mother told me she won't read to me again."

"She never said that."

"She did, too, and she tore up my book."

By this time I was backing away from him. He looked very angry and walked toward me, repeating that my mother had not said those things, could not have. I stepped back again, repeating what I'd said.

We were now by the cellar door that opened into the large garage under our house. My father grabbed my arm and hurried me through the enormous cement space to the outer door. He put me outside where I could see the dark driveway that curved down to the street below.

"You stay out here until you can learn to say nice things about your mother." He shut the large heavy door with its high knob.

It was dusk. I waited by the door that I couldn't open, bewildered by this new problem and the empty world I found myself in. I'd never been outside alone in the front of our huge palace-like house. Even Louise couldn't help me with my whimpering out here as I waited for the minutes to go by.

Suddenly, I saw Joe coming up the driveway. The big man crouched down in front of me. My hand immediately shot up to the burning wound on my head. I wanted to share it with him. He didn't spank me or swipe my hand away the way my mother did whenever I rubbed or pointed to a painful place on my body that had been hurt. He scooped me up in his strong arms and opened the door, marching through the garage, into the cellar and playroom, then on upstairs to the pantry by the kitchen and down the hall, right into my father's study, where he stood with me on his shoulders so high I could almost touch the ceiling.

"Mr. Davidson, I've had enough with what I've seen you do to this child." He lowered me down as his fingers probed my silken waves to find again the gash with its dried blood, showing it to the man. "What can you be thinking of, putting this baby outside at this time of night—and after you hurt her?"

My father stood up, his face reddening.

"Listen here, you stupid nigger ... you mind your own business!"

My hero put me down and backed away. I watched him walk away without saying anything. I felt bad for him hearing that nasty word "stupid" said to him when he'd been helping me.

My father bent over to look at the cut on my head, lifting away my hair to do so. He went to the bottom of the stairs and called Susie to come down.

"Did you do this to your sister?"

"Yes."

"Why?"

"Because our mother said she wasn't supposed to read again."

My father sat down. He stared out the window by his desk, into the woods at the side of our house and the black night.

We waited. We both waited for the correction, the words of criticism to Susie for injuring me. She had always been my father's favorite, losing that place only temporarily to me at Christmastime, when I had become his "Little Angel." But still, she must have expected a word of reproach from her usually reserved father, and I hoped she would be taken to the playroom and beaten with his belt.

Whatever mysterious and fascinating world he was looking at out of his black night window, it kept our father's attention longer than we sisters could bear. Our tension broke out at each other.

"You did it, you hit me!" I said.

"I did not!" she yelled weakly against my fists and nails. "You weren't supposed to read!" she screamed, finally getting hold of my arms and keeping me away from her face.

Thunder boomed from the window. "Both of you get out of here!"

We ran, as always, to the kitchen, to the comfort waiting for us, though we knew that this was serious business; this was not a Grace-problem, it was a Jessie-problem!

We fled down the cellar steps, hardly bothering to enlist Grace's help, our fury with each other exploding. I got to the playroom first, grabbing my precious pages and holding them to my chest, huddled against my sister's oncoming attack. Susie went after them, pulling and punching, scratching my arms until I cried out for Grace who climbed down the stairs after us.

She grabbed my sister and pulled the furious girl off me.

"What you think you doin,' Miss?"

"But Daddy said she shouldn't be writing yet, and she's been writing something."

"Honey, tha's between her an' her daddy. Now you go on upstairs right now this minute and you tell yo' good daddy you sorry you hurt yo' li'l sister."

Grace sat down on the same wooden stool Joe had used one month earlier and reached out her hands toward me. I stood my ground, still clutching my drawings and letters in my fists, my arms bleeding from Susie's scratches. I stared at the person who had pushed me another time into the arms of the dangerous lady.

Suddenly my vocal chords reached down deep into my waist area for their scary volume as I let out a screech of rage at Grace and my father! My sister had not been punished for bludgeoning me on the head with a book! Now she had scratched the skin of my forearms into red streaks and not been spanked for it!

Grace tried to hush the alarming sound of my screams, as she glanced upstairs, but she didn't stop me. When my cries became sobs, she gathered me to her, my chest and heart next to hers until the sounds became whimpers. I pulled myself from the tight arms that held me and fell over onto her lap, my tummy giving up its final heaves against her great thighs. My head and legs hung down limply, the papers falling from my unclenched hands.

I never saw my letters to Jesse again.

Grace must have picked me up and carried me upstairs to the bathroom where she washed and dressed my wounds. I remember the fragrance of Witch Hazel, a scent I came to love. Then she gathered me up for our nightly rocking and songs, but I was asleep before she had finished one verse.

Louise felt the same way I did about my mother. She tried to help me make new letters for Jessie. We would get up in the middle of the night and creep down to the playroom to write together, but I don't think she mailed the papers as she promised. I didn't pester her about it because I began to think Grace would be able to help me find safety again, just as she had comforted me in the playroom

And she did, for a while.

When my mother returned from the hospital, I felt the lady wasn't any nicer than before she'd gone. Grace and I had a heart-to-heart moment as I sat one morning on the little two-step stool, my favorite spot in the kitchen.

I asked, with great solemnity, "Why can't my mother get fixed?" I couldn't understand why the doctors couldn't get her better the way Grace had fixed my book—she had painstakingly glued the pig story back together before it got burned up.

The answer came with equal solemnity, "Oh, Honey, Ah guess some things jes cain't be fixed."

I looked at her. I had never heard such a serious deliberation from Grace about the lady I feared so much, nor had I ever felt so grown up. The brown woman was putting a chicken in the oven to roast. I walked over to her, visualizing with a calm finality that the fat bird in the pan was my mother.

As Grace closed the oven door, I turned to her with trust, confident in my decision to formally claim her as my parent. Any disappointments in her earlier failure to agree with me about the lady who was supposed to be my mother vanished from my heart due to her honest appraisal of my parent's condition and the respect shown for my plight.

"Grace, Ah loves you."

"Ah loves you, too, darlin'."

We hugged, the large-bosomed woman leaning over to gather me in her arms, and I, a skinny child, reaching up to gather back. A rush of good memories from earlier, of green grass and the wonder in spring that Grace and I had loved together, as well as the concept of God's beautiful world she had shared with me as a toddler swept over me.

I didn't need to write Jessie another letter. I had Grace.

Chapter 14 – Joe Saves Me

My mother must have been listening behind the swinging kitchen door, because she burst into the room.

"You let Grace do her work!"

The jealous woman grabbed me by the arm and pulled me over to the cellar door, throwing me head over heels down the stairs to the playroom. It was probably the halfway landing, as well as the relative softness of the wood, that saved my life. Even so, I felt as if I had died as I crouched at the bottom of the stairs, my pain pushing tiny sounds out of my closed throat.

Grace was not allowed to come to me. When I could hear again, it was *her* voice I heard, crying. My mother stood on the stairwell's landing, looking at me. She didn't move. I didn't move.

Like a squirrel that watches to check if its world is motionless again, having just seen a human face in the window, I waited. I don't remember whether it was the flick of my mother's eyelid or vibration of a syllable that sent me into motion. I fled, this time to the corner of the room, where I could watch any movement from the stairs.

Grace's crying and pleading did no good. My mother didn't let her bring me anything, no food, drink, or warm clothes during the long hours I waited in my cold corner, fighting the intermittent attempts by my mother to approach me. I was a strong child—at almost four—and had enough curled-and-slashing strength to foil her.

She must have begun to worry about my father coming home and finding me in my corner, a cold ball of anger and purpose, waiting to show him the living proof of what his wife was capable of doing to me. My father had been my last hope, but my plan was foiled when Joe came walking through the door from our garage into the cellar, arriving for his after-work visit.

My mother ran to him as he stood in the laundry room staring at me. She begged him to pick me up and carry me to my bedroom, which he did, avoiding my bites and kicks with his iron arm around my waist holding me firmly against his hard body—as if my twisting was no more to him than that of a fish in one of my father's fisherman's nets. But Joe was not able to stop my screams until he came to my father's study and went inside to look around at the book-lined walls.

"Look at all these books, and the man is a fool! All his big-shot learnin', and he don't know what's goin' on in his own house!"

I stopped my yelling because I agreed with what he was saying about my father not believing that my mother was hurting me. Then we went on with our battle, up the stairs and down the hall to my room. Joe told me to put my pajamas on and stay there. Then he closed the door.

I waited a few minutes and then crept out of my room, determined to get back downstairs to my corner in the playroom where I could finish my protest in the shape of a wounded ball. As I rounded the corner from the upstairs hallway, I saw my mother standing on the halfway landing.

"You get back to your room where you belong!" she yelled up at me.

Standing strong and tall above her, my two legs wide open and defiant like boys I had seen on the playground at my sister's school, I shouted back something like what Jessie had confided to Susie and me a few days before she left, "You get back to the hospital where you belong!"

The irate woman screamed at me and flew up the rest of

the stairs, chasing me into my bedroom. She grabbed me by the armpits, lifted me up, and started to smash my head down on the round wooden globe that topped one of the bedposts, when Joe, who had zoomed back upstairs, snatched her arms and saved me from oblivion.

He carried me down the hall to my mother's bedroom. Shutting the door, he sat me down on her dressing room table where I begged for water. I remember confusion and hearing the two of them talking in the bathroom, then seeing Joe return just in time to catch my fainting fall.

I woke up, held high in Joe's arms, out of reach of my mother. He was standing in front of the closed door of her bedroom. There was a golden light all around him and me, filling my chest area as well as in my mind. It was as if Grace's God was speaking to me saying "Something good is going to happen." Held up high as Heaven it seemed, I felt safe, loved, and certain that I would be all right.

Joe was moving me from one side of himself to the other. Then I saw my mother holding a huge pair of silver scissors from her dressing table, and she was trying to stick me with the thin, gleaming silver that was as long as one of my arms! Joe looked down at the flashing points, which had begun to jab *him*, and switched his hold on me from two hands to one!

I lay flat, holding myself still and perfectly balanced, my stomach held up by his palm and outstretched fingers. Joe reached for the doorknob, but the awful lady stuck him, so he changed direction. Never taking his eyes off my mother and her hands, my hero edged his way over toward the chaise lounge and set me down on the long chair. Lifting his foot up, Joe pushed me backwards toward the farthest corner of the comfy blue furniture.

"You stay there!" he growled at me. Then he grabbed the long pointed scissors from my mother and walked her back through the dressing room into the bathroom. I heard water running and words like "prison" and "I know what it's like" and "Do you really want that?"

I may have fallen asleep, but I remember being carried down to the end of the hall where Grace waited in the doorway to the maid's quarters. She was leaning against the heavily hinged wooden door to keep it open, knowing that she shouldn't be in the White part of the house for no reason, but also figuring that she might be needed.

"Joe," she said softly, for his ear only, "Should I go on down an' git Misus Strong?"

My mother came up right behind us. "I'll fire you just like Jessie if you go to Mrs. Strong or if you tell anyone about this!"

I still didn't understand what *firing* meant, but I had no time to think about it. Joe took me into my bedroom and closed the door on the two women, putting me gently down on my bed as Grace called from the hall.

"Joe, she done had nothin' to eat since nine this mo'nin'!"

He told her to be quiet and undressed me carefully, putting on my pajamas and laying me down under my sheet and blanket. He looked tired. He rested his face on his folded arms that lay next to me on the bed while I put my head down on my pillow, exhausted.

The fight was over. There would be no message for my father when he came home, even if I could remember what it was. A new problem had been added, but my brain could neither comprehend nor contain it.

As if Joe had been standing on the grassy bank in front of our house and caught me under the window the night I feared being thrown out of it by my mother, Grace's boyfriend became my next mother substitute. I felt not only deep gratitude but great love for him.

I was not the only one. My mother and Joe became lovers, though I didn't know it until a month later. I did think it strange that he began putting me to bed and at a time when it was still bright outside. I didn't realize that my mother needed to get her lover upstairs early enough so that he could return to the kitchen before my father came home.

I didn't like being put to bed when June sunshine poured through my western window, feeling that I was being cheated from a longer chance to play. After all, I had gotten used to staying up to greet my father. Yet I fell into a deep sleep the minute I lay down, as if I had been drugged, as I well may have been, a suppository slipped into my bottom during my bath. It wouldn't have been convenient for my mother if I'd suddenly jumped up from my bed and run down the hall into her bedroom.

Chapter 15 – Sunshine

My mother began a strange reversal of roles, taking on my care and forbidding Grace to come near me. I suspect that my *brown mother* had been just as scared of my mother's jealous attack as I had been, for she kept far away from me.

I was told to stay in my room in the mornings. Once my father had left for the office and my sisters for school, the scary lady came into my room and told me to get my clothes on. She waited until I'd dressed myself, while she kept watch for Grace out in the hallway. Then I was taken downstairs, made to eat something, and all but tossed into the basement playroom.

I didn't see my Grace anywhere. I was kept below the whole day, though sunshine burst through the small east-facing windows at the top of the white stucco walls during the mornings, and cold air filled the black-tiled room after I'd eaten the lunch brought down to me by the unfriendly lady.

After Grace did laundry behind the closed and locked cellar door, the overworked woman was forced by my mother to carry her basket of damp clothes outside rather than through the playroom. She had to walk down the driveway then back up our back path of twenty-five slate slabs to the kitchen yard in order to get to the clothesline. Only when Grace was busy cooking dinner in the kitchen was I allowed to play in the rest of the house or outside.

My sisters were nowhere in sight. I was sure my mother had sent them to their rooms because she didn't want me talking to them, but now I think they'd been farmed out for dinner with our cousins, a friendly family who had been asked to help many times, being told that "Margaret needs a break."

Though I missed the fun of playing with my sisters and the sunshine, I had my own form of both. Late in the afternoon, every day for the next month, except on weekends and on Grace's day off, Joe arrived at our house. After feeding me, my mother took me upstairs, bathed me and brought me to my room, where Joe was waiting for me.

There I was played with, sung to, danced with, and charmed, in a way that filled me with enough joy to get me through the next day's emptiness. Joe became the sunshine of my life. Sometimes he brought me a pretty flower he had picked up on the way. Then he'd put it in my hair with a barrette before closing the door on my mother and beginning our wonderful playtimes. He tossed, swung, and whirled me in a frenzy of activity and commotion.

Sometimes he held me up with one hand. Exhilarated, I floated above him in a circular motion, looking down at his concentrating face, our four eyes registering the pleasure of this peaceful moment as we remembered the other time he had held me like this after my mother had attacked us. Then he would lower me, take my ankles and turn me upside down until my brain felt full and my face burned. I would put my arms up to be rescued, and he would, to my squawking delight.

"Shh," Joe said. "They'll come in and we'll have to stop!"

As my blood raced back down from my swollen face, I glowed with delight. Sometimes, Joe grabbed my knees and pulled me closer to him. "Let's get away from those nasty bedposts," he said as he twirled me harder. My hair flew away from my head, while I hung as far out as I could, feeling free and safe at the same time, and thrilled to be alive. With Joe, life seemed to be filled with warmth, tenderness, delightful sensations, excitement, and safety.

Each evening when we were finished playing, he pulled the

chair over by the window, and we rocked together, cooling our sweaty bodies in the early evening breezes coming through my windows. The full green leaves of June waved to us from the maple tree outside my window, the world outside and in giving me a sense of peace and comfort. The bottoms of my feet hugged Joe's shoes as I rode his walk over to put me into bed.

My companion came to mean more to me than a conveyer of fun and pleasure. He fixed me mentally, too. About my mother hitting my head on the bedpost, he said, "You weren't doing anything wrong. She's bad. She's a bad lady." These remarks lifted me, just as Jessie's remarks about my mother had the year before. They meant that I was good.

Joe had solutions for how I could survive. I shouldn't try to fight my mother. I should expect her to be bad. When I asked him why my father couldn't do anything to stop her from hurting me, he said, "He doesn't know what to do about your mother." And that was that. When I was near my father and annoyed with him for not doing something about my situation, I thought, *Oh, I feel sad for him, he doesn't know what to do*.

I learned from Joe that I should accept how things were in my family, even though they weren't good. This concept of resignation gave me strength, and I blossomed under his care, as if I were a gigantic sunflower, big headed, strong, and high above everyone else. With all of Joe's thrilling influence stimulating my brain and my body, I felt that I did not need my own family anymore.

Nor did I hunger for Grace's company. My mother couldn't have found a better way to complete the separation she had started between my brown mother and me than to arrange nightly playtimes with Joe. I suspect that she told Grace I had asked him to put me to bed, because I sensed a kind of hurt in her face whenever I did catch a glimpse of her. In some ways I didn't care, feeling angry with Grace for letting "Misus

Davidson" come between us.

I explored everything about my new substitute father, amazed at the difference between him and my real one. He had dirt on his shoes, whereas my father's polished footwear was spotless. I would look up from the ground at Joe's dark pants and feel them, the soft and worn cloth clinging to his legs, whereas the crease of my father's trousers separated the cloth from his. The tunes Joe hummed while he rocked me made me relaxed instead of jumpy—the way I'd felt when being danced around by my father.

Brown, always the color of the word love for me, now became the color for the word "truth." Joe spoke the truth and stood for what was true in my life. I would finger the buttons and frayed collar of his shirts and look under the sleeves at his dark arms, smelling him with pleasure because it was the same odor as Grace's, though stronger, the smell I had first learned to associate with love.

Chapter 16 – Dreaming

One evening, Joe seemed sad when he came to put me to bed. I tried to comfort him but he continued to be gloomy. Sometimes he complained about my mother.

"That Bitch!" he said when he talked about her. But then he stopped speaking to me and sat reading his newspaper as if I weren't there. It was painful for me to be ignored. I tried to make him notice me, asking him questions or singing happy songs. Sometimes I could get him to share what he was reading, though hearing about fighting going on in a place called Europe was scary until he promised me that the war wouldn't affect us. But then he became cross, as if annoyed by me, so I learned to sit quietly, leaning against him and loving that at least I had his presence next to me.

One night after Joe left, the voice of my mother sounded soft and kind through my bedroom door. My brain swam down into the creamy, comforting sleep that I'd become used to, my mind dimmed by the lime-colored light coming through dark green shades that had been pulled down over my sunny windows, and I dreamt that my life was safe. The tenderness in my mother's voice meant to me that, now, she was going to be good.

When I woke up, I was so certain of this change in her that I didn't think she would mind if I ignored her rule to stay in my bedroom until she came. I chose a sundress, knowing that I would be allowed to play outside on Grace's day off, and dashed down the back stairs to the kitchen, where my cereal had been left for me.

I was excited as I ate my breakfast, looking out the windows at the bright summer sunshine and thinking about all the things I would do with my freedom, both in the house and outside. I liked that my sisters had left for their summer camps, because they might have pestered me in my choices. I felt reborn and ready to try out my White family again.

I swung open the pantry door into the dining room to look for something fun to do, and there, on the table, were crayons and papers and books. The possibility that they had been left by my mother confirmed my idea that she was a changed lady. I ran to them, picking up one after the other like a famished person who isn't sure where to begin the meal.

Suddenly I heard a noise from the hall. It was Joe's voice, as if he were singing. I looked up, and couldn't believe my eyes. I went over to the doorway of the dining room. Down in the middle of the hall, at the part that faced the front door, my mother knelt on the floor, facing Joe and holding a part of him in her hands. I thought he was making her do what she was doing, and I didn't like it. I would have to tell my father about this.

I turned away from them to go back to my things, but before I could touch anything, I was grabbed and set up on the dining room table. Joe looked at me and asked what I'd seen. I didn't want to say it, but he slapped my face, so I did.

"My mother was on her knees and you were hurting her."

He grabbed me and sat me in the chair by the door to the porch. He put his foot up on my chest and asked me again what I'd seen. I started to describe it but he pushed so hard I couldn't get any words out. He pushed more and asked me again, until I wasn't able to breathe.

Then he said, "That's right. Nothing. You saw nothing!" I struggled for air, but he wouldn't let me go, his shoe against my stomach, my breakfast collecting in my throat. "And if you breathe one word about anything, you won't ever catch your breath again, you hear?"

I fell off the chair and crawled past the door to the porch out to the lilac bush that sent its perfume to comfort me as I threw up on its roots. With the food went my idea that my mother had changed. She had not stopped Joe from hurting me, as a good mummy would have. I stayed under the large green leaves of the protective bush until I gained the strength to crawl away. Once I reached the brick foundation of the house, I dug a cool hole in the sand and hid.

There was a terrible ache from the pain in my chest, both physical and emotional. I felt humiliated and betrayed. I had thought Joe loved me. Apparently he did not, this person who had helped me survive a scary mother, and who had made living a fun thing as well as explaining my family to me! My sunshine man had become a gray cloud in my overcast sky. I vomited again and crawled farther along the sandy soil beside my house.

No one came to get me until late in the afternoon when Grace, called back from her day off and cross about it, carried me inside and pushed me into my pajamas. Furious at her lack of insight into my situation, I slammed the door on her fingers, as she tried to close me in for the night so she could run back to her freedom.

That summer I hid myself away, literally, in a hole next to the red brick foundation of our white house that faced our back yard, dug into sandy soil that molded itself to my body. I never saw my parents, because they left our house soon after my sisters had gone to camp for their month-long vacation in the mountains. Joe had disappeared also. No one bothered me except Grace, who fed, bathed, clothed me, and brought me into the house for naps, rescuing me from the afternoon summer sun that would find its way around to the western side of our house and my hiding place.

Often at midmorning, Grace enticed me inside for a cookie. She knew I would eat nothing that wasn't sweet, which was perhaps an unconscious way to medicate myself. I may have been trying to get rid of my memories by eating only sugar-filled starch and blowing out my brains with the slowness of thought and sleepiness that such a steady diet of carbohydrates causes.

Sometimes Grace served the snack as if I were a princess, at the dining room table where she sat with her black coffee, loving it in a slurpy way. Perhaps she thought coffee would help wake me up, because sometimes she served it to me in a special pink-flowered china cup and saucer on a pretty doily. I drank my sweetened light brown liquid, watching my books and crayons that had been set out to entice me, but I always wandered back outside to my resting place. There I curled up next to the house, watching the ants sharing my sandy home as they scurried around, until I fell asleep in the heavy humid air of the summer morning.

Occasionally I felt a twinge of guilt for not talking to Grace or thanking her for saving me from the hallucinating brightness of the sun in the afternoon and carrying me into the kitchen. I would smile in joy at the thought of reconnecting when I heard the mantra that accompanied her approaches to me, "Po' Lamb, Po' Lamb."

Because I knew from my picture books that lambs were "white as snow" and because I was angry at Joe, my idea that I was the little White girl of a White family became stronger, with Grace as my doting nursemaid who would do anything for me. Though tempted to show my love toward her for taking care of me, I let the moments of longing for closeness pass, fearful that if I talked to her I might break Joe's restrictions. I kept my mouth shut, forgetting even the hope of warmth between us.

Towards the end of the summer, I began to think of myself

as a male child. Just as I had thought it would be better to be and act like a strong boy when around my mother, I now decided that I would be better off in general to be one. Boys were strong. Boys fought. Boys talked back. They controlled. They didn't have to sit and take the bossiness of other people, as I'd seen Grace do with Joe and as I'd done in the dining room chair while being yelled at.

When my sisters returned from camp, Louise came to greet me in my backyard home. She had a sad look and tears in her eyes at my plight. She begged me to come with her, and I did.

She swung me around and around in the middle of the end-of-summer-burnt-grass lawn, but after our moments of joy, she confided, while we walked to the porch, "You know, I understand why you hide. I hate coming back here, too."

I looked at her and fled back to my warm place in the soft sand, resting my head on the ground. The intensity of my sister's clenched voice had reinforced my own feeling of hopelessness.

In the desperate pleading of her words, as she begged me to leave my sand and come with her, I heard her grief and anger with herself for spoiling what she had almost achieved. She made it up to me later, once I had decided to come inside, by giving me a golden September of rocking and the sound of camp songs in her deep smooth alto voice—with lots of passion and the love of nature in it—up in her room, both of us squeezed tightly into her bedroom rocking chair.

Susie was sent out to "get Anne to talk," but her coaxing and tickling did not succeed in getting me to open my mouth.

However, out there in my lonely yard, with autumn winds hinting at their approach from across the field, I knew I had to give up my outdoor refuge. Finally, I trudged back into life, lugging my enormous secret deep inside me, never, ever to be told to anyone for fear of the shoe in the chest and not being able to breathe.

Chapter 17 – Saying Goodbye

I returned to the kitchen as my hang-out place. One night I stopped in the doorway because I saw Joe sitting on his chair in his usual place. I had forgotten all about him. He said something to me, a remark that was complimentary and flirty, but he must have been talking to the sweet child I'd been, that little girl who was outside safe where I had left her in my hiding place. I was angry, and according to a nursery rhyme we'd often heard, girls were sweet and good while boys were nasty and bad—so I was doubly sure I was a boy.

I didn't answer Joe. I hadn't said one word to anyone since he had threatened me in the spring.

He could see that I was taller, but he didn't know that I'd changed my gender. Feeling full of my new boy-strength I lunged at him, my fists hard and fast, digging into his chest as I silently yelled "Bad! Bad!" Then I lowered my head and banged into his breastbone, exactly where his foot had pushed against me three months earlier.

He didn't stop me, but sat there looking down at me hitting him. Exhausted, I glanced at his face while panting and then stole a look at Grace. She wasn't paying any attention, yet I didn't dare ask Joe in front of her why he'd hurt me. Instead, I pounded him with my fists again, the intensity of my attack asking him, "How could you have caused me so much pain when you had been my best friend?"

Still furious but fatigued, I sprawled over his lap. Then he lifted me up in his arms and held me, rocking both of us as if to say he was sorry. And that's when the tears came, silently, because I didn't dare to let Grace hear me. I hid my face under his arm, smelling that smell again that meant love.

So we got back together, in the way it had been at first, with Joe as someone in the kitchen to play with and love, the strong person I could hold onto when scared, and the member of our household who took my side and who said what was true. Only now I felt like a quiet boy instead of the talkative girl I'd been the spring before.

And I was brown in my mind, not White. Feeling loved by Joe again and ignored by my war-preoccupied parents, I came to believe that I was truly the child of the brown family whose home was in our kitchen.

During that fall of 1941 I spent every evening sitting on Joe's lap after he came from his work at the factory, identifying with this man who had been fun but who now grew more sober every day. Instead of music and serials the radio told us about the war in Europe. By mid-December we heard that our soldiers would have to go *over there* because of an awful thing called *Pearl Harbor* that had happened somewhere very far away.

One night, as Joe talked with Grace before going home, I heard him say that he was going to Virginia, to "help build ships for our war effort."

"JOE, YOU CAN'T GO!" I ran from my chair.

"Hey, Grace! She started talkin' again!" Joe swept me up, setting me on the kitchen counter, near the sink where Grace was washing up the dinner dishes. Then, gently he confided to me, "Honey, I don't want to go. I have to go. And don't you think I'm not scared! I'm plenty scared. But I got to be brave and you got to be brave just like me."

He turned away from an unhappy Grace, and started down the cellar stairs with me galloping after him, the sounds from the kitchen radio fading behind us. I grabbed at him, catching his pants as he crossed from the playroom into the cellar.

Allowing the little-girl part of me to come back, with all the verbal energy and emotion that had been stuck inside her all summer, I yelled out my love.

"JOE, I CAN'T LIVE HERE IF YOU GO!"

The big dark man bent down to hug me and then was gone.

A few days after Christmas, he left our house for good. I was enraged that I, the one who had been most attached to him, of all my sisters, was not to be included in the group escorting him to the railroad station. My father was to drive, with Grace, Louise, and Susie going along, leaving "no room for" me. My mother, who had returned from her sister's house a bit nicer, held onto my hand as we stood on the cement balcony, watching.

"I'm little! There's plenty of room!" I yelled out through the iron railings at the group that had descended the circular front steps. "It's *not* too late!" I screamed my answer to Susie's taunt from the driveway below, as I squirmed to free myself from my mother's grip. What could they all be thinking? Joe had been *my* lap, *my* comforter, *my* confidant and now, *I myself*, was not to be allowed to go with him to the train!! And I was being left with this lady I didn't want to be near.

She wouldn't even let me wave through the storm glass door though I yearned to share in the excitement and stretch out my goodbyes. Furious, I ran past her up the stairs to get away. But my mother, the person in our family who demanded that others leave her alone when *she* was unhappy, could not accept that I needed the same thing. She followed me and found me curled up and sobbing on the dark red oriental carpet in the upstairs hall. At her touch I turned, my shoes and arms striking out at her, my desperation at her interference turned into a tantrum.

When I remembered this scene as an adult, long after I'd finished dealing with most of my memory recalls, the pain I felt was so fierce that a psychologist I phoned had to lead me through a visualization process to release me from its hold.

"Think of a woman you consider a wonderful mother. How would she have acted at that point?"

My children hadn't had tantrums, so I'd had no experience with how to handle them. Then I remembered how both Grace and Joe had dealt with mine.

"She would have waited and watched me flail around," I answered. "When I became exhausted I might have recognized her patience as an attempt to help me and gone to sob out my grief in her arms." I thanked the therapist, Renee Rocklin, and hung up the phone, restored to balance.

I understood that my mother, now returned a nicer person from her visit with her sister, had wanted to comfort me, but she didn't know how. The youngest of ten children and raised by siblings, who likely had also been neglected by their hardworking parents, my mother had not learned these skills.

To be the one assuaging pain instead of giving it should have been a golden opportunity for her. If she had treated my grief with respect and understanding, it could have been a peak moment for change in my childhood, providing a way for me to start transferring my trust of Joe onto her. But my mother had not returned home *fixed*, as Grace and I'd hoped, and she was unable to act in a way that could have surmounted the bad history between us.

Instead of waiting for me to calm down, my mother became angry and threatened me. I jumped up and squeezed by her, hurling myself down the stairs for a mad dash to the kitchen, a hurting animal seeking solace in my own time and space.

When I realized that the lady was coming after me into my comfort-corner (the farthest reach of the kitchen, and of the house, with its wall only fifteen feet from the kind neighbor's rose-covered fence) with no one else around to help me, I let loose a blood-curdling scream. My mother stopped suddenly. My scream's message of unbearable terror and wild hatred had pierced her self-centered mind and reverberated there.

She sank down into one of the kitchen chairs, actually Joe's chair, turned around, as it always was, with its back to the kitchen table. He could sit there and survey the situation, teasing Grace lightly, joking with a loud laugh, or turning his charm on whichever child was lucky enough to be around. When he wasn't feeling too beat, or too full from the delicious dinner he would have been lucky enough to find ready for him, then he'd stand up and hold me up high 'til I shrieked with delight hard enough that Grace would make him put me down.

I woke from my reverie to realize that my mother was still sitting in that chair, and that *she was not moving*!

I got up and tiptoed around in front of her. She was looking off into space. She didn't see me. I asked what strange way of acting this was, and she answered, not looking at me, not moving a muscle.

"They call it a depression." I thought that was a funny thing. I did a little dance in front of her, taunting her, even poking her immobile form, without being able to change the dazed focus in her eye. I realized that I was now the one in control, and that I, with my *own* voice, had saved myself!

I decided I could do anything I wanted, and I did something I had always wanted to do—punish my mother for all the bad things she had done to me. I would copy my father's way of punishing me the spring before down in the playroom when he had kicked me.

But first, I had to change from my grieving little-girl self back into my boy-personality, because Grace had told me many times that little girls didn't hit people. I tiptoed around in back of the statue-still lady and climbed silently up on the kitchen table, so that I was standing in back of her. Then I lifted my leg, with its foot still clad in its hard daytime shoe, and jammed it with all my strength down onto the back of her head, striking the exact spot where the scary lady had hurt me on the changing table. She fell forward, but to my amazement, recovered herself, and swiveled around, grabbing my leg and sending me crashing to the floor.

As I fled to the doorway, she caught me, tightening her hold on my shoulders and shaking me as she asked me to say I was sorry. I couldn't speak.

"You're a bad girl!" she said and began to twist my shoulders back and forth, until my eyes flew like two blobs of light, whistling from side to side inside my skull, my neck becoming putty for the whirling globe above it, the words "How dare you!" lost as they crawled through her gritted teeth. Then she picked me up, and with all her might and fury, flung me careening through the air toward the overhanging edge of the kitchen counter, the one between the sink and the corner, and the one I had sat on the night Grace had protected me from the awful lady's knife.

It was a repeat of the andiron incident, my mother's backhand being apparently her strongest one for throwing. And this time, she did not rush to interfere as she had in the living room, cupping her hand between the side of my head and the mantel. The counter edge, slightly sharp, cut my cheek and ear.

I fell to the ground, but staggered up. I had seen a knife, not a big one, just one to cut an apple, sitting on the chin-high counter as I flew past. I reached up and grabbed it, holding it out in front of me and edging my way to the doorway, never taking my eyes off her the way Joe had moved in her bedroom while protecting me months before. When I reached the doorway, I ran down the hall to my father's desk.

I sat in his large wooden chair, looking through the smooth round sticks that formed the hard and bony back at my mother coming for me. I stuck the point of the knife through the space between two gracefully carved dowels.

"Don't you come one step closer to me," I said.

She tried to take the knife. She was so slow and I was quick. I struck out at her and she pulled back. Everywhere her hand was, mine was, as quick and sharp as she had been with her silver scissors months before, when I'd watched, secure in Joe's arms. Now, this day, I felt safe and supported in my father's fortress chair with the desk behind me to support any falling back I might have to do.

The violent lady stood back, telling me to leave the chair. This was definitely not a scene she wanted her husband, who might be coming back any minute, to see.

"I'm staying here until they come back, so I can tell them that you threw me across the room," I made the mistake of telling her.

"WHAT? You want your father to find you with a knife? What do you think he would do to you? That's a crime, you know. He could put you in prison."

She had attended well to Joe's lecture in her dressing room after trying to kill me with the scissors, but now she added the cruel lie that my father would imprisoned one of his children.

"Listen, I'll make a bargain with you. If you don't tell him about the kitchen counter, I won't tell him about the knife."

I dropped the knife on the floor. We went to get Band Aids for the gashes on my cheek and ear. When my father came home, he heard the same lie as when I was two.

"She fell."

Only this time, I, with my willing silence, lied, too.

I returned to the state of quietness I had adopted the spring before. I could not trust that my tongue, once allowed to move, would not say what had happened the night Joe had left our house, and get me sent to prison.

Grace stopped talking also, unless she had to deal with the practical details of our lives, her sadness taking all of her attention. I think she was also preparing for her departure by withdrawing from me.

When I was told that she would be leaving in May to marry Joe in Virginia, I pretended not to care. On the day my brown mother left, my father gave her a ride down to the railroad station. In order to fit everyone in the car, I was allowed to sit on Grace's lap. Feeling separated from her already, I leaned forward.

"Hold her tight, Grace," my father said, as he swung the car out of our garage, "I'm taking a chance with a child in the front seat like that."

At the station, I stood on the platform apart from my family. I saw my skin color the same as the sycamore tree outside our kitchen, basically, a light color, but with the mottled look of tan and brown patches. Perhaps this complexity in my self-image created the love I felt for the bold, black, metal monster as it clanged and thumped its way down the railed tracks towards us. Its mouth seemed moved by the wheels, and its personality was shown by the panting it did even at rest, as if its eagerness to eat up the travelers disappearing into its sides was hard to control. Or maybe I loved the train because it reminded me of Joe, the bold man whom I had loved and then lost and to whom Grace was now going.

With all hugging completed, the person whom I had thought of as my mother climbed the stairs. She looked beautiful in her lilac suit, which smelt like those flowers that had bloomed in our backyard the spring before. Hands waved above me. Mine were in my pockets. I took one out and moved the fingers up and down just so I wouldn't be noticed for not waving. But in my mind the words echoed loud and clear:

"Saying goodbye is no problem for me. I'll be fine. Goodbye!"

The monster roared and thumped again, and I realized that what had been its mouth became its rear end, wiggling at us as it pulled away, like a "Sassy ass whistling Dixie." Grace was not going to South Carolina where her mama and sisters were, but she was going back down in the direction of the south, which I knew gave her great happiness.

And she were glad to be goin'. Tha's a fac, I said to myself. *She be glad to be gwoin'. Not like mah own fam'ly.* I looked up at them. *They was, all of 'em, cryin'! An' me, not a drop. In Grace's eyes they wasn't no tears, neither, not a one, no way, no how, no Ma'am.*

The strangest thing had happened. I'd begun, in my head, to talk like my idea of Grace's dialect when *she done firs' come to us from some place she done called the Souf.* It was as if now that this older and moody Grace had left, I was free to remember the other one, the one who had taught me life was fun and who had given her love openly to me *like sompin, no way!* The one used to *bounce me, an' sing an' smile to me, an' laugh an' talk to me like no one you never did seed, no way.* Then the tears flowed.

I wasn't laughed at on the way home, as I slithered off my mother's lap, hiding my sorrow down under the glove compartment and pressing against the automobile's walls, which were colored a dark brown like my Grace's arms, to merge my groaning with the gruff sounds of the car's engine noise.

In the month after my brown mother's departure, I discovered that the child inside me who cared about living wanted to leave also. She didn't dare stay around without Grace in the house. Even though I had stopped communicating with her very much, I'd needed to know that she was bustling in the kitchen, holding it for me as my place of refuge.

One afternoon before my sisters came home from school I stole money from Louise' piggy bank and walked two short blocks and one very long one down to the bus stop. When I told the bus driver I was on my way to the train station he wouldn't let me get on "without your mother." I slipped into a country estate Grace and I had once walked through. Its white wooden gates had a small door built right into them that I pulled open and climbed through. A Scottish gardener—Grace had told me where he came from when we had visited before—found me, just like Peter Rabbit, among his strawberry patches.

"Hey, there, Lass," the stocky man bent down to me, "what be ya' doin' here now?" he asked, his kindly eyes looking down at me from a rosy-cheeked face. I immediately loved him, trusting anyone who spoke with a dialect. I sat on his lap, enjoying the earthy smell of his gray overalls, as I told him how I'd planned to go find my brown mother.

"Well, now then, Sweetheart, it just can't be like that today. Mebe, how 'bout, mebe it'll be tomorra that you be finding her. How would that be fer ya?"

"Oh, yes," I said my eyes finding his and glowing with joy.

"Well, listen then, me little beautie, this is what we better do right now, today, eh, mi darlin'?"

I found myself on a brown leather seat in a huge black coach, not drawn by horses, but it might have been for its strangeness to me. I felt tiny in the back seat as Mr. Raymond, the "chauffeur," drove me down the mile long curving driveway, out past the bus stop and back up the long hill I had walked down.

I was lucky it was before my father got home from work. The baby sitter begged Mr. Raymond not to tell, but I think he did, because we never saw her again. I found it strange that my father never punished me and even more puzzling that I didn't feel betrayed by the Scottish gardener. I still loved him for listening to me and suggesting that "tomorra" we would find Grace. Nobody had told me I had Scottish genes, but my heart knew.

After a while I forgot him as well as my plans to go away. But the little girl inside me still wanted to leave, so one afternoon I went out to the back yard and buried her—the part of me I associated with feelings of passionate love and terrible anger. I watched her disappear in the freshly dug earth of my father's new Victory Garden, like our grandfather had done, according to Susie who had told me the year before about how he had been put in the ground. Later I went to the oak tree and struggled to scrape enough of a hole in the hard dark soil so that I could bury my little brown-girl self, though I think I was burying Grace, too, because she had not come back as she had promised.

A quality of dreaminess enveloped me. Our good neighbor, who lived in the yard on the other side of our fence and whose garden was responsible for the climbing roses, invited my sister and me on a weeklong vacation trip to the same islands, where the beautiful shiny white boat had taken us as small children. She reported afterwards to my mother and father, "Anne would forget her head if it were not attached."

Still, I kept my mind on what happened around me sufficiently to watch how I behaved. I had figured out that since my mother liked my father, she wouldn't hurt me anymore if I was like him, so I copied his mannerisms, at least the work-week-daytime father who didn't drink his *stinky drinks* as Louise called them. This father was scrupulously neat, punctual, and polite to everyone, and my efforts were hard work, but I was determined to accomplish my goal in order to feel safe around my mother.

I remember the sweet Irish girl, Cathy, with the tight brown curls carefully arranged around her concerned face, as she stood in the doorway of my bedroom telling my mother that I had crumpled all the dresses she had put out for me after my nap, and why was that, did she suppose? From now on I would fight being dressed in any item of clothing that didn't have pant legs—with one exception. I had been given a little suit of Scottish tartan, an orange-red and yellow skirt, vest, and jacket I would have slept in if allowed, its bright colors warming my body on fall days and its name reminding me for a second of someone I had loved, now deep in my lost files of memory.

My eyes joined the effort I had begun, that of changing my personality to be like my father. My right eye took over all the work of seeing, as if it were telling me only to do what was *right*. My left eye stopped being used, and turned inwards again, as if unable to face the fact that Grace had *left* me. With it went any bit of feeling or memory from my earlier life.

Because my parents didn't like how my face looked by the age of six, my unused eye having slid over by my nose, I was made to wear a black patch on the good eye, in hopes that the other one would straighten. But I wouldn't allow it to. I had become terrified of the rage I sensed I would feel if I started to use the left eye again. The doctor and my mother gave up and allowed me to abandon the patch.

My relief at being allowed to see and feel only what I wanted came close to happiness when I realized that my mother had come to like me. She even gave me a new name.

"Sonny suits you better," she told me, saying that it went with my last name, but I knew she was referring to the boyish mannerisms I had copied from my father. The name also suited how I looked.

Shortly after saying goodbye to my brown mother, I had sat in a chair in the backyard where my mother had told me to go for my haircut.

"Grace spent too much time brushing this." She had lifted up the golden locks that had bounced down past my shoulders and sheared them off. She called it a *Dutch boy haircut,* and the sudden change turned my hair straight and brown.

I was happy my plans had worked out, the only sense of what I had lost coming to me at night before bed when I had long conversations with a friend called *Sandy*, his name formed from the combination of *sad* and *Sonny*, a phrase I repeated to myself every night the year I was six.

Sandy helped me bridge the next twelve months of loneliness until I discovered that my private grade school made me feel safe enough to relax and have friends. Even so, as soon as I left the playground for home, I changed back to my other personality, perfecting during the walk home, my imitation of the quiet, unemotional and passive way in which my work-day father conducted himself. This borrowed skill helped me cement connection with my classmates as time went on, because I found myself negotiating within the calm center of their arguments, an easy position since I had few strong opinions of my own about anything.

At eleven, an operation straightened my eyes in a cosmetic way. It looked to others as if I saw straight, but I continued to use only the right eye, a habit encouraged by my increasingly studious life. Sent to an all-girl boarding school for the last part of high school, where I felt as if I'd been put in prison, I nevertheless opened a gate to my future with the strong academic work I did there. Accepted at an excellent but gigantic university, and surrounded by the stimulating energy of students, professors, and town residents, I found the freedom, safety, and time to begin asking myself who I was.

This journey of self-discovery, begun in my late teens, reached its peak at the age of forty, when the rich treasure of insights my flashbacks had spawned propelled me farther along toward recognition of my deepest and darkest roots.

Part Three – Truth

Chapter 18 – PTSD and Tranquilizers

I missed Felix's classes and decided that I would start teaching my own. At first, I thought of giving creative dance because I didn't think I was good enough to instruct what my teacher often referred to as Soul dance. Though I told myself that five years of study hadn't loosened my body sufficiently, my reluctance to teach a style that I'd learned from a Black person in classes where many students would be of color may have been a hangover from my childhood.

Though I'd felt like the child of Grace and Joe when they'd been a part of my household, after they left without a follow-up word or phone call, I felt insecure not only about their love, but also about my right to feel my love for them. Similarly, as a young adult I had been frantic to work in a record store where I could hear the music of Motown that I knew I would need to teach my dance classes, as if there would be no other way to be connected to it. My desperation about that job had been influenced by my forced separation at age five from the Black world that I'd loved and my sense that I would never know it again.

Now, as I began to think of teaching in Felix's style, similar doubts about not being able to enter a world where I was not supposed to be—and not wanted—made me hesitate to start working with the kind of dance I loved. I didn't understand all of this interference from the past and asked myself simply, "Will my Black students bristle at my attempt to teach Soul dance?"

Suspecting that the answer would be *yes*, I decided to try creative dance instead. Yet I felt that one week's training in

Adrienne's style at the summer workshop I had organized had been insufficient.

I was at an impasse.

Suddenly my life did not look as cheerful and promising as my summer successes had made it seem. I had turned forty and hosted a birthday party, which my husband had to miss because of a conference in America. My age weighed on me like a powerful warning that I'd better move forward and fast in my career. Yet I couldn't seem to begin. In this state of concern, I lost interest in the creative work I had been doing in my studio.

At the same time the distant astonishment I had at first felt at discovering that my mother had wounded me many times moved into a state of shock and disorientation. I had assumed that my life in a wealthy and privileged New England household had included an uneventful childhood. I knew that I'd grown up shy and lonely, dropping out of college twice. I remembered that I'd gone to a psychological treatment center for a while, but I had never questioned the reason for my *nervous breakdown*, as it was called in those days. Nor had I ever questioned why Grace's departure had been so devastating for me.

Now with my childhood amnesia breaking apart, I understood: Grace had felt like my true parent because I'd felt unsafe in my own home! I had identified with her, imagining that all I needed to do was eat enough raisins or chocolate for my true brown skin color to come through so that my birth parents would realize who I was and send me where I belonged. Perhaps my endless hours of sitting in college cafés drinking black coffee had been for the same unconscious purpose!

Living in The Netherlands, at a safe distance both in time and place from when and where these events had occurred, the truth of my early life coalesced into clarity. I began to recognize that certain events from my school-going life had been clues to my early childhood story.

At ten I'd seen a movie called *The Search* about the desperate search of a child who had been separated from his mother in a concentration camp and then released at the end of World War II. I sobbed through the film, but was able to keep my reaction secret from my parents since I'd gone to the movie with my sister Susie, and she chose not to tell them. Yet my response had been so vivid, it could be repeated at the slightest glance back to the film, so I had to make sure I was alone when I allowed this reflection. I became fascinated, for a short while, with this tool I had discovered toward locating some intense feeling in my life, but its connection to my own story of loss and yearning for my brown mother remained unconscious.

At twelve, I did not keep my tears to myself. Coming home from the play *Member of the Wedding* that a friend's family had invited me to, I sobbed for hours without being able to shed light either for myself or for my mother on why nothing was able to stop my tears. Carson McCuller's play combined many of my own themes: a young girl suffering from loss and alienated from her family finds comfort as well as guidance from a Black cook. Yet neither my mother nor I made the connection to my early life.

Certain words and phrases had contained a special magic in them. The word *adopted* had mystified me with its importance if I ever heard or read it. Now I knew it was connected to Joe telling me I should be adopted by Grace and him and come live with them when they had their own house. The word *rude* had interjected its way into my thoughts any time I'd picked up a book for a relaxed read, and I connected it to what my father had called me when I had tried to tell him my mother had torn up my book and said she would never read to me again. *Proof* had also seemed special for me during my life, and now I understood that it described the frenetic need with which I had rushed to find the book my mother had torn up so my father would know she had lied to him. As with all of my memories from my early childhood traumas, I'd forgotten the significance behind these words by the time I was five- and-a-half.

I remembered the pig dream from my work in Jungian therapy and realized that it had told me of the rage I'd felt as a small child when my guardian-angel sister Susie had hit me for disobeying my mother and teaching myself to read.

The day I recalled that my father had fired Jessie for taking me down to his law office and showing him the marks my mother had made on my back, I began to have difficulty speaking to my parents.

I stopped looking at their letters. Zach suggested that they communicate through him at his office.

"Don't tell them about what I've recalled," I told him. "It'll be too upsetting for them." My parents were both in their mid-seventies, and I thought at their age it would be better for them to wait until I got over my anger. With time to heal my shock, I would be able to forget all of this early stuff and start communicating with them again as if nothing had happened.

This break in communication with my parents was painful to me. Triggered by the hurtful separation, another brutal incident flashed back to me when I remembered that my mother had thrown me across the kitchen the night Joe left our household. In my studio I'd felt the flight to be thrilling and spiritual, even heavenly, but, later, in the hallway outside of my practice room, when the truth hit my conscious mind, like the metal counter-edge hitting my temple as a child, I cried out in shock and loathing. My daughter heard me and asked what was wrong. It was difficult to find a way to answer her.

My memories had left the studio as their gateway to my conscious mind and were jumping at me at any moment they wanted. So shocked that my mother could have hurt me right in the middle of the Christmas holidays, I felt compelled to call off the Thanksgiving dinner I had planned for my husband's American colleagues and their wives, as well as a planned trip to my parents' house for Christmas. My light-hearted attempt to play the game of downloading my subconscious through dance, in order to solve the reasons for my body's pains, had begun to affect me and my family in ways I had not foreseen.

At this time, the mid-seventies, in different parts of the United States and in Europe, dance teachers were experimenting with plumbing emotional truths through movement either in private sessions or in groups. These experiences would develop into healing techniques taught as dance therapy in academic settings and as Authentic Movement or Contemplative Dance in private studios.

But because I, as a jazz and Soul student, had lost contact with this experimental aspect of modern dance, and because I'd stopped reading, I had remained unexposed to this exploratory work so similar to what I had been doing. I therefore had no idea about the essential ingredient that pioneers of Authentic Movement—Mary Whitehouse, Janet Adler, and Joan Chodorow—required as part of their practice: the presence of a trained witness, leader, or therapist during participants' sessions.

It had never occurred to me that I might need a guide to help me with my attempt to plumb the subconscious in my studio. I had been so energized after leaving Austen Riggs Center, I never thought I would ever have to consult a psychologist again.

My ability to forget my emotional difficulties had given me great pleasure. I had loved being in The Netherlands, where no one knew my past, as if I'd taken a kind of vacation. It gave me a thrill to be known among our Dutch acquaintances as the "American woman who loves our country so much she may want to stay here, and by the way she's a dancer and speaks fluent Dutch, has two lovely children, and a brilliant research scientist for a husband."

But in keeping my history a secret from others and myself, I had forgotten that the doctors at my final conference had said, "You might need help later, once you've had children." I had never taken the time to search out a psychotherapist I liked and trusted in case of need.

Now my memory work had gone too far, and I didn't know how to stop it. I had heard of a treatment center not too far from the Dutch town where I lived called Centrum '45, created to help adults who were remembering their childhoods in concentration camps. These men and women had been able to live normal and satisfying lives, but now, in their forties and fifties, they could be walking through the park with their children, or in the middle of teaching a class, and suddenly get a flashback from the early years. Over time the memories would accumulate until mental focus became impossible. I knew about this clinic, but I didn't feel it appropriate to ask advice from those working with real sufferers from World War II.

As the darkness of December descended I heard that Felix was taking his professional company to the United States for good. Because I hadn't been in close touch with him, my understanding was skewed. If I had talked with him, I would have learned that his trip was to be a trial run. Instead, I was faced with the agony of losing my close friend forever. My sense of doom triggered the terrible memory of Joe's departure from our house. I projected out onto the world my feelings of dark despair, the strange idea coming into my conscious mind that the whole of Europe was at war.

If I had turned to a trusted and engaged therapist,

crackerjack smart like Dr. Deikman, fully engaged in his ability to wield the tool of verbal psychotherapy against confusion and worry, I could have been guided into safety.

> "Hey, look at this!" he might have said. "That incident with your mother you just remembered, about the flight across the kitchen—that happened in December of 1941, right? What was going on in Europe back then?"
>
> "Oh my God! How *meshugeh* I've been!" I would have responded, seeing how the past had taken over my present life, making me feel that this Europe of 1977 had become dark with the suffering of World War II. Suddenly released from this horror I would have joked, using the Yiddish word my husband had taught me for crazy!

But this period in my childhood when I had felt alone and without help had taken over my mind, and I didn't think of looking for a therapist. I was therefore unprepared to handle the night I stood in my brightly lit kitchen remembering an evening thirty-five years earlier when I had felt squeezed in a similar room by a large person leaning against me. I sat down and began to shake. My hand went up to the corner of my left eye, and looking inward, I saw the scene of Grace's body holding me and blocking my mother's assault. I pushed my hands into my chest to try and calm the pounding of my heart.

"You really won't believe this one," I stammered to Zach who walked into the room. But when I told him the story of the night Grace had rescued me from my mother's knife, instead of relief, my panic grew worse, the fright I'd felt as a four-and-a-half-year-old flooding my upper body until my chest felt it might burst.

The next day a call to Mary Ann gave me no greater help. I phoned Dr. Vandergroot, our family physician, and told him about the avalanche of horrible memories that had descended on me. He prescribed a mild tranquilizer that held me together for a while.

Dance—and my loving daughter—helped in this rescue. In the kitchen one night, while listening to Motown songs on the radio, I began to move rhythmically, something that had always helped me, no matter what mood I had been in. As I broke out into the fun of jazz steps, all horror fled from my mind. Sarah saw me.

"Mama, you are good!" she exclaimed. "I wish you'd teach me and my friends."

And so, I did. On impulse I entered a music store several evenings later and found the whole Motown section on sale. I bought every recording they had, jumping at the thought that I'd been stuck in my teaching career not because I wasn't good enough or the right person to teach Soul dance, but because I hadn't had the right music! Felix had once told me, with amazing modesty, that seventy percent of his success in teaching had come from his choice of music. Especially in Europe this was true, where jazz and American popular songs were treasured.

I began a small class in January and enjoyed combinations to Motown's rhythms as much as did the girls I was teaching. But this jumpstart of my career didn't last. Terrible thoughts and worries muddled my mind whenever I was neither teaching nor doing choreography. I'd been told by my Dutch neighbors and friends about the German occupation. Now I heard sounds like Nazi boots in the streets; I imagined a German officer walking into the café where I had stopped for coffee. I worried about my son if he was five minutes late from school.

Without knowing it, I had begun to experience PTSD or

Post-Traumatic Stress Disorder, a state of mind caused by memories that seem real. This kind of recollection engulfs the mind so much that an event from the past appears to be occurring at the current time—the sounds, sights, smells, and touch of a former moment vividly present. A former soldier thinks he is running through the woods, feels the crack of broken twigs under his boots, and hears the deafening yell of his comrade, fallen beside him. He is racing beyond the sight or sound of help or hope.

So was I.

Zach called Dr. Vandergroot, and asked him to drop by. I told the physician that I didn't know what was going on with me.

"Let's get you something stronger," the gray-haired, neatly dressed doctor said and bent over the kitchen counter to write out a referral to a psychiatrist who would prescribe heavier medicine. "You really need to get rid of these thoughts," he said to me.

I don't remember if Zach or I called to make the appointment, but while waiting for it I phoned the therapist in America I had consulted about the job in the record store.

"You should go see a Dr. Frances Remming in Rotterdam," he said. "She is a child psychiatrist and a friend of mine. See what she says."

The next evening, Zach and I took off for the two-hour drive to visit the doctor whom the therapist in the United States thought was very good. The large and sturdy-looking woman with blond hair, gray-tinged at the roots, *was* very good, warm and responsive. She listened for three hours while I poured out my stories one after the other, tying my memories into the chronological whole I had organized into thirty pages the week before. I never sat down, my need to talk so great that I had to pace around the small living room on her third floor in order for my vocal chords to work.

Dr. Remming said only two words the whole time, "Poor Anne, poor Anne." My husband sat patiently downstairs in the main living room of her home. I thanked the therapist for her understanding and time and indicated that the session had been an amazing help to me. My compliments pushed Dr. Remming to clarify her situation.

"I'm sorry, Anne, that I, myself can't be your therapist. I wanted to give you time tonight because my friend Dr. Stein said it was urgent to help you with your decision. But I need to tell you that I have just retired and can't take any more patients. I agree with your plan to go on stronger medication, but you must insist that your new doctor provide you with talk therapy also."

Dr. Remming's words disappointed me, as I had taken for granted that I could continue working with this woman to whom I had told my entire life story. In my confusion at feeling betrayed, I forgot to ask for a referral to someone whose manner would be similar, a tragic result of the depressive state I'd slipped into. I would find out back in America that, just as with research on and treatment of visual pain, cutting-edge psychological help for emergent early traumatic memories was being offered right at that moment in Rotterdam, this most modern of Dutch cities. Ah, for the Internet and easy access to information!

Though I felt relieved at having unloaded my story to a compassionate listener, I remained anxious. The new doctor that my family physician had recommended listened to my frenzied story and agreed with me that medication would be a good idea. I took the prescription and made an appointment for a session of talk therapy the following week. I never returned for it.

The tiny circles of white I swallowed the next day, the same sized pills as the ones I had used for a few weeks at Austen

Riggs Center but fifty times stronger, swept away all trace of my memories. Similar to my childhood switch in personality from a verbal and engaged little girl to a child of emotionless passivity, the medication shook my head free of the past and in the process wiped away any capacity to feel. The doctor had said that the pills would allow me to function as a wife and mother, yet I could not manage to be the engaged person my husband and children had known.

My eyes closed in mid-sentence when I read to my five-year-old son at night.

"Mama! Mama!" Kenny screamed, looking up into my face until my lids flickered open. He waited to make sure they stayed that way. Then my normally peaceful youngster returned his attention to the story, only to shout his defiance of my stupor every time it happened. Finally, he gave up on me as a satisfactory reader or player of games.

Sarah missed me, too. She asked questions about the change in me that I could not answer. Then the strong girl adjusted to the necessity of making decisions on her own, using the help of teachers, her many friends, and their compassionate and generous *mamas*.

The heavy drugs stole from me not only my chance to communicate with my family, but also the opportunity to talk with a professional about what I'd remembered. According to Dr. Larry S. Sandberg, a psychoanalyst and co-author of *Psychotherapy and Medication: The Challenge of Integration*, drugs by themselves cannot make the lasting changes in the brain that occur from talk therapy.

Decades later I described these events to a former colleague of my husband.

"That heavy medication sounds to me like a kind of punishment," he said.

Yes, I thought to myself. Just as in childhood I had been

punished for talking about the truth, the whiplash I had received from the brain-washing dose of medicine was like a slap in the face for having looked at my truths and then having dared to voice them to others.

Chapter 19 – Saving My Marriage

I wrote in my journal at this time, "Sweeping the floor is like sweeping the world." Living the role of mother and housewife in a foreign country while on leaden tranquilizers was hard; teaching dance felt impossible. My fire was gone.

The medication began a long hiatus in my development as a dancer. With some exceptions, not until discovering the flare I showed while learning swing dance later in the States did I return to the spirit and vitality of expression my daughter had witnessed that night in the kitchen.

Yet I persisted, encouraged by a wonderful Dutch woman, Annika, the mother of my daughter's best friend. She asked me to begin a class for her and a group that she would assemble. These mature students didn't notice my lack of speed. I brought in a younger teacher to help with my classes for the children.

Dr. Vandergroot sat across from me with the report in his hands. I would find out later that the psychiatrist he had referred me to had written, "The patient imagines that her mother tried to murder her." My family physician told me the psychiatrist had concluded that if I still wanted treatment, even after going on medication, it should be to see a *behavioral psychologist*. I had no idea what this kind of therapist would be like, but I followed the psychiatrist's suggestion.

The strict clinician, a young man with dark hair and thin face, helped me make a list of what I should accomplish each week. I felt as if I were picking up and discarding loads of bricks while working down the items that he and I agreed on.

In the end, I managed to refinance the house and receive a loan for a much-needed new car. I hired a contractor to dig up the downstairs hallway floor and repair the drainage pipes that had leaked unpleasant odors. His team of workers restored our hallway to a pleasant place, the painters releasing the carved wood of banister railing and dowels from their four layers of old paint so that we could see the beauty of stained wood grain as we climbed the eighteen steps to our upstairs hall.

One day I said to the counselor, "Isn't there going to be any chance to talk?"

"Not without your husband," he answered.

"Well, you'll never get him in here." Zach had refused to be included in any follow-up therapy.

"Really?" the psychologist replied. "Then that is something that should get looked at, isn't it?"

I got Zach to come, but within minutes, he'd stormed out, saying this was nothing to do with him. The stern young man put his papers down and looked at me.

"A husband and wife with your level of miscommunication should consider filing for divorce." I got up and walked out. Divorce? From the man I'd said "until death do us part" to? Was he crazy?

Through the haze of my tranquilizers, I hadn't noticed that Zach's bad moods were back. After the crisis of my emotional breakdown, in which he had responded to the challenge with strong and gentle support, Zach had withdrawn into a repeat of his twelve-hour work days, leaving all decisions about house, children, vacations, and friends to me. If he became involved at all, it was to complain in a loud and sarcastic voice about the decisions I'd been left to make on my own.

My male company became the team of workers who invaded our house for three months, filling it with noise and bustle. My family waited through a cold fall while our downstairs hall was traversable by stepping over two-by-fours slung across an enormous ditch. I had to stand by my bed while being lectured by my contractor.

"A bedroom is more than a place to sleep," he had said. "For instance, don't you want a built-in television?"

"No, I don't," I said, relieved that he was not about to teach me other uses of the bedroom. But I agreed to plentiful and useful shiny white cupboards as substitutes for built-in closets that were not common in Dutch houses at that time. The contractor and I papered one wall with sunny flowers facing the three others covered with a textured hanging matching some of the flowers' beige petals.

We chose large, full-length drapes along the northern side of the room that looked out on a balcony, not used much by us because of the soon-to-be-fixed faulty railing. The curtains were a dark salmon color that shut out winter's black night, which had glared through the enormous French-doors and their flimsy gauze coverings to greet me with its cold and unwelcoming look just before bed. The salmon became peach in the early summer mornings of this northern European country, as it tempered the sunlight that had robbed us of sleep at 4:30 am. Nine years later, when Zach and I sold our house, we had people waiting in line, and it was this bedroom that made one woman beg for us to sell the house to her.

The following spring, just as I was entering the final phase in my year-long regime of pill reduction, I was cheered by an invitation from my middle sister Susie—now called Susan—who lived in Florida.

"Come visit me. All of you deserve to have some fun in the sun," she wrote. I'd written my sister that I'd remembered her hurting me as a child, and I had received a letter from her saying, "I don't remember anything, but if I ever hurt you in our childhood I'm terribly sorry." That apology had been enough for me to keep our communication open and our relationship strong.

Even more moving to me was a new memory that came to me one day in my studio after my memories had started to come back into my unclouded mind. I recalled the unwinding of my back after my mother had beaten me with a hanger, which Susie, at five-and-a-half, had watched me do. I wrote my sister and thanked her for taking such good care of me afterward, saying, "I guess you knew right then that you would be a nurse."

We accepted Susan's invitation, even though I looked scrawny, weight-loss having been a bi-product of the medication. I decided to pack the thirty pages of notes on my memories I'd written up in case I got a chance to read them to Susan and my oldest sister Louise, who planned to join us after her summer course.

Zach refused to go on this trip with the children and me, saying he had too much work to do. Sarah, Kenny, and I spent three weeks in my sister's large and accommodating house, enjoying her generous hospitality and beautiful garden that included a large swimming pool. Susie's children, older than mine, indulged my son and daughter with attention and fun. We played in the sun, visiting amusement parks and eating ice cream daily.

When we returned to Europe, it appeared that my husband hadn't used the time for work, but had moped, and he continued to do so after our arrival home, complaining to me and the children in a loud voice whenever he came out of his shell. I was surprised and disappointed. I had come back yearning for a reunion with the charming husband who had written me three love letters of longing while I had frolicked in the sun.

My reaction to the renewed unpleasantness at home was the sudden realization that I hadn't been yelled at for three weeks. I said this to Zach.

"Why do you think that was?" I asked him. "Do you think I was a different person in Florida? Do you think, maybe, just maybe, I didn't and don't deserve to be yelled at? Perhaps I'm a good, kind, decent person who is trying to do my best for my family and myself!"

Zach seemed stunned and speechless, but his behavior didn't improve. I began to think about the trim-looking, quiet-voiced man who had come up to me after my dance workshop's performance two years before and complimented me on it. He had written me several cards and even a letter asking if we could get together sometime to discuss dance and the possibilities of more workshops. There was a phone number, but I hadn't responded. Coincidentally I was planning to attend a weekend dance workshop near where he lived, and I called to say that I would be glad to meet him when my class was finished. After dinner we spent the evening chatting and roaming through his town, a pleasant place in the south of Holland. We arranged to meet again. I don't know what would have happened if he had not broken the date.

"I think you should consult a real counselor, not one of those pill-happy guys," Mary Ann told me when she heard about the total breakdown of my marriage and what it had driven me to do—or think of doing. "I've heard of a former priest who people seem to think is wise and helpful."

When I discussed my marital problems with Mr. Vogel, he summed them up by referring to Zach's moodiness as homesickness: "Anyone who has lived this long in a foreign country without learning the language is most definitely suffering from homesickness."

This thought about Zach had never occurred to me. He'd never discussed with me any doubts about signing the university's contract for tenure. I confronted my husband with the direct question as to whether he wanted to go home.

"I'll go back with you if you really want to," I told him.

"No, I want to stay and make something of this job."

In spite of his answer, I suspect that my inquiry touched him, but his withdrawal from me and our family life continued.

The departure of my close friend, Mary Ann, was weighing on me. In one month she and Gary were going to America because of a new job. I began to think about going with them.

When Zach could think of nothing he wanted for his birthday except to play a few games of Ping-Pong with Kenny at his workplace, and then cancelled that, I made my decision. Strengthened by the insights I had gleaned from remembering my childhood abuse, and armed with a fierce awareness that I would never allow unacceptable behavior again in my marriage, I was ready to make changes.

"Please come home because I have something important to discuss with you," I said on the phone to Zach and sent my children off to a friend for the afternoon. In the upstairs television room, cozier than the large space downstairs that combined both living room and studio, I began.

"I'm sorry to say this, but I'm leaving you. I'm taking the children and going back to America to stay with Gary and Mary Ann until I can get settled."

Zach sat down, saying he couldn't believe what he was hearing.

"I can't live with someone who doesn't let himself enjoy life and then takes out his unhappiness by hurting everyone else," I explained.

To my great surprise, my husband, who rarely drank more than an occasional glass of wine, went down and retrieved a bottle of gin from our cupboard. He came back upstairs and drank it while begging me to stay, saying that he would do anything I ever wanted him to do.

"I will never survive another divorce," he told me, while

downing the whole bottle as he paced the room, tears falling down his face.

Zach had never cried in my presence. I was unprepared and disarmed, his sobs increasing as he walked the length of our television room until I thought he would fall while leaning over against the wall. I suspected that his sadness had to do with grief at losing his beloved friend Gary, but I think now that Zach was letting go years of sorrow, maybe even going back to the death of his father at age seven.

My husband must have been ready and waiting for my announcement because he changed immediately. As we wandered the North Sea beach twenty minutes away from our house at sunset, I recited the list of what I wanted him to do. It consisted of ten items that ranged from a cessation of his loud and scary outbursts to increased interest in the house, children, and planning vacations, as well as more tenderness and nuance in our intimate relations.

I joked to myself that these were my "Ten Commandments," and I checked the list in my head every year on the anniversary of Zach's birthday to be sure he was sticking to his bargain. He kept to it for the rest of our lives together.

Zach's most important promise to me was to start family therapy, something which the former priest had suggested because he was leaving his counseling work and wanted me to have a follow-up arrangement. Zach had refused, but now he accepted the idea.

The first recommendation of our new Dutch family therapist, Deidre, was to take our dinner meals at the University's Dining Hall. She had picked up immediately on an old symptom of discord—Zach's irritability at dinnertime. Deidre was certain that communal eating would put an end to our tension.

She was right. Because someone else prepared the meals, I

couldn't be blamed for making Zach eat what he didn't want in the forceful way his strict Orthodox Jewish mother had used. I tried our therapist's trick later on, announcing new recipes I prepared as coming from sources other than me. At the first sign of Zach's return to the projection of his restrictive mother onto me, I mentioned the name of a friend he liked and said that she had given me the recipe for what he was finding on his plate.

Some of the dissension between us had been caused by our differing attitudes about raising children. Deidre often used the Dutch word *consequent* when talking to Zach and me about good parenting, because she couldn't find a satisfactory English translation. Consequent is a combination of consistent and relevant, Deidre's point being that one needs to exhibit other qualities than the ability to be consistent in order to be a good disciplinarian. A parent has to be attentive to the details involved in the transgressions of a misbehaving child. For instance, when Kenny exploded with anger at the age of eight and kicked a large hole in his bedroom door, our counselor suggested that he be made to replace it.

"How can we enforce that?" Zach asked. "He can't drive."

"He has a bicycle," Deidre answered.

It must have looked strange to passersby, the three of us, Zach, Kenny, and I, walking the two miles from a supply store with an enormous wooden door balanced on the seat of my son's bike. He and his dad carried it upstairs and removed the hinges of the old door so they could put on the new one. My son did an excellent job of prepping and painting the bare wood, having learned the process from watching Zach and me finish off the renovations in our downstairs hallway.

After five months of counseling, Deidre announced that she would be stopping our work. I felt abandoned and saw the same look on my husband's face. She leaned forward and looked into our eyes, "You must CHANGE!" she said. My husband and I stared at each other as if to ask what she meant, and then we knew, because Deidre had said these things in her very good English many times.

Looking at Zach, she had said, "You must become more involved with your children." Turning to me, she had often told me, "You must stop mentioning the recalls to your childhood." To both of us, she had warned, "You have to start listening to each other so that your decisions about your son and daughter can become unified, definite, and reasonably consistent." It took us time, but gradually our small family became stronger than it had ever been.

My success after communicating my feelings and intentions to my husband in a strong but calm way gave me the sense that I was back on track with my life. I plunged into teaching, helping my children navigate their preteen years and enjoying my husband's new sociability. Our circle of friends grew, our house again a place for foreign visitors on holidays, and our imaginations stimulated by jointly-made travel plans.

It was time to use the same directness toward my parents that had been so successful with Zach. When my husband asked me to write them my first letter in a year-and-a-half, stating exactly what was going on with me and why I had separated from them, I agreed.

Chapter 20 – Losing My Parents

Ten months before, on my last evening with my sisters in Florida, I read aloud the thirty pages I'd written about my childhood and asked for their help concerning the difficulties I was experiencing with my mother. She had been pressuring Zach to get me to talk to her, and I suspected I would end up telling her what I'd remembered. I wanted to know if Susan and Louise thought I should do this.

At first, they thought it was a good idea because they felt my mother's apology would be important for my healing. We fantasized about the giant hug and weeping that would occur after my mother begged me for forgiveness. Then all three of us began to worry that it might give her a heart attack to be reminded, since such terrible things had happened. We concluded that she shouldn't be told.

I continued to keep my distance from my mother after returning to Holland, but my anger at what she had done to me grew. I became anxious in October, when an invitation came from her inviting us to visit at Christmas. We had gone the year before, and I'd been unable to sleep at night, even while on heavy medication.

"You shouldn't force yourself to go," Mr. Vogel told me, soon after I began counseling with him. I remembered the concept of *moratorium* used by Austen Riggs Center for difficult relationships. This method for family repair combined temporary separation with the hope of reunion after psychotherapy.

When we went to the United States at Christmastime, I

stayed with my close friend Ellen for two days, while Zach and the children went to my parents' house. Then the four of us visited friends for a week. Just before returning home, I met with my father at his club.

He and I had the strange experience of talking about events from his childhood I had never heard before—as if there was nothing problematic going on. I learned how at twelve he'd been forced to take the Staten Island ferry from his home to get to school in Manhattan, and how cold it had been on those early mornings. I wondered if the tuberculosis he contracted that year had been caused by exposure to the wet-cold of that ferry ride. We departed from each other peacefully without any questions or complaint from him that might have made me feel pushed to come and talk to my mother.

As far as I knew, a peaceful hiatus had been established.

Sometime in January, however, during an early-morning telephone chat with her mother, Louise spilled the details of what I'd remembered. My sister had a warm heart, and she said later that the upset woman had confided how desperate she was to know why I wouldn't communicate with her. But Louise's action created a maelstrom between my parents and me. The peaceful moments I had enjoyed with my father were forgotten as the surprised man changed from a peaceful acceptance of my separation to anger at the *reasons* for the break.

To my sisters' and my amazement, both of our parents vehemently denied the truth of everything that I'd remembered. My disappointment was severe. My father began a relentless campaign to persuade me to retract everything and say that my memories had been fantasies. Again, I asked my husband to take over the correspondence with my parents. I didn't realize until two decades later, when I read the letters my father had saved, the amount of pressure Zach endured to protect me, even a suggestion that he should arrange a lobotomy for me.

I hadn't been particularly close to my parents in my teens, but I'd loved them and depended on them during my twenties when they'd been emotionally supportive and extremely generous financially. It hurt to be separated from them, yet my fury at their denials kept me from connecting.

In my depressed state, I enjoyed MaryAnn's presence as a ballet teacher of small children in my studio. During the fall I had asked my friend to work with me privately on my technique, hoping that my dance ability would return. Perhaps it was this weekly training and the return of my body, literally, to balance that made possible my sudden ability to read. I asked Mary Ann to lend me books that would get me out of my down mood.

I gobbled up the message of hope for the future in Carl Sagan's *Dragons of Eden:* evolution is occurring right now in our brains to help us adapt to the daunting, thousand-fold changes in our societal and environmental world. I was cheered by Freeman Dyson's *Disturbing the Universe*, in which the author declares his belief that Earthlings will someday create pockets of civilization throughout the solar system. Perhaps I loved the idea of escaping the earth because of the East/West umbrella of nuclear deterrence that hung over our heads, especially haunting, it seemed, to those of us who lived in Europe.

Another reason for my delight was Dyson's recognition that the societies of earth—like me—needed the "expansion of spirit," which finding a new frontier to explore would give them. This caring mathematician, physicist, and visionary predicted that the investment of time and money necessary to transport future space citizens to their new home would come from the business sector. Today, proving him right, Elon Musk, founder of the company SpaceX, speaks of manned flights to Mars—the first of them planned in ten years—not for a visit, but for the purpose of establishing civilization there. The Dutch nonprofit organization Mars One has already signed up thousands for a one-way ticket.

By the time I tried Bronowsky's *The Ascent of Man,* my reading ability had petered out, but the title itself lifted my spirits. All of this reading did the job I had needed: positive messages about life counter-balanced the horrors I had been dealing with for too long.

But my husband suffered because of the pressure by my parents that he had taken onto himself while I regained my spirits. In the spring, he asked me to try and write a letter to my mother.

"She's been begging for you to come visit her."

To please my husband, I wrote the letter, stating my position as clearly and directly as I could.

> *It will be very hard for me to come visit you or even to write or telephone, if we can't talk about these things that I've remembered and which you have denied.*

The answer came a month later. I read my mother's short note while seated on a park bench overlooking a pond where a waterfall danced, my Dutch bicycle parked beside me.

> *Please come see me, but don't talk about those things.*

The thought of going back and being polite to her, as if I hadn't remembered the traumas of my early childhood, made me feel sick. I tore up the letter and bicycled back home to inform Zach that I didn't want anything else to do with my parents.

"Why couldn't she have said what Susan did?" I asked him. "It would have been so simple for her to say that she didn't remember anything but if she ever hurt me, she was terribly sorry."

My disappointed husband, stymied in his efforts, had no answer.

My rage built, not only from my parents' refusal to believe me, but because of the abuse itself. I had looked forward to my mother's apology to melt my anger, her tears of pain to create reconciliation, and the warmth of admission and forgiveness to bond a family tie so strong that compassion and understanding for her, as the severely sick woman she had been in my childhood, would have billowed out of me. Instead I felt left alone, blown farther away from my familial roots by the cold winds of family disapproval and suspicion that traveled across the ocean.

In Florida, my sister Louise had tried to teach me about the transformative therapy that I should now be starting. Before coming to Susan's house, she had gone to see Dr. Arthur Deikman, my first psychiatrist at Austen Riggs Center and a personal friend of hers. Six months before, I'd sent Dr. Deikman my thirty pages, asking if my memories fit in with what he remembered about our work together at Riggs. Louise had visited him to get his answer.

"Yes," he told Louise, "the incidents fit with that therapeutic experience. But more important, she must do aggression therapy. She must get the feelings of anger out of her and release them in physical form."

Louise had brought notes from this conversation and read them to me one day at Susan's house.

> You have to take a tennis racket and put a pillow
> on a bed. Holding the racket with both hands,
> you must visualize someone you are very angry

with who hurt you, and bring the racket down on the pillow, as if you were hitting that person on the head. You need to combine this with breathing so that your whole body becomes involved, exhaling as you swing the racket down and breathing in deeply as you straighten up. You have to get all worked up and sweaty doing this so you really get into your feelings and can release them.

Louise demonstrated with great enthusiasm, including the deep and noisy breathing I would need to do. Just as in childhood, I felt comforted by my oldest sister's efforts to help me, but I didn't do the exercises when I returned to Holland. Their violence didn't fit with the gentle two-hour philosophy sessions I enjoyed one evening a week with the retired priest.

But once Mr. Vogel had stopped giving counseling and referred us to Deirdre for family therapy sessions, the support I received from their success allowed me to face my feelings of anger without fear or shame. I dared to *think* about doing the aggression-release exercises my sister had taught me, and I was imaginative in creating other scenarios.

I gave into my fantasies, fully confident of myself as an artist to confine my thoughts of revenge within my imagination. During one of my free-flowing daydreams, I boarded an airplane, went to my parents' house with cans of gasoline, spread the fuel around outside, and lit it. I imagined standing back and watching the flames fly into the air, as the house, with its "lies about love and good care," a sentence I dared to whisper out loud, burned down. Then I breathed a sigh of relief that I lived one great ocean away, so that this acting-out would never happen, and returned to my current life, relieved temporarily from my load of rage.

I didn't remember the other message my sister had brought

from Dr. Deikman: "Art says you have to be seeing a therapist when you do this violent kind of inner work." My life was going relatively well, I was teaching regularly, and I had managed to increase my profits by arranging for another instructor to share my studio for more hours than Mary Ann had needed.

But family therapy was not sufficient for what I was going through. A friend tried to help with my anger by mentioning the practice called Primal Scream, telling me that a therapist probably could be found in Amsterdam who used this healing method. I recalled a black and white movie I'd seen in my childhood, where a distraught teenager stands on the side of a railroad track and teaches his companion how to scream under the cover of a passing train.

In the freedom of my car out on the highway, with windows up so that I wouldn't be heard, I allowed myself to let loose the blood-curdling scream I had just remembered making at four-and-half after my mother had tracked me like a hunted animal into the kitchen the night Joe left our household. She had stopped on a dime, and I was able to agree with the teacher of my new self-defense course that loud sounds are a woman's best defense. He taught us that swear words work the best, and I had a wonderful time screaming *"godverdomme!"* and other Dutch expressions at the top of my lungs with my classmates. Our throats were sore for days.

In the fall, one year after my conversations with my sisters, just as my family was finishing up our therapy sessions, Zach passed on to me an urgent message from my father.

"I'm running out of patience," he had written. "I need to make some decisions." We suspected that this referred to a final version of his will.

I told Zach to say that I didn't know what the future held, but that right now I couldn't accept the changes he wanted me to make about what I believed and whom I could visit without discussing my memories. I had no problems with the children coming to see their granny, I said. The thought of denying her the pleasure of her grandchildren because of my difficulties about what she had done thirty years before, when she had been a different person, seemed a mean and unjustifiable thing to do.

Zach wrote my father back. "As sad as it is for everyone, I believe Anne, on the one hand, and you and Margaret on the other have irreconcilable views as to what transpired at home when she was a young child. Regardless of what really happened, no amount of arguing on either side seems capable of changing any minds. If you can accept a very limited relationship, and some possible hope for the future, that is all well and good. If your patience has reached an end, then it will be a loss for which Anne has been trying to prepare herself for a long time, and I, too, will regret."

These words are almost word for word what I read later in a letter from the doctors at Riggs written to my parents in response to their demands for help in getting me to recant. My husband had done a wonderful job, with one exception.

At the end of his letter, Zach reassured my parents that "We both want very much for your contact with the children to continue." But he did not include the requirement—and I did not think to suggest it—that these visits of our children should only happen when he came along, in order to prevent them from being pressured to take sides in the family argument. I comfort myself that the geographical distance and my mother's developing ALS kept contact between the children and their grandparents—without their dad's presence—to a minimum.

A month later, my sister Susan begged Zach to ask if I would speak to our father or come to see him now that he had become terminally ill.

I told my husband that I could do neither.

Susan called him back again. "Dad wants to know why

196

she's so angry at him."

"I think it's because he didn't help her when she was being hurt as a small child," Zach answered.

When I found out about this answer years later, I was touched. My husband had understood me, believed me, and chosen to say the truth, though he knew it would be difficult for the father-in-law he had come to enjoy and even love.

Deidre had warned that I would feel guilty when my father passed away, and she was right. Four months after his death, I was overwhelmed with uncertainty about what I'd done.

I missed Mary Ann, who had left with her husband and young family for the States. I needed her intelligence and grasp of what made sense. She would have cut through my endless second-guessing and said, "Look, it doesn't matter who left who or why. Whatever caused the loss, you're going to be sad right now. Death is hard. You're in grief. Give in to it."

But Mary Ann wasn't there, and I didn't hear her words. Our separation had been complete and painful due to the overwhelming demands of her new, fast-paced life in America that included a switch of rental houses and resulting change of telephone numbers, as well as her inability to write letters, for which she apologized when we finally saw each other again.

I went to Deidre's office, begging her to continue working with me.

"I'm not trained to do person-to-person therapy, Anne," she said. I wonder to this day why she didn't refer me to a colleague, but it was the look in her eyes that hurt most. I had the feeling that she was *afraid* to know more about my childhood stories.

I began to slip back into the idea I had received as a young child that I shouldn't tell anyone about the things that had happened to me because they were too horrible for others to hear. Turning inward, I stopped mentioning my memories to friends and, in time, suppressed them yet again from my own mind.

This mental vacuum left me vulnerable to the guilt that drove me to believe I was a terrible person who had caused my parents unbearable unhappiness at the end of their lives; and worse, I was an ungrateful daughter who had not gone to see her sick father before he died. A friend of mine at Riggs had told me, just before being discharged, that she'd learned her family difficulties had not been her fault. A good psychologist would have reassured me that the rupture with my parents was not something I had caused; my mother and father had brought it on themselves through their flat denials. Yet I never thought of going back to my family physician and asking for a referral to a talk therapist.

It is possible that guilt, with its powerful and destructive force, caused me to reject the information that my life had taught me: psychologists can be helpful in resolving confusion and uncertainty. If, as some people think, guilt is really a cover-up for anger, then it may have been rage from the hurts of my childhood that blinded me from making a good decision. Perhaps I wanted to punish myself, believing that I didn't deserve the relief of finding a therapist who would let me talk and help me find balance and happiness in my life again.

Whatever the reason, I muddled along, my creativity as a dancer and choreographer diminishing. As if my father's ghost had walked into my house and repeated his message from my childhood, that I was forbidden to grasp the truths of my life and speak out or act on them, my artistic development gave way, my classes becoming more exercise than dance.

Some relief from my malaise came four years later, when I received an envelope from my mother that enclosed two blue pieces of paper, an unusual color for her letters. At the top of the first sheet, she had scribbled a note that this letter had been written by an elderly cousin before she'd passed away.

In a neat handwriting, the relative wrote to my mother.

> *"My dear Margaret, I feel the need to confess something to you and to apologize. I must say this to you before I die. I'm sorry that I didn't treat you well the summer I took care of you when you were two-years-old."*

It seemed to me that my mother was acknowledging what she had done to me, by letting me know that something similar had been done to her. It was because of that letter that I went back to visit her.

"Why have you come?" she asked.

I had promised her, through my sister Susan, not to speak of the childhood memories, so I didn't know what to say. I hadn't gone to my father's funeral, and I felt a need to restore some connection.

"I guess it's a matter of roots," I said. I couldn't bring myself to say that I loved her or felt any close bond, or to thank her for her care during my tough young adulthood. But at least I had visited. My eleven-year-old son Kenny accompanied me on this trip and helped with his gentle influence to make it successful. Together we took the sick woman on a sunny drive in the country and to a restaurant where we sat at a table in front of a picture window looking out over a creek and small waterfall. That summer Zach and I rented a house in the country not far from my mother's assisted living residence, and we were able—all of us—to visit her before she passed away.

Two years later, my husband found a job in the United States, a perfect one for him, which the children and I, though fond of living in The Netherlands, couldn't ask him to refuse. Sarah, now in college, decided not to go back with us. She warned me about returning to the United States, as coincidentally, the new job was near my hometown.

"Mama" she said, "all your memories will come back and you'll feel awful again."

"Oh, I'll be fine," I said. But even if I had known she was right, I would have chosen to leave the half-life I'd been living. I was eager to grab at the emotional reality I suspected I would achieve once back in the United States.

Energized but conflicted about leaving Holland, I turned to the song "America!" from *West Side Story* to inspire a dance combination for my classes. The music's counterpoints expressing praise as well as criticism for the United States were perfect for what I was feeling.

My dance contained fast turns, quick stops, and changes of direction, as the song declared the singers' contrasting views:

> *Rosalia: I like the city of San Juan.*
> *Anita: I know a boat you can get on.*
> *Rosalia: Hundreds of flowers in full bloom.*
> *Anita: Hundreds of people in each room!*

Because my classes were small, I took part in this dance, and after the song was finished, I dropped to the floor with my students as we panted and laughed at the wonderfully smart lyrics.

> *Immigrants go to America,*
> *Many hellos in America,*
> *Nobody knows in America*
> *Puerto Rico's in America!*

Yes, I was ready to go back, whatever was to come, one of *my* counterpoints being that I would miss my oldest child and the warm-hearted country of The Netherlands.

Chapter 21 – Home

We arrived at the end of summer. Defying my visual handicap and determined to find a return to the area where I'd grown up interesting and challenging, I signed up for two courses in the political science department of a nearby university, doing most of the reading for it and one of the exams.

I loved sitting alongside students half my age in the weekly discussion groups and getting a chance to hear their opinions about the United States' role in the world. I enjoyed the appreciation of our graduate-student teacher when I spoke up and described my work as an anti-Vietnam War activist.

But the overuse of my vulnerable left eye during this four-month period of study caused a return of terrible pain. I ignored the constant hurt until the excitement of studying was over.

I remember one day in late January when I happened to be in my hometown to do an errand. I parked my car a distance from the stores to enjoy my walk along the tree-lined street, but my stroll turned into a nightmare. As I looked up at a telephone pole, I fantasized that blood was pouring out of it. All of the streets and buildings around me appeared darkened with red as if the thick fluid were pouring out of my own eye. The town felt like a war zone, with a bomb about to strike me at any minute.

I rubbed my eyes and recovered my normal vision, but when I got home, I called the Gesell Clinic in New Haven, Connecticut, which I had planned to visit anyway. Back in the seventies, I'd heard about a study in visual development that had been done at this clinic. It involved children between the ages of six months and five years, and it showed that those who'd missed the crawling stage were more apt to have visual problems later on, the implication being that the crawl's contrasting arm and leg movements were essential to the ability of the eyes to focus together. I'd wondered if my determination to study the Graham and Dunham dance techniques, that combined contrasting moves for arms and legs, had been an unconscious effort to give my eyes the therapy they needed. I had thought that this clinic might have the answer. Now I wondered if it could help me with my current dire situation.

After a long drive to his office, I met Dr. Richard Apell and discovered the name for the kind of eye doctor I had gone to in Pittsfield Massachusetts, when my left eye had bounded with joy back into life. A *behavioral optometrist*, Dr. Apell did not put me in front of a revolving wheel with a yellow ball on it, but he used exercises to help my weak left eye.

The doctor seemed intrigued with my case, calling up a colleague in the middle of our appointment to tell him about my *anomalous correspondence*, my left eye's refusal to see, even after it had been surgically pulled away from its turned-in position during childhood. Some peripheral vision had kept me from bumping into things as a young person, and after my emotional release at Riggs and work in Pittsfield, the left eye had become active in an intermittent and alternating way with the right. But much of the time its vision had been turned off, similar to the *lazy-eyes* of children whose eyes are misaligned, except that in my case my surgery had masked the truth of what was going on!

After four weekly appointments, in which Doctor Apell tried to get me to complete his introductory exercises and couldn't, he complained, "I can't work with you. Your eyes won't relax." As a child of six, my eyes had likewise refused to loosen up enough to benefit from using the stereopticon, a handheld optical device prescribed to help children synchronize two half-pictures into one complete story. Even the wish to make a dog jump through a hoop had not enticed me to let my left eye move out of its determined lock.

A book on visual development I found in the Gesell library at this time told me what I had learned experientially, that good vision in an infant and young child is dependent on the child's desire to take in the sight of the world around her. Now, as an adult, I was balking at the reemergence of my left eye's vision, just as I had in childhood because of my unwillingness to face the terrible emotions that I feared would surface if I used my left eye in a consistent way.

"You can't do my exercises because you don't see black when you palm," Dr. Apell added. Each week he had asked me to cover my eyes with my palms and stare into the blackness. He had wanted my muscles to relax so that they would be able to respond to the visual therapy that would stretch and strengthen them.

"But I don't see black," I'd told him.

"What do you see?"

"I see the cook, Jessie, holding me on her lap. I'm three years old, and I'm telling her that my mother cracked my head on the changing table."

Each week, when Dr. Apell asked to report why I hadn't seen black, I reported a different image connected to child abuse. One day he stood back and admonished me for not realizing what was going on.

"You know, you should be talking to someone about these flashbacks," he said. "The fact that they're there right up-front in your mind means they're calling for attention. You should go to the psychologist up on the third floor."

I didn't agree. I felt better one month after the end of the political science courses, and the visual therapy had done a bit of good. My reemerging flashbacks didn't seem to bother me, except when doing these visual exercises. I was content to let them float around in my mind while I lived my life.

Meanwhile, my doctor used a simple but effective trick to encourage my left eye to remember to look straight forward. He put a half-moon-shaped patch on the nose-side of my glasses' left lens. I remember the Sunday in May, when I sailed down a street of the town near where we were renting a house. I couldn't believe the joy of moving in a consistently clear three-dimensional world.

A sign that I might otherwise have missed, placed on a lawn to the left, caught my eye, a *For Sale* notice on a house from whose porch I could see part of a large lake. I had asked my real estate agent to find me something near water because living in The Netherlands for so long had made me feel lost without it.

"I'm sorry, Anne, but there's nothing available," she'd said, "at least in the town you want."

I walked into the Open House that same afternoon and committed the transgression of signing up with another agent because of my elation and eagerness to grab the perfect house that my new eyes had found for me. When the sale went through, I thanked my eye doctor for helping me see the *For Sale* sign. But this was to be my final appointment with him. He said there was nothing more he could do.

It was at this time that my gynecologist suspected I had a pituitary adenoma, having picked up the signs of it from my high prolactin count. She sent me to an endocrinologist, and he confirmed her suspicion that I had a small tumor. He began to ask me questions.

"Yes," I answered him, "I stopped menstruating around the age of forty-three. I didn't think anything of it and don't really remember the exact date. In my busy schedule of teaching my gymnastic form of dance and raising children, it was much easier not to have to deal with my period."

"Well," my doctor said, "you probably should have looked into it. You'll have to start on medication."

Alarm bells rang in my mind. "No! No medication."

He said to think about it and come back in a month.

I began to wonder if there was a connection between the suppression of my recall memories, first from the heavy medicine and then from my inability to deal with them, and the pituitary adenoma. If this was so, I reasoned, and I went into psychotherapy as Dr. Apell had suggested, perhaps facing the emotions that had been created by my flashbacks would stop the growth of my relatively small tumor.

At my next appointment, I asked the endocrinologist if we could keep a watch on the tumor's size by means of prolactin checks every few months. I promised him that if the levels rose, I would begin the medication. He agreed, and I pledged to myself to find a therapist.

A few weeks later, I became nervous at the idea of accompanying Zach on his trip to Canada for a conference. He was going to be staying with Gary, who had moved there from the United States. I decided to stay home because Mary Ann would not be there and because I didn't want to be reminded of the months that had been so difficult around the time they left The Netherlands.

Upon my husband's return, I felt sad and annoyed with myself at my weakness, hearing what a good time he'd had. One evening, coming back from the movie, *A Fish Called Wanda,* which had bothered me because of scenes involving cruelty, I trashed an old piece of furniture in our house. Looking at the broken wood in my hands, I decided to go for help.

The next day I took the long drive to the Gesell Clinic to see the child psychologist who had been recommended to me by Dr. Apell. Within a few minutes of meeting Dr. Keith Alstedter,

I knew I had found the person who could assist me in getting the annoying memories of my childhood out of my head for good. In answer to my doubts about choosing a child therapist, he reassured me, "We are a perfect match, because all of your troubling memories are from your young childhood."

Together we began the treatment program I'd hoped to start in Dr. Remming's third floor living room ten years earlier, before both the white pills and guilt over separating from my parents had washed my undigested memories out of my conscious mind.

Chapter 22 – Keith

I will be forever grateful to Dr. Apell for sending me to Keith, just as I am in debt to my eyes for taking me to the Gesell Clinic in the first place. The hurt in my left eye had moved me towards the truths of my life while doing creative dance in Holland. Now my eyes had taken me to the healer needed to complete my journey. After the shock of my recall memories and then the storage of them in the ice chest of forgetfulness, I needed someone gentle and warm like Keith to thaw me and draw me out.

My new therapist was calm and receptive in his responses to everything I told him. No longer did I have to hide my story, as I had in family therapy sessions or as I had in childhood. In contrast to my work with the former priest, I was not dealing with philosophical questions about life and the existence of evil. I was digging into the emotions imprinted on my soul from my abusive childhood and *de-cording* myself from them, as Keith described it.

The expression, "It's easier to tell the truth because you don't have to remember what lies you've told," describes the flow with which my memories came back to me. My recalls spilled into my conscious mind without change or confusion of detail, clothed in the same colors, sounds, and words they had exhibited a decade earlier, only enhanced by the addition of a few new events and by added clarity to some memories that had been fuzzy ten years before.

My therapist lifted my spirits with his voice as he accompanied me, consoling me with his words when I talked about the worst ones. It is not that I entered therapy with the conscious intention of discussing these childhood incidents; the memories arose by their own power, triggered from disappointments in my daily life, or by scenes in books or movies. As Dr. Apell had said, they lay just under the surface of my thinking, waiting to be dealt with. At the end of our sessions, Keith found ways of reminding me that my life, in the present, was sweet and good.

One day, at home, I drew a picture on translucent paper of a small child cart-wheeling down a flight of brown wooden stairs, her head hitting the edge of a step. On the other side of the paper I drew the stairs as seen from the bottom, with a child toppling down to the playroom from above, as if there had been a pause in the fall. By flipping the paper from its front side to its reverse side, I witnessed the spill I had taken at four, after my mother overheard me telling Grace I loved her. The turning of the page represented the flat wooden landing in the middle of the stairway where it, and I, changed direction.

For the first time I was able to accept the reality of my fall down the cellar stairs, one of the recall memories that had remained hazy to me. Some months later, when I found this drawing again, I drew a large, adult-size hand, fingers straight as if letting go, not curved as if trying to grasp, and then I was finally able to absorb the fact that my mother had intended, with every fiber of her body, to make sure that I lost my balance enough to fall all the way down to the playroom.

I began to do the aggression exercises, which Dr. Deikman had told me to do. I would think about the person who had hurt me and use my tennis racket on a pillow. Then I would unload my rage onto this inanimate substitute while using an enormous amount of imagination and obeying what I jokingly called the *Psychological Golden Rule*: "You do unto others what has been done to you."

If I felt like screaming, I'd go into my closet and bury my face in my clothes to let the horrendous sounds out. After these exercises, in which I'd been absorbed in my anger and then in the harmless release of it, I would feel refreshed and changed. I would emerge from my house and go out for a walk, greet my neighbors, and enjoy their gardens.

I began to understand why Dr. Deikman had suggested that it was necessary to be in treatment while doing aggression therapy. I needed a defense against the feelings of shame at acting privately in a way most people would consider crazy, and others might interpret as dangerous. This negative attitude toward how I was managing to release a lifetime of rage could have made me feel isolated if I had not had the understanding, trust, and respect of my therapist. Also, it was important to have a professional involved with my progress to keep me oriented in the present, so that I would stay within safe boundaries. Otherwise my increasing clarity at realizing what had been done to me would have dragged me down into self-pity and despair, just as it had done in The Netherlands.

To my delight, Keith and I did dream work, reminding me of the discussions I'd had with Dr. Bennett, the Jungian therapist I'd seen in my twenties. I was thrilled to share with my new friend the loneliness and terror of a nightmare that had occurred frequently ever since my period of memory recalls.

In the dark of night, I stood on a long and swinging narrow bridge, at the midway point of it, half-a-mile above a dark and rapidly flowing river, wider than the Mississippi. From the bridge I could see the black waters swirling below.

While working with my therapist, the recurrent nightmare changed by steps. At first, the time of my dream changed to daylight, and my location moved closer to shore. After a year of therapy, I was standing on land at one side of the bridge. Later, I was comfortably walking along bright, new train tracks next to the river. Finally, perhaps after four years, I dreamt of riding in an open car, out in the sunshine with other travelers, as if on a sightseeing tour.

Because I'd been told by my Jungian therapist that water represents emotions in the subconscious, I knew that the original dream had expressed the emotional trauma I'd felt in The Netherlands, when emerging memories had overwhelmed me. I recognized how lonely I'd felt on that shaky bridge, the half-mile between the river and me representing the empty space between my emotions and my consciousness that the too-heavy medication had created.

Having reached common ground, quite literally, with other people in my latest dream, and feeling more engaged with normal life, it became possible for me to register the fact that I'd lived more awful experiences in my first five years of life than most people experience in a lifetime.

One day I brought into my therapy two dreams from recent nights. In the first, my tongue was a bunch of dried, broken, and knotted rubber bands. I was trying to pull them off from the rooted part of my tongue, using both of my hands to get some threads out; but there were continually more to pull. In the second dream, I was able to get the crowded and useless dried rubber-like bands out of my mouth, but then found that only three blood-red spines of the tongue were left hanging out from its roots, as thin as birds' feet but vibrantly warm.

On the way to relieve myself each of these nights, I had stopped to stare at the dreams while standing outside the bathroom in the cold hallway, and enjoying the quiet breathing of my husband and son in their rooms. On the second night, during that moment of midnight serenity, I dared to remember what had happened late on a December evening when I was five and had tried to tell my father what my mother had done to me "when I was little."

My father had become furious, telling me never to say those things again. But when he made me go back into my bedroom I dared to tell him that I was too scared to do that, because I had just remembered how my mother had "tried to kill me right across the hall in that bedroom!" I pointed at my sister's closed door, where the changing table had been. In the cold and lonely hallway between the children's bathroom and my bedroom, my father had given me an order.

"Stick your tongue out." When I did, he took my chin in one hand and the top of my head in the other and clamped the two parts of my jaws together. I thought I would die from the pain, gingerly testing my mouth to see if my tongue was still there.

"If I ever hear you tell me again that your mother tried to kill you, I'll cut it off all the way." My father concluded his conversation by pushing me into my bedroom and closing the door.

Together Keith and I grieved over my physical pain and the loss of my ability to talk with honesty after that. My feelings of guilt about not going to see my dying father, which had literally hobbled me as a dancer and choreographer in Europe, transformed itself into horror and rage. My regret at having failed to visit my ailing parent evaporated.

Not even the argument I had given myself before, that my father's punishing behavior was caused by the heavy drinking he did before dinner, helped to temper my anger, after I remembered this abuse. At 11:00 at night, not only a large meal but an evening of work would have canceled the two double Scotches he had needed to relax after work.

Nor did my life-long and powerful need to excuse a parent who had been loved, seize another chance when a friend reminded me of the great stigma against mental illness in the 1940's. If my father had committed my mother to a mental institution, and my mother's behavior had become known, his rapidly rising career as a prominent lawyer could have been put in jeopardy.

Likewise my knowledge of psychology did not change my reaction, the recognition that people tend to repeat what has been done to them unless they are changed through therapy or religious transformation. I knew my father had lost his mother as a baby, then had been left in the country with a grandmother whom he adored until the age of five, and taken back to the city by an emotionally distant father to live with a stepmother who treated him badly. It is quite possible that my grandfather had punished my father as a small child for talking about what the stepmother was doing to *him*.

None of this reasoning worked to stop my anger's transformation into the calm acceptance that I no longer needed to feel guilty at not having visited my ailing parent before he died.

The relief I received from my work with Keith and feeling safe while dealing with disturbing emotions encouraged me to believe that my life had a chance of becoming good again, not just on the surface, as in my last six years abroad, but in a deep and genuine way.

Keith helped me recover from the rawness of our hard working sessions by telling me that it was good to be kind to myself with special baths or a massage. He encouraged me to learn meditation, telling me that he woke up an hour early to have time for it. I couldn't believe that someone would sleep less in order to meditate. Now I do the same.

I discovered acupuncture, given to me in a gentle way by a Chinese woman, born and trained in her own country. My tolerance of pain was so low that she had to reject her teacher's dictum that "the stronger the signal, the more the patient will feel she is getting her money's worth."

During the half-hour lying on my stomach, my senses rich with stimulation, I remembered how, as a child, I'd pretended that the dark bed I was sleeping on was Grace. When I breathed, the mattress seemed to breathe under me; I could feel again the comfort of my brown mother's bosom as I was rocked to sleep, my unconscious mind telling me that she had never left.

In spite of moving through difficult psychotherapy, I found this to be a happy period. Though transitioning back to the States had been difficult for my son and me, Zach had been filled with delight. Kenny—now fourteen and called Ken to fit into the more macho culture he had found among American high school boys—bonded with us in a new way. My son may have regained some of the family warmth and attention he had missed during the periods when his dad hid himself away at his work place in Holland, and I seemed distant because of medication or depressed in spirit from guilt at the break with my parents.

After working for several years in a small family-run bakery, which reminded me of the aromatic neighborhood Dutch stores I had loved so much, and for which I was homesick, I began to teach dance again. I had figured my classes would be popular in America, but they were not a success. This was 1989, a time when many dance/exercise students looked at their watches and counted their heart rates. If the number was too low, they quit. I felt forced to change my direction into teaching aerobics.

Sarah visited often and eventually joined us in the United States, transferring to a university not too far away. I was able to stay in frequent communication with my two older sisters, even though we lived miles apart. Making my re-entry into American life complete, I returned to the activist political life I had led before leaving the country in the late 1960s. My children did very well in the universities they chose, and their graduations were joyous occasions for Zach and me.

I graduated, also, in two different ways. My endocrinologist said goodbye to me and admitted that it had been "interesting" to have watched my pituitary tumor disintegrate without medication. After five years of hard work with Keith at once a week and one year at twice a month, we said goodbye. I knew that in need I could always call him.

Chapter 23 – Phyllis

The emotional release I had achieved in therapy allowed me to start working with my left eye in the ways that Dr. Apell had wanted, the stretching and strengthening of my eye muscles. Under the care of Dr. Phyllis Liu, a behavioral optometrist also associated with the Gesell Institute, I was ready to do visual therapy in spite of the disturbing emotions I continued to feel while doing it. Just as I had with Keith, I travelled the many miles to every new location where Phyllis opened her offices for weekly therapy, a great deal of it fortunately paid for by my insurance.

I had heard about an optometrist on Long Island who used prisms as a corrective tool for eyes like mine that couldn't focus together on close work. I figured if the left eye could be lifted up to the same level as the right one, then maybe the two could see the same close-up image. When living in The Netherlands, I had visited this doctor at his office one summer, but he had not been willing to work with someone at long distance, saying that prisms without exercises were worthless. My eyes would demand a constant increase in the prisms' strength and thickness. I hadn't realized that my eyes were not only off horizontally; they were out of alignment vertically, also.

Dr. Liu, to my delight, used corrective prisms in her treatment, and she was able to maintain their level of thickness in my glasses because of our regular visual therapy sessions, even reducing their strength over time. My nearsightedness also improved, as if the realignment had made a difference in my ability to see at a distance.

As my eyes improved in acuity, I wondered if I had been born normal-sighted.

"Was my nearsightedness caused by the fall on the andirons?" I asked my doctor one day?

"Since there is no history of nearsightedness in your family, I am thinking that the accident may have been the cause, but there is no way to be sure. I am certain that the fall caused your eyes' misalignment." For a long time in my work with Phyllis, I had referred to this event as my "accident" rather than "abuse."

Now I called it for what it was. I recognized, for the first time, that the horrible visual pain I had been dealing with for so long was directly due to the injury by my mother. My mind had skirted the direct cause-and-effect aspect of my eye problem out of the need to avoid the strong emotions involved, my fury at recognizing that my mother had created the agony that had interfered with my happiness, as well as my ability to be the calm mother I would like to have been. My own mother's murderous message had been sent down the years in the form of a hurt so great, that once, in The Netherlands, I had thought of completing her intention by ending my life, wanting to get rid of the hammer-like pounding at the side of my left eye for good.

As I faced the truth, my resentment sparked the paranoiac suspicion that the splendid treatment in Pittsfield had been stopped by my parents when the doctor questioned if my eyes had ever been injured in childhood. But, then, I let it all go, delighted that I knew I would soon be reading again. Phyllis had assured me of that.

I asked my doctor why the turn-in of my left eye had not bothered me after the operation at eleven. I suspected that part of my adult pain was due to the cut muscle that had been shortened in order to pull my eye away from my nose, yet I remembered no pain as a child.

"Children's muscles are much more pliant and flexible. I think the pain you have had since your late twenties has been due to the difference in age," my doctor answered.

After a decade of work with Phyllis I began to reach a new level of understanding about my visual history. I recognized that, indeed, the dance techniques of contrast between arms and legs as well as use of the diagonal—so that at times my eyes were looking in opposite direction from different parts of the body—had been a form of home-grown visual therapy for me. I realized another magic quality of dance: the stimulation of all parts of the body at once causes a healing in grounding and awareness. I began to understand why I had felt most alive, most intelligent, most insightful, most disciplined, and most sensually aware all at once when involved in my dancing.

My insights continued with every month: just as monocular vision had removed me from an unwanted awareness of my surroundings as a young child, it had interfered with my ability as a college student to think in an engaged way. Since critical and reasoned thinking corresponds to the left brain or right eye, and the emotions as well as intuition connects to the right brain or left eye, inputs from both visual pathways are necessary for the best combination of grounded and imaginative thinking. One of the many reasons for school children to have the coordination between their eyes checked is that their thinking can be improved by the active use and involvement of each eye stimulating both the left and right brain.

I have learned to delay any important decisions when I have temporarily lost my left eye's vision due to fatigue. I have occasionally forgotten this truth while writing *Finding Grace*, pulling whole chapters out for deletion at night. The next day, after a good sleep and regained binocular vision, I have put the chapters back, realizing that the right eye's dominance had enforced a removal of material with unusual, genuine, and imaginative or innovative ideas. My sense of humor has improved with binocular vision, my left and right brain more able to share and surprise each other into laughter at similar unexpected switches of mind.

From the patients I met in the office at Dr. Liu's private practice, I discovered that I was not the only adult with difficulties in visual coordination, and that the problem for many of them did not come from a lazy eye whose treatment had been neglected in childhood. People who had been in automobile accidents or students who had lost the correct position of an eye through sports collisions had been suffering from changes in the visual cortex of the brain just like me. I had never heard my problem referred to as a brain injury. I felt less alone and different from other people, less out of place in what was mainly a children's doctor's office, when I realized that my situation could now be simply stated: I received a traumatic brain injury—or TBI—as a child, and I am trying to repair the visual damage fifty-five years later.

A common sense friend had asked me in Europe, "If it's the left eye that's bothering you so much, why don't you just cover it up?" I had thought this was a great idea until I tried it. Even when covered, the left eye fought to be part of the action. I recognized that this proved my problem came from a brain disorder rather than a question of physical alignment. Apparently, once my brain had received the message that binocularity was needed and desired, the left eye refused to be *left* out again.

But Dr. Liu told me I could use the patch idea if I alternated the eyes and then included a no-patch period in between. This seemed to calm my brain into acquiescence. For the first time since my twenties I began to read again without pain.

I found the flow of immersion in books I had known as a child, when I had escaped into another world through the right eye. I amazed myself by wending my way through eight hundred and forty-eight pages of David Payne's *Confessions of a Taoist on Wall Street* in paperback small print. I was fascinated with the hero's journey, which paralleled my own leap between cultures. America had felt like a cold, uncaring, vast, and complicated place after seventeen years of living in The Netherlands where, for instance, I, as a forty-five-year-old woman, had received a letter from the government reminding me to get a pap smear.

However, my beginning methods of reading were time-consuming because I had to alternate the patch between my left and right eyes every page or two, and then remember the no-patch period in between. I was fussy, using my precious reading time and energy only for the books I wanted most to read.

They had to be real, by which I meant either nonfiction or told in such a historically accurate or emotionally true way that they felt real to me, such as Erica Jong's *Fanny,* which I had managed to get through, even with the eye pain, in The Netherlands. Women authors like Anita Diamant, author of *The Red Tent*, were my favorites, as if I were trying to fill in the years I had lived in gender neutrality. But I also loved Nicholas Evans' *The Horse Whisperer* for his understanding of feelings, both in women and animals, and Dan Brown's *Da Vinci Code.*

Until I read this enriching thriller, which was also a history of the feminine sacred, I had never considered the possibility that God could be feminine. I was now beginning to feel the taste on my tongue of women's liberation—specifically, a release from the belief that *masculine* means better—about thirty years later than my college peers.

I remember the day when Phyllis asked if I wanted to work part time in her office, where I would be doing computer tasks.

At first I refused, but then accepted a trial period. My left eye immediately acted up, and I fled in agony. Yet with three more years of monthly sessions I found that I could manage long hours of writing on the computer. It was discouraging, however, to find that I needed to use the alternating-patch method for revisions until my doctor told me that the *fine-point* work of computer use was creating misalignment problems even for people with normal vision!

I have had company during my journey with misaligned eyes, though I did not know it until recently. Now that I have become able to describe my visual situation accurately, I have learned from casual conversations with other adults that perhaps one out of twenty people suffer from this condition and have adapted to it with different tactics. For instance, some use one eye for far and one for short distance. The most interesting— and famous—example is President Lincoln, who had to deal with a visual handicap similar to mine, had some of the same symptoms, and dealt with it in similar ways.

According to an article in the April 1952 *A.M.S. Archives*, *Abraham Lincoln's Organic and Emotional Neurosis*, President Lincoln's wayward left eye, its muscles thought to have been weakened by a brain hemorrhage from a horse's kick in his tenth year, could suddenly drift upwards, causing double vision in the former president.

At these times, Lincoln would drift into depression, just as I would when the sudden turn-in of my left eye created the sense that I had lost a part of myself and my ability to think in an organized and well-rounded way. My deep sense of loss would then be intensified by a trigger back to the physical wounding as well as emotional pain at being hurt by my mother, just as I imagine the sudden loss of Lincoln's ability to see and think clearly may have triggered his original shock at being physically hurt by the horse as well as grief at the death of his beloved mother, which occurred in the same year.

Friends of Lincoln would report that after periods of glum silence and rest, the president would suddenly jump up and burst into laughter. Was this change to joy similar to my thrill at my left eye's activation through dance? Did President Lincoln go from gloom to this sensation of joyous repair just as I did when my left eye slipped back into use? After all, the left eye connects to the euphoric side of our brain, the artist, the dreamer, and the part that plays with ideas. Just as important, he could have felt the relief I have experienced from gaining access to my whole range of thinking, by finding himself better able—with both imagination and reasoning—to grasp the total picture of any matter at hand.

After over twenty years of work together, involving hours of take-home easy-to-do exercises as well as regular office visits and frequent adjustments to my prescriptions, Phyllis and I have been able to get my eyes back to their original design—their ability to work as a team and at a low level of acuity correction. I owe my renewed ability to read, a reduction in eye pain, and my career as a writer to a conjunction of talk therapy, prisms, corrections by a chiropractor, and skillful guidance by my intuitive behavioral optometrist.

Chapter 24 – Transition

Five years after returning to America, Zach survived a heart operation successfully, and I thought major sickness was behind us. But he must have known better. Never having been an observant Jew, he joined a synagogue near us, his reason being concern as to how I would handle his leaving me. "I want to give you a place where you'll be able to cry when I go." Six years later I lost him to cancer.

I had not realized how dependent on my husband and our relationship I had become. As I floundered, my rabbi recommended Victor Frankl's *Man's Search for Meaning*, which helped, but I returned to Keith for a year and a half to get help with my grief. I had learned my lesson, not to wait until darkness took me over.

I also found a new form of dance, organized around the *chakras*—centers of energy in the body. Our teacher played tapes of music that resonated with each *chakra* area, and we were asked to move to the sound while thinking of the color that was associated with that particular center of energy. The tender music of a string concerto accompanied the heart *chakra*, stimulating me to dance out my grief, as I thought of the color green and melted into an awareness of how much my heart had entwined itself with my husband of thirty-one years.

I missed the sexual relationship I had enjoyed with Zach and developed incontinence, partly, I believe, because the muscles used in intercourse lay still, unused and weakened. I turned to a clinic doing urinary control biofeedback in Danbury, Connecticut, a delightful place with understanding, well-trained female technicians who fitted my vagina with a device that stimulated my pelvic floor muscles. I returned home so horny that the broom handle inside the kitchen door looked good to me. When I graduated from the clinic, much improved, I was given the device I had used for four months to take home and enjoy, which I did.

After a year and a half, I became involved with a new partner, who is still with me today. I consider myself blessed in finding Stan, not only as my life companion, but also because he is the practitioner who was able to finish the healing of my eyes, which could flare up into tense spasms from emotional stress or with extensive computer use. A chiropractor with training in kinesiology and emotional release therapies as well as in the use of an activator rather than hands-on manipulation, Stan was able to lessen my residual eye pain by realigning my neck.

He led me through an emotional repeat of the fall on the andirons and in the process, conditioned my muscles not to react to the memory. He told me that my neck had been injured along with the eye during the fall and therefore was equally vulnerable. If my eye was pulled out of alignment by fine visual work, the vertebrae in my neck would lose placement, and, conversely, if the neck was thrown off through physical activity involving twisting or through lack of sleep, the eye would be thrown out of alignment. With timely neck adjustments, visual exercises, and a device called Eyelights, a pair of dark blue glasses with tiny red lights—set to flicker at certain intervals in order to take the eye muscles out of spasm—we were able to put an end to the pain that had plagued me for two-thirds of my life.

My new husband encouraged me to continue my use of integrative medicine (a combination of medical and alternative care) for the stomach aches I'd been having. Keith had recommended a naturopathic physician, Dr. Debra Gibson, who had connected my habit as a child of eating only sweet foods with the sickness I now had in my gut called Candida.

I had been able to compensate for this imbalance in bacteria for most of my life, but I could no longer do this at my age. She told me that the mental fogginess I complained about that had caused me to fall asleep at the wheel for a second, as well as the ringing in my ears and discomfort in my abdomen, would vanish when sugar and refined carbohydrates were removed from my diet. My great number of infections would lessen also because sugar suppresses the immune system. She added that we were never meant to eat all the fruit that is available now. Two pieces a day is sufficient.

My new naturopathic doctor's extremely difficult solution for a person addicted to sugar, as I had been during my period of malaise in Europe and while working in the Swedish bakery in America, was to give it up.

It took me about ten years to completely accomplish this feat, and I still slip when enjoying a dessert after a meal out or take a glass of wine. But now I know to take an antihistamine—an alternative one, which means a pill based on herbs and without side-affects—to counteract the inflammation that the sugar has caused. The solution has had to be a drastic one: I do not keep sweet foods in the house, having scanned—in spite of eye pain—the labels on everything I buy for the sugar content. But a more difficult job has been steering clear of sugary spreads at meetings and parties.

I am grateful to Keith and Dr. Gibson for starting me on this path to health, and to Stan and Dr. Sherry Stemper for helping me stay on it. The results have been exactly what was predicted: the reduction of stomach discomfort and number of infections, as well as the enjoyment of a clearer mind from my mid-sixties on than I had enjoyed for the previous twenty years.

Just before I married my second Jewish husband, I

converted to Judaism, finding in the Reform branch of that religion clear and sensible directions of how to live. I had accompanied Zach to services, but now I took on the commitment for myself.

I had come to see the Jewish religion as earthy and practical, having experienced the common sense involved in many of Reform Judaism's customs. I'd noticed the affectionate way parents cuddled their children at services, and I felt there was a chance in this religion to avoid the prudery and hypocrisy about *the flesh* I had found in my Christian upbringing and which my parents had suffered from in theirs.

I delighted in the trilogy called *Rashi's Daughters*, especially *Book I: Joheved*, written by Maggie Anton. According to this author and scholar, traditional Jewish teachings not only referred to sexual intercourse as a spiritual act to be enjoyed often, but also considered the pleasure it offered to women as well as to men, so important that special instructions had been given on the subject in religious writings. Such spiritual appreciation for the delights of feminine sexuality helped me erase any remnant of my mother's Puritan message that love and the enjoyment of her sensuality was nuclear sinful and forbidden unless accompanied by the anxieties of secrets, fear, and shame.

The sentiments I gleaned from reading *Joheved* echoed the ideas I'd enjoyed when reading Erikson's *Childhood and Society* while at Riggs. On pages 238-239 of a chapter called "Reflections on the American Identity", Erikson describes how the delights of the senses—not only the sensuality of sexual relationships—came to be suppressed in American culture:

> Puritanism, beyond defining sexual sin for full-blooded and strong-willed people, gradually extended itself to the total sphere of bodily living, compromising all sensuality—including

marital relationships—and spreading its frigidity over the tasks of pregnancy, childbirth, nursing, and training. The result was that men [and women] were born who failed to learn from their mothers to love the goodness of sensuality before they learned to hate its sinful uses. (p. 293)

The book *Childhood and Society* was published in 1950. In 1956, as if confirming Erikson's analysis of America's cultural malaise, Grace Metalious finished her excellent and richly written work of fiction that describes the pain and dysfunction in the lives of New Englanders who suppress their feelings of sensual pleasure. In *Peyton Place*, the author portrays the difficulty many women have in expressing their sexual feelings. But once they do—and Metalious shared here a secret about New England's women, who at that time were considered in popular culture as staid and stiff—given the chance, they find that their sexual passion is every bit as strong as that of men.

Jewish humor, another facet of Jewish culture that resonated with me, reflected a delight in chiding mainstream culture, similar to the jokes about "White folks" I remembered hearing in my childhood kitchen. The Jewish characteristic of poking fun at society's hypocrisies reminded me of the refreshing attitudes Joe and Jessie had shown towards my dysfunctional family.

The message of kindness on a public scale, or social justice, taught as one of the most important parts of Judaism, on a par with the reading of Torah and prayer, resonated for me. My sister Susie and I had learned strict lessons as very young children from Jessie and Grace about consideration, decency, fairness, and respect for one another.

I was happy at being allowed by Jewish law to date as soon

as three months after my husband's death. This practicality and understanding of the human heart reminded me of the common sense and practical way of thinking I had come to know when living among the Dutch. The ancient Jewish restriction of three months had been for the purpose of being certain who a new child's father was. The importance for me was the fact that I did not have to wait longer. I had thrived on living with someone I had loved, needed, and enjoyed, and I wanted to repeat the experience as soon as possible.

To my delight Stan loved to dance, whether at home or out in the middle of crowds. My ability to dance creatively flourished with jitterbug. Eight-count swing brought out of both Stan and me the desire for leadership and need to compromise, conflicts that paralleled our personal growth as a team. After all, we had lived lifetimes with certain behavior patterns that we did not want to give up but which were not appropriate for our new relationship, and changes needed to be made.

Again, dance was giving me help in solving the pressing questions of my life, this time assisting me in figuring out how much I wanted to remain the independent self I had been for two years versus how much I wanted to accept the joy of following someone else's exciting moves.

Chapter 25 – Learning to Write

Just as I had looked for a new partner when Zach passed away, I longed to live in a place far from my childhood hometown. I had even gone back for a few weeks to The Netherlands to test it out, but came back when I realized that my chances for finding a partner were better in the United States. I'd decided on a move to the south just before I met Stan but had been forced to give this up when my fiancé was offered the job of his dreams nearby. I could not refuse him his wish to stay in the north.

To answer my need for a change, we settled on a small town in the green and hilly countryside an hour from where I had grown up, one whose old-fashioned village streets had only been known to me in glimpses as I'd passed through them on trips. I figured that I would see a lot of my husband since our new house was closer to where he worked, but I soon learned that twelve-hour work days for him were common. Even Saturdays were without companionship because my fifty-six-year-old husband, who had thrown all of his energies into his exciting new work, needed the day to sleep and recover.

At first I was disappointed, and then I recognized that I had been handed a gift: forty hours a week of free time with no financial pressure to go out and teach my classes! I began to think of it as a chance to get back into the creative dance work I had left behind in The Netherlands, and I started looking for a studio to rent. I checked out classes in order to get back into condition but could find nothing that came near what I'd enjoyed with Felix. Hearing about an all-Black dance school in my hometown that had classes for adults, I called up but found myself too shy to attend, even though the woman on the phone was friendly and welcoming when I asked if it was okay for me to come.

For two months, I attended a class for women my age taught by an elderly Black male teacher in the African American Club at a university not too far away. Ecstatic, I thought I had found Felix again, but when the group began to perform, I dropped out. I was convinced that they wouldn't want one White face in the middle of the stage. Later I met one of the women and she looked at me strangely.

"Why did you drop out? You were so good and you seemed to have such fun." I told her the reason and she replied, "Oh, Honey, come on, no one would have thought two minutes about it."

I wept when I was by myself, realizing that I'd missed out yet another time on joining the Black community due to my insecurity about whether I had the right to be in it. It saddened me also that I had lost the possibility of making friends. I had come to feel lonely in turn-of-the-century America. Giving my aerobics classes to women of my own age had been a kind of substitute for friendships; now that this kind of teaching was over, I felt a lack in my American social life as compared to what I had known in Holland.

Coming back to the States at age fifty, I'd found that women my age had little time for friends, most of them busy with the full time jobs they had grown used to while their children grew up and college tuition made demands on them. In The Netherlands, the pressure for a two-income household had not been as strong as in the United States, due to unbelievably low university charges and reliable non-job-related low-co-pay health insurance. I had enjoyed many friendships with other women who had been interested in meeting for lunch, coffee, or an early dinner.

I began to look back with longing to my life in The Netherlands, remembering my excitement in living before the tranquilizers.

Yet I had wanted to come back to America. What had that been about? Was it that "one never feels fully at home in a country whose native language is not yours," as my sister Louise had told me when she returned for good from her home in Scandinavia? Or was it something to do with the arts, as if here in America, I had expected to find more creative juice? Then I remembered the Dutch choreographer and head of the Netherlands Dance Theater, Jiri Kylian, and his magnificent *Stoolgame* that used the children's game of musical chairs on a dramatically lit stage to teach a point about social cruelty. Why was I in such doubt, and where was I going with all this?

I called Keith.

"Look" he said, "you've gotten in touch with many feelings that you kept under wraps for a lot of years. Why don't you join a speakers' group or drama class where you can express some of them?" I thanked him.

To my surprise I found an acting class in my own town, whose vibrant weekly sessions changed everything for me and put my American life back on track. First of all, I made a friend, my first one who was neither a neighbor nor a student. I was finding out that mid-sixties was a better age to develop female friendships in northeast semi-urban United States than fifty had been.

Moira was a retired school teacher one year older than I, with the good pension and marvelous health insurance given to all teachers by our state's legislature. She had decided to enjoy the time ahead of her by doing everything she had never had the leisure for. Laughing and sharing stories filled our hours together.

She and I preferred the improvisational exercises our class

231

did to learning from a script, partly because, coincidentally, both of our short-term memories had been compromised by bouts with Lyme disease. But we also liked them because we were equally charged with a need to be creative and tell, or work out, our own stories in a dramatic way.

My lively and outspoken friend had lost her husband during the Vietnam War, not because he was killed but because he came home violent. There was little understanding of PTSD in those days and, terrified for her baby's safety, she was forced to ask Martin to leave, which he did, respecting her judgment in the calm of day after the night he had picked up a knife and walked toward their baby. She had raised her son alone while teaching. Now it was time for her to play.

One day in class, I acted out, in mime, the scene in which I had gone to a park in The Netherlands and sat on a bench to read a very important letter. It was my mother's note, written after my flashbacks but before our long-term separation. She had asked me to come visit her but, she had added, "Please, do not talk about those things you think happened."

I had a lot of fun exaggerating my emotions, mimicking my arrival on the bike, high with pleasure at the beautiful spot I had chosen and my cheerful expectations about what I was to read. The gradual but crushing shock of disappointment was followed, of course, by the proverbial destruction of the letter before I swooped up my bike and tore away. My teacher and classmates loved it.

I went home to write up this little drama and added it to my collection of short stories, as I thought of them, scenes from early childhood that I had dashed off over the years, written in the third person to protect my family's privacy if I ever published them. Soon I was compiling chapters and realized that I was writing a book. As I turned my creative drive to language instead of dance, I remembered other dancers who had done the same. While in Europe I'd struggled through but loved Agnes de Mille's *Speak to Me, Dance with Me* about her passionate life as a young dancer in 1930's London. It delighted me to think that I was now in good company.

For the next two years, I lived a similarly passionate life, working with eagerness toward the finish of a story I was certain would be of great interest to others and a success. I did not know about the publishing market of 2004, but I discovered the truth soon: it was, in one word, *TOUGH*.

I learned that memoirs had to have themes, the message clear and easy to grasp, and they had to be uplifting. I was told that the events of 9/11 had sobered the American reading public so much that even adult fiction had begun to follow the format for children's stories: a basically happy individual faces problems and challenges and is able to solve them—with smart thinking, moral courage, and help from others.

"So you are saying that no one wants to read a book that tells about child abuse?" I asked an agent at a writers' conference.

"You're too late," she told me. "The days of memoirs like *A Child Called It* are over." I checked this out and found that Dave Pelzer's riveting memoir about his abuse-filled childhood was still selling, but everyone in the writing world told me the same story.

"Dark memoirs are out," one agent told me at still another conference.

"But I don't see my story as dark. I see the warm light of stunning rescues by a community of women—until Joe came to add his help—including my siblings, who were kind and strong beyond their years in their attempts to help me. And some of it is funny, seeing how children manage to have fun no matter what, and with my mother being so peculiar."

"I don't think most readers would see it that way," she

concluded the three-minute session.

I thought that perhaps Austen Riggs Center would be interested in my project, and I made an appointment to see the director. He encouraged me but was unable to guide me as far as publishing went. Thinking that I might be able to get a position there teaching dance to the patients, I began a series of trips to the center, but this effort was interrupted by something far more important.

During my drive on an autumn day, I suddenly had a flashing thought about Grace, who I knew was living near the town where I grew up, but whom I had seen infrequently since coming back to the States. Before I knew what was happening, I had turned around and headed back home, the certainty in my heart and chest that something was wrong.

Part Four – Black Roots

Chapter 26 – Saving Grace

At nine years old, I'd hardly noticed when Grace came once a week to help my mother in the house after she and Joe had returned to our town following the end of the war. I was a human being whose soul had gone off to another land. All memories of anything or anyone meaningful to me from my early life had vanished from my mind. One day, however, Grace looked so sad while washing dishes at the sink that I asked her why.

"Oh, I've gone and lost my watch," she said in a despondent way, fingering her left wrist with a soapy finger, and looking out of the window.

"Oh, you can get another one," I said trying to be helpful, but some message from inside told me that I was being insensitive.

She looked down at me. "Well, but you know…you know, you get attached to the one you have…" She seemed disappointed in my inability to pick up on her sorrow.

I realize now that I was saying to her, "Well, it was no problem, was it, for you to leave me? You just went and got yourself another family with another child, so now you can just go get yourself another watch. It should be no problem for you."

I was unconsciously walking slipshod over her feelings, just as I thought she had walked over mine. We didn't exchange meaningful words again until after I entered Riggs in my twenties.

The last day of a visit home from the treatment center, at twenty-four, I shared a morning with Grace. After retiring from a job at the local hospital, she had come back to work for my mother once a week. Neither of us had much to say to each other, though we had the house to ourselves, but when Joe came to pick her up, I remember a warm feeling among the three of us as we stood in the empty kitchen. I had no conscious memories, at this time, about Joe. I just knew he had been around in my childhood.

I mentioned that my mother, with her impatience, must have been difficult for me, and for all of us, to live with. Joe answered, "Horrible!" to which Grace did not disagree. I was surprised to hear from her no correction of Joe. I had received the impression as a child that my brown mother had felt only respect, compassion, and something like love for my mother. But, of course, as a little girl I had not understood the relationship between employer and employee.

I didn't see Grace much over the next twenty years, partly because I was preoccupied with raising children and pursuing my dance career in another American town, and later in Europe. Yet, even when back for visits to my parents' house, I dropped by her house only at Christmas time, and then I felt guilty about it, especially if I'd told my mother where I was going. I hadn't yet remembered that my mother had thrown me down the cellar steps for telling Grace I loved her, but the terror it had caused was probably the strongest, though subconscious, reason for delay in renewing connection with my brown mother.

I had kept in better contact with Grace when I was in Europe, writing occasional letters and sending birthday cards. The September of 1976, when most of my early memories came back, I made a photo album for Grace. I put in captions, so that she could follow every step of the way as my children had grown and played in our foreign land. That album turned out to be more extensive than any I'd prepared for my own mother. Though she had many nieces and nephews, Grace had no children. I felt as if I were giving her a chance to experience grandmother-hood.

Once I was back inside the United States, living in my old hometown and involved in the deep therapy that revisited the dark scenes of December 1941, I kept away.

If I called her on the phone, I would hear how nervous she was.

"Why are you nervous, Grace?"

"Oh, I don't know why, I'm just shaking inside all the time."

Grace had a psychic side and she may have sensed that I was dealing with that scary night when she had saved me from my mother and run across our huge lawn to carry me to safety. She may also have been suffering from exhaustion, at seventy-six having just finished taking care of her older brother before he passed away and now doing the same for Joe. Later she would refer to this time of going from home to hospital and back again, bringing homemade food to substitute for hospital fare, as "runnin', runnin', runnin.'"

Grace was kind and supportive when Zach died. She had rallied her strength after Joe passed away and looked good at eighty-three. I made efforts to resume contact, inviting her to my house for lunch several times, with the first invitation being the last she accepted even though she praised the hearty soup I'd made. Later I heard that she'd been scared of my dog. This tendency of Grace to keep silent instead of expressing her needs got worse as she got older, showing up in a refusal to let me know how sick she was getting.

One day, during a trip to The Berkshires, my body froze, panic driving me into a diner to call her. There was no answer, and I raced back home. In desperation, I phoned the daughter of Grace's best friend, Sally, who had cared for Susie and me at one time. I had not seen Sally's daughter, Janine, since we were tiny children, but I'd heard about her all my life. Grace would never let me visit her if "Janine and her mama comin' today," her personal rule about keeping Black and White families separate becoming clearer to me later.

Nervous that I was overstepping boundaries into a world where I was not wanted, I stammered that I was worried about Grace, whom I couldn't reach. To my relief, Janine seemed happy to hear from me, telling me that Grace had been lying in bed unable to breath but had managed to call 911 for the help that got her to a hospital. She was being kept for observation, put on blood pressure medicine, and told to eat more potassium-rich foods like bananas when she got home.

From that day on, Janine and I became a team in handling Grace's care. Strangely, we discovered that we lived a mile away from each other in the same small New England town where I had moved with my new husband.

For months, I came twice a week from my condo in the countryside to Grace's house. They were not happy visits, except for the food I would bring and watch her enjoy. She didn't talk much, except to tell me one day the sad tale of losing a baby in her only pregnancy while in Virginia. The surgeon had taken out the fetus when he'd removed a large benign tumor that had formed around her waist. I'd heard stories about southern doctors and what some of them had done to Black pregnant women under the guise of other medical procedures.

"How awful, Grace. I'm so sorry." I hoped that telling me and seeing the tears in my eyes did a bit to heal her pain.

During the next few weeks, I had the feeling that Grace was keeping herself guarded from me, watching everything she said or allowed me to see, so I wouldn't know she was doing badly. She kept me out of her kitchen, so that I wouldn't notice she didn't use it. Grace suspected that Janine and I would make her move out of that house, which we ended up doing.

I think that she forgave the two of us for making her say

goodbye to the dwelling Joe had built for her and which she had enjoyed for forty-five years. She seemed to like her small nursing home not far from Janine's house and mine. The attendants and mostly White other residents would give Grace compliments on how she turned herself out, Janine's impeccable taste supplying her with a constant supply of alluring and snappy slacks, jerseys, and jackets. The visiting beautician enhanced her beautiful long fingers with auburn or mauve nails.

Grace had been able to pay for this comfortable nursing home with Social Security payments and the pension from her former job as a Dietitian's Assistant in a hospital nearby. I believe that this ability to take care of her finances herself gave Grace great satisfaction, if not second thoughts on how she had always presented herself to others when Joe was alive, as a meek woman, dependent on and subservient to her husband.

I would visit her for dinner in this pleasant place. She had her own large room on the third floor, accessible by elevator and heavily curtained, because she liked it that way. A southern Black woman in the small building's kitchen fulfilled her every request.

"Well, what've you fixed tonight for yo' dinner?" Grace would begin our familiar chat in the dining room, to which question I would lay out my entire menu, soup, salad, main course, all cooked from scratch, and she would nod, while chewing arduously to enjoy what she could of her own dinner.

"And fo' dessert?" she asked one day. My brown mother was keeping me in line.

I swam with good feelings as I drove out of the parking lot, having experienced my bond with Grace as something still young and fresh, as if there had been no interval since the warm conversations at lunchtime in my birth family's kitchen after my mornings at nursery school.

As we became closer both physically and emotionally, I

needed more and more to close the gap and say, "Grace, you know you were my real mother and it hurt me so much when you left that I almost died."

Of course, I suspected that she knew this, because every time I leaned over to kiss her and say "I love you" before I went home, she would explode with a wavering wail, saying, "Ah loves you, Ah loves you…" with a choking and terrible sorrow in her voice. The fingers of one hand would stroke those of the other, as she held her hands down in her lap. I wonder now if she was remembering the day I had been angry with her as a young child and slammed the door on those beautiful long fingers.

I knew from past experience that if I asked her about my mother, she would change the subject and go on to some cheerful memory about how much fun she and I had had together back then. But I seemed to do better over the phone, and once I asked if she remembered a time when I was two years old and had been made to wear a white bandage over my left eye.

"Oh, yes," she said.

Shocked at striking gold, I said, "Grace, I don't mean the black patch I wore at six to straighten my eyes, this was earlier after some kind of fall in the living room and the doctor came."

"Oh, yes, Honey, I surely do."

This was what I had needed to hear ever since my flashbacks, to connect with someone from back then and hear another person confirm what I'd been saying. I had discovered, after Zach's death, through conversations with my sisters, the sad truth that even he had doubted my memories because the pressure from my parents' denials had been so strong.

"Grace, my mother had just thrown me into the andirons," I dared to add.

There was silence.

"Yes, Grace, she did that, right in the living room, and she told everyone I fell."

"Oh, Honey, no!" She began to cry.

Grasping at a possible deeper nugget of shiny treasure, I chanced the question, "Grace, do you remember how my mother threw me down the cellar stairs?" I waited. "And how you cried?" I helped her to feel that I was not blaming her for not coming down to help me.

"Yes," she said. I could hear her weeping.

"You do?" I was standing in the kitchen at my condo, holding on to the edge of the table. All these years of feeling alone, with only my therapists able to believe my horrible stories, everyone else doubtful, pressing their questions into my ears: "How could you think that of your mother...?" or "No, I can't believe that..." all this time of being told that I couldn't be right, all redeemed!

"Grace, you remember that?" I asked her again, not having heard very clearly because of her tears.

"Yes, I do, dahlin'," she managed, her voice gravelly from her sobs.

Then I persisted yet another time, but feeling certain that she wouldn't recall such weirdness of behavior. "And Grace, she kept us separated?"

I could hear the sound of her tears.

"Grace, Grace, do you remember that there was a time when my mother kept you and me apart? You remember that, do you remember that, Grace?"

"Yes, Honey..." her voice swam with the tears she had been forced to swallow and hide from her employer sixty years before.

Then I knew, I had not dreamt it, my mother had kept me away from my brown mother for one month, though it had seemed like forever, because Joe had silenced my tongue with his threat after that.

I couldn't believe my good fortune.

Grace, someone who had lived in that house and at that time right along with the young child that I had been, had confirmed the truth of my early life!

I flowed with this information into a luminous and friendly mental space; a lonely part of me said goodbye and drifted away.

I was tempted on other days to ask more, but Grace wouldn't accommodate my burning curiosity. Long drives by coastal beaches with her joyful comments: "Oh, look at those flowers!" and "Oh, what's that child doing now?" would end up with my not having started the questions sitting on the edge of my tongue.

One day I did manage to say that I forgave her for leaving me and not writing or even sending a card. Janine worried when I mentioned talking about the past with Grace, but I know that this lady, at eighty-nine, had not been hurt by my talking the truth. She'd been healed. The words "I forgive you," that had slipped from my half-unwilling lips, pushing themselves out before their time, just in case she should leave this earth before I had another chance, had helped her. From that day on, Grace never uttered those troubled and despairing sobs as she said, "Ah loves you" when we parted. She had been forgiven, and her message of love was sent out to me in flowing, eager tones.

One month before her death, Grace was sent to the hospital for a tightening in the muscles that controlled her ability to swallow. She was put on a feeding tube. Janine and I felt she was being well cared for when we left her side at dinnertime, but around ten o'clock I had a sudden wave of anxiety and jumped into my car, racing through the late spring night to the hospital. As I burst out of the elevator onto her ward, I could hear Grace's voice, and it was unusually loud. I hurried to the room to find her trying to get out of the bed, all tangled in her lines.

"They comin' to get me," she explained, tugging at the lines. "I got tuh get out of here! They don' know what they doin." I pressed the button for the nurse.

"No! They gonna come get me!"

"Grace, you need water! I'm getting it for you!" I grabbed at this idea even though I couldn't believe what I was saying. Was the line actually hanging free? I pushed the call button again.

"Nobody should be treated bad..." and she looked around with accusations at the hospital room and machines. Then she managed to get a leg over one side of the bed. "I jes goin' to get mahsef out of heah..."

"Wait, Grace. They'll be here in a minute. You'll feel better in a minute!" I banged on the button, thinking I should go to the hall, but Grace was fumbling with lines and trying to yank them off her. I tried to stop her. She looked up at me, desperate in her pleading.

"You know they shouldn't have tried to stop her!"

"Who, Grace, who?"

"Rosa Parks, an' she got on up an' got on that bus, like you never saw no one do!" I had never, in all of the thousands of hours I'd spent both as child and adult with Grace, heard her say anything political, historical, or racial.

"That's right, Grace, she was a great woman, and a courageous one," I agreed.

"Yes, she was." She seemed quiet for a moment, but then went back to her struggle to get herself loose.

"Grace, they'll be here in a minute to fix your line and get you hydrated."

She looked up. "An' you know yo' daddy gonna hep me."

"My daddy, Grace?'

"Why yeh," she insisted, seeming annoyed that I didn't know what she meant. Then she gazed intently at me. "Yes, yo' daddy would have give it to 'em, yes he would...."

She was having trouble mouthing her words because of the dryness in her mouth. I leaned forward to hear her clearer.

"Yep, he gonna he'p me. I'm a goooood girl!" That word "good" took a long time in the saying of it while Grace looked earnestly into my face. Some confirmation was being asked for. Like a mother, I agreed.

"Yes, Grace, you are a good girl," I said, realizing that she must have felt as if the nurses were punishing her.

"Tha's right, tha's right, a goooood girl." Her emphatic way of saying the word seemed like a little girl who has been chastised by her mother but is definite in knowing that she has not been bad. Her physically weak body sat up straight with the energy from this defiance, her arm up straight to clench a fist if she could have gotten the strength to do so.

The nurse came to fix her IV drip and all reverie stopped. I wondered if there would be more unusual words coming from her, but Grace relaxed back onto the bed, the sweet waters pouring into her and telling her that it was safe to stay where she was. When I was sure that she slept, I left, but not before receiving an explanation—and apology—from the nurses who had forgotten to reconnect the hydration line after a procedure. I shook and shivered as I walked to my car, the experience having moved me with its urgency and what Grace had shared with me.

My Grace had allowed me to see and comfort her about personal struggles that lay inside her, meshing themselves with conflicts from the civil rights years. Somewhere in her personality was a little girl who had been told she was bad, and that little child had never quite grown up after that.

246

The next day, Janine had her own moment of pride-in-rescue. Together we had agreed that Grace was not getting the tender care she needed and seemed—though very unlike her—to be demanding. Janine called a friend who happened to be a manager over the wards in our part of the hospital. Gladys came down to see what was going on. The three of us agreed that Hospice would be a better place for Grace. Janine's friend pulled so many strings that we got a transfer arranged for the following day.

After Gladys left, Janine and I stood side by side at the foot of the hospital bed, our arms around each other's waists and laughing, proud at what we had accomplished. Sally had asked her daughter to care for her good friend after she passed away, and Janine had taken on the responsibility as if Grace had been her own mother.

"Hey, Grace, I bet you never thought Janine and I would become friends!" Pale but proud, her elegance increased overnight, in spite of her sickness, our lovely Grace sat propped up against her pillows. We could hardly hear her astonished mumble, "No, I surely didn't…"

During one of my last conversations with her at Hospice, I tried to give one more gift to her, my childless mother.

"You know, Grace, that without your love I wouldn't have had any. You know that, right?"

Her protective mind allowed only a tiny bit of a nod, her need to protest, out of loyalty and deference to her former employers that they had loved me, too, stronger than her ability to give back to me what I wanted.

Once, Grace had said to me during an afternoon outing in my car, after I had asked if my mother had really wanted a son, "I don't believe your mother was ready to have a third child at all." Yet she had difficulty being honest about the fact that she herself had been my mother substitute. It saddened me that our social and economic roles had prevented her from claiming the goodness of having had a child who loved her as if I had been her own.

Grace's difficulties with swallowing had been a problem for years and were accompanied by a benign tumor in the esophagus. However, I couldn't help but wonder if the increased tightness in her throat had been partially caused by her vocal chords' civil war, the fight inside her to be allowed to talk to me, to confide in, to cry, and to hug the *baby* who had known her so well and who had forgiven her for disappearing without a word. But she did not trust me enough, and quietness won.

Her throat did relax enough to sing her gospel music, softly, however. I brought her a tape of gospel music Sarah had picked up during a trip through the south when she had visited a Black history exhibition in Atlanta. Grace mouthed the words with a high thin voice, gently touching the ends of her long slim fingers together in half time, a life of choir singing sending the tunes to her willing but tired vocal chords.

Her lack of directness to me hurt. Once again I asked myself the question that had bothered me much of my life: Had Grace really loved me or had we been tied together only by job, money, and duty on her part, and love mixed with gratitude on mine?

Stan's mother lay terminally ill in another city. I felt obligated to accompany him. When I returned, Grace lay still with eyes closed—the stage when Hospice nurses say, "Talk. She can hear you." I took her thin hand and leaned over her still beautiful face and said, "Grace. I love you and I always will."

Did I see the lines in her face smooth a tiny bit, or was it my imagination?

At Grace's funeral in May, I was surprised by the name a church choir member used when talking about her. "Oh, Baby?" she began to reminisce, "She was a singer! Why, she had a beautiful voice and she never missed a Sunday!"

"Baby?" I said.

"Oh, yes, that's what I called her, ever since the first time she came to our church. It just seemed to suit her. I don't care about all that cooking she did—and they loved her upside-down pineapple shortcakes and cherry pies, yes they did. No, for me, she was just 'Baby'."

In my mind, I agreed. Grace had been a baby, hard working as a bricklayer, yet a baby. It was not just that she was "peaceful as a sleeping infant," and she was that and beautiful as well, her pleasant personality matching her pretty face. She had perseverance and an overall strength to endure and see this life through, with God's help, but in her relationship to other human beings, she had seemed to be as weak as a baby. She had appeared to be a timid soul—except, of course, for that horrible December night when she saved my life—and, strangely, except for her last days when she began to speak up for what she wanted.

A family member told me that once Grace married Joe, she became a vassal to him, choosing his wishes and needs over anything else, even family connections and female friendships if he didn't like her choice.

Grace had told me how well she'd taken care of Joe before his death.

"I nursed him at home a long time after most folks would've, carryin' trays with everything he liked and arrangin' for neighbors to come on over an' lift him up."

"And I hope he was appreciative, Grace," I said.

"Oh, Honey, I don't know about that." Then, in a rare streak of independence she'd said, "Well, no, you know, Joe didn't never thank me. The one who did was Robbie," and she went off singing her praises of the brother whom she had taken care of at home before Joe. But while her husband was alive she had not complained, as she could have, by using comparisons to her brother to make her husband shape up. This timid behavior gave me an answer to my persistent question— whether my beloved adoptive mother had truly loved me when she left our house and never let me hear from her again.

Yes, I was able to answer with relief. Grace had truly loved me, but had acted out of fear of my mother's jealousy in not writing me or sending any presents on my birthdays, not even a card. And in turn, I'd stayed away from *her*—even as an adult— because of old, still-unconscious fears about my mother's punishment. When I remembered not only the terrifying fall down the cellar steps, but also, months later, the shape of the hand that had pushed me, bringing my mother's jealousy and her sound intention up into adult consciousness, I found myself looking up Grace's street on a map of her town and realizing how easy it was, after all, to get to her house.

As a child of three I had, one afternoon, called Grace "bad" for something she'd done. She had apologized to me for her behavior. Then she'd shared a deeply reflective moment, for which great wisdom I will ever be grateful.

"When people acts wrong it jes mean they's scai'ed," she had told me, teaching me for life that the way to communicate with children is to treat them—and their intelligence—with respect.

Chapter 27 – Psychosynthesis and Feeling Black

The summer after Grace passed away, encouraged by the therapist, Shamai Currim who had helped me deal with Grace's illness and death, I began a study of psychosynthesis, a branch of psychology that among other things emphasizes the importance of spiritual health in a patient's ability to heal completely. There are many centers for such training, including one in Florence, Italy. I chose the Synthesis Center in Amherst, Massachusetts, deciding to stay for a total of nine nights over three weekends at a motel several miles from the center.

I liked coming back to my unadorned room in the late afternoon after the full-day sessions had ended. My front window looked out across a grass lot to the motel's swimming pool and toward the western sky beyond. I used the pink-clouded sky for inspiration but never went to the pool. I didn't have time.

Pages of notes scribbled during the day's fruitful sessions looked up at me from the round wooden table I placed by my room's large window. I knew if I didn't look at these papers and clarify the abbreviated revelations I'd noted from the day, that the nuances of what I learned would be lost. The most important lesson I received from this summer at the Synthesis Center was one that life had taught me twenty-five years earlier, but which I hadn't been open to at the time.

Roberto Assagioli, the great Italian psychiatrist who founded psychosynthesis in the middle of the twentieth century, taught that most of our psychological pain is caused by the conflict between our sub-personalities, or parts of us that feel different from each other. It was rumored that Hitler had Jewish blood in his ancestry, and that he hated it. A corollary for Assagioli's theory is that we do damage to a centered sense of ourselves when we obliterate from our conscious minds the parts of our personalities or lives that we don't like.

I had done this when living in The Netherlands. Relishing my new life abroad, I had blocked out any memories of my withdrawn youth and time at Riggs. I even forgot that I'd ever suffered from psychological stress. I therefore had no idea that working with flashbacks by myself might trigger mental problems. When the accumulation of memories from my devastating childhood caused emotional overload, I was caught unaware with no support system in place.

From my work with Didi Firman at the Synthesis Center, I learned how to accept and bring into harmony the two parts of me that had been in such great conflict with each other that one part had completely forgotten the other. One of Didi's exercises involved placing two pillows on the floor representing the "patient's" personality parts and asking a participant to name them and then go sit on one of the pillows in order to stimulate the voice of that sub-personality.

During an afternoon session with a fellow student, I named my two pillows *Strong and Doing Things* and *Weak and Empty*. *Strong and Doing Things* was the part of me that had flourished after my treatment at Riggs and served me well for most of my time in The Netherlands. *Weak and Empty* was the part that had been withdrawn and passive during my school years and again in Holland when on tranquilizers, as well as after separating from my parents. *Strong* disliked *Weak* so much—because of her separation from living—that I needed to place the pillows a distance away from each other on the carpet of the small counseling room.

The classmate with whom I had been paired asked me, if I

minded speaking as *Strong* first. I said I didn't mind and went to sit on one of the pillows.

"May I ask *Strong* if *Weak* has ever been of help to her?" my fellow student asked, practicing the training protocol we had learned that morning.

It took my somewhat arrogant part a few minutes of thinking and verbal exchanges with my therapist-in-training, but eventually, *Strong* admitted that without *Weak*, she might not have survived her childhood. "If my personality hadn't changed to a passive one, empty of emotions," *Strong* said, "I would have gone on fighting my mother and possibly been killed by her."

"Does this mean that you, *Strong and Doing Things*, can appreciate *Weak and Empty* and therefore like her better?

"Yes," *Strong* said.

Empty was asked the same series of questions and answered, "Yes, I can appreciate *Strong* because passivity didn't always work. Sometimes I had to end up fighting anyway in order to survive. And *Strong's* life was much more exciting and satisfying than mine. Though peaceful, I was bored and lonely because I couldn't understand or sympathize with anyone who was in pain since I didn't feel anything, myself."

"Does this mutual respect mean that the two pillows can be brought closer together?" my classmate asked, finishing our standard protocol for negotiation between personality parts.

"Yes," I said, and got up to move the pillows. To achieve closure after this experience, I returned to my original chair and reflected with my Higher Self—now a more unified self—on what had happened. I realized that through playing a kind of game, I had stepped up onto a new path to healing. I'd been able to synthesize two heretofore disparate images of myself, creating one picture of myself that could allow for both parts of my personality to coexist.

I received an unexpected benefit. *Strong* hadn't liked the

feeling of being depleted at the end of the day because it reminded her of *Weak*. Over the years, I had developed a habit of puttering around the house until two in the morning, not willing to admit my fatigue until I dropped with exhaustion. Now that I had learned to accept my feelings of weakness and emptiness as just one part of me—without being afraid that I had lost my strong side permanently—I found that I could recognize when I was tired and give in to it by going to bed at a normal time.

The winter after Grace passed away, I began to sense that a part of me felt as if I were a Black woman, similar to how I'd thought of myself as a Black child in my childhood. This early self-image had apparently not died, but had hidden itself deep down in the diamond mine of my various identities. During the first stages of my discovery, I played a game with myself similar to the pillow talk of Psychosynthesis, and for my first step, I wrote out a list of anecdotes and comments that voiced my Black side:

At a writers' conference in New York City, I chose to sit next to an African-American woman, her head wrapped in a colorful turban. I had felt drawn to her. During the day, after some of our life stories had been shared, I confided that while sitting next to her I felt I was "with my people." I thought she might be offended by my putting her in a category, but she accepted my tribute to her race with a warm welcome.

I have observed a tendency in myself to gravitate to Black women, sitting near them on trains or at concerts and in music halls or in movie theaters. I tend to call out in response to speakers when among these women in the same way that they share their responses freely with whoever is up on stage, just as I'm sure Grace did every Sunday at church.

The friend I feel most comfortable with, and the only one

to whom I say "I love you" at the end of phone calls, is Black. I love when Janine and I laugh at the same things during a stroll downtown and when she wears clothes with my favorite color, orange, sometimes with pink next to it.

The dance moves I love most, after all of my studying, are African based. The music I prefer for dancing is the sound of soul, African drums, Motown, and salsa. Moving to these rhythms draws my feelings out, touches my heart, and asks the most from my passions and physical engagement.

As a twenty-nine-year old, I formed my plan for study and teaching from my love of African drum music and a summer working with Black school girls who used Motown for their inspiration. I was unable to find dance classes using African drums in my American town, but delighted in finding a teacher of Soul dance in The Netherlands. I identified with the girls from Curaçao when they complained, in my creative dance workshop, that there could be no organic and genuine dance without the stimulus of rhythmic music. I had shared that belief, having experienced the joy of communication and mutual stimulation between African drummers and the dancers they were playing for.

My second choice in dance is to move from within, the silence allowing my motivation to come from inside me. One day, as a three-year-old, I had watched Grace dance with ecstatic abandon in the middle of our kitchen. Minutes before she had received a phone call from her sister saying that Tom, their beloved older brother had been attacked with a knife. Though he had survived without severe harm, he lay in the hospital. Susie and I watched Grace move into a trance, consoling her heart with the rolling rhythm of her body as she connected to some kind of outer and inner energy that healed her worried state. Perhaps I gained the ability to listen to my body years later in my studio from having witnessed Grace dance the feelings of panic out of herself, and the emotions of love and reassurance back in.

Today I have joined a religious choir, just as my Grace did. In the experience of singing and bringing meaningful sound to life, I know what Grace felt as she hummed her way through our house. I do the same with my own choir music. Grace gave me my spiritual roots, her efforts to teach my sisters and me kindness having been one of her strongest gifts to us.

I love pictures of African clothes and have a painting in my front hall showing African women, dressed in batik-dyed cloth, standing with pots on their heads, regal in their statuesque posture. One of the first pieces of art I bought as a newlywed was a portrait of women from the South Seas islands by Paul Gauguin. It was not the one I had originally picked out. This had been sold between the time I'd chosen it before dinner during my honeymoon in a Provincetown gallery and the time we got back. No comments from my understanding and practical new husband, that it had been a print and would be available somewhere else, could stop the depth of grief in my momentary sobbing, as if my last chance to become what I was meant to be had been taken from me.

I am delighted that I was able to rock my babies to sleep and stop their crying in minutes. I have been astonished to learn that many young mothers don't know that crying babies need motion as well as static holding and caressing. From window to door and back to window I have walked with an infant, accenting my rhythms with humming, feeling the small body relax as the child senses again the motion of intra-uterine life and the syncopated rhythms of the heart he had come to know in his earliest and most safe existence. I hear again the sounds of Grace singing her gospel music, as I comfort a grandchild while moving to my songs.

I relish any chance I get to speak the southern dialect that I heard as a young child, as if it were my own native language, my skill so great that my children, when little, begged me to stop, because they thought their mother had left them to become another person. Where did I get my love and gentle ease with language, able to grasp a basic, utilitarian level of Dutch within a few months' time? Neither of my parents spoke a foreign language. Did this skill come from my exposure to the language of southern dialect that I had switched on and off with northern American English as easily as if I were changing clothes?

A friend advised me not to include Grace's accent in this book, for fear of making her seem to the reader less intelligent than she was, but I have decided to use it. It belonged to Grace and I loved it, so I have included it, lessening the dialect as her speech corrected itself while she lived with us, and almost dropping it in reports of our conversations at the end of her life, unless she felt distressed.

When I enter a room of Black people, I feel happy, as if I am now allowed to be myself, with a chance to let go. I feel as if I have come home. I dance as if I had been born with blues and slinky jazz in my bones, only needing the beat of drums to stimulate this part of me. I am in awe at others who can sit at a swing band concert without moving a muscle. At a weekend of Spiritual Dance, I wowed those gathered to watch, including my husband, by whirling in fast and rhythmic ecstasy with other Black women to the sound of Haitian drums, the musicians entreating us to give them everything we had.

My White self laughed, so possessive of me she was eager to attack her Black sister's arguments. "How can you say you feel Black? You've never had to know the sting of prejudice except when you hear it from White people around you who are speaking freely because they don't know they are offending your inner identity. Your claim to be a person of color is nothing more than Blackness Lite!! Look at all the advantages you have enjoyed because our wealthy parents were considered by our society to be from a privileged class."

My would-be Black part wailed, "You're wrong! You're wrong!" desperate to convince her debater of the truth in her heart. "Yes, I didn't get the sting of prejudice, but when I became Jewish I felt some of that. And yes, I did get the privileges of great education you mentioned, but I could have gotten along without them. With hard work at a fine state university I could have achieved more success than my White self, sick at heart from the unhealed loss of her real parents, was able to reach at an elite and private one!!!"

My would-be Black-self turned away, as if disgusted with me, confident in her sense that I would never know the suffering of being the member of a minority of color. "I refuse to talk another minute with you."

My White part yelled at her, "In fifty years, Blacks will be the majority in this country! There is not such a difference now between us. You should appreciate how much I love my Black self!"

My Black sister turned around, her mouth open at my bending of the truth, the majority not to be a Black one, but one of all non-Whites. But she let my exaggeration go.

My mouth dropped also as I looked at my debater. She had become brown-skinned, and she seemed to be a little gentler and slower of pace than the White person who had pretended to speak for her. My split personality had formed into even more parts.

The dark woman stepped toward me. "Perhaps what you really love about me is what I bring from the farm that reminds you of Grace." She sat down, wrapping her arm around the back of her chair and looking into my eyes. "How I take the time to enjoy life, and 'smell the flowers,' as White folks say, how I can move into a song or dance any time I feel like it, not in a class but as part of how I feel in my body, raised with the homegrown joys of country living."

"Hey, girl, I got you, now!" The African woman stood up. She seemed taller as she towered over me and said, not unkindly, "Now I understand why you loved The Netherlands so much, that country of cows, flowers, and green pasturelands stretched out between every town."

"And the smell of fresh baking," I agreed. Then I added, with a twist, as my friend clicked her high heels into action, "Hey, but I got bored there too. I wanted the city just as you do with your smart shoes and walk!"

I had stopped her, but she didn't turn around. I gazed at her long red nails at the end of a hand that waved me away. I wondered for the umpteenth time how such a woman can work a computer or more importantly touch her boyfriend's cheeks, with such hard and long, fang-like fingers, but I stopped my thoughts. I knew that I was really unhappy at feeling like White trash next to her, a country bumpkin in my shabby clothes glancing at a city sister who feels disdain and has put me in a category.

I saw again the hopelessness of my life to ever become what I was meant to be, a Black woman who was not hated by her tribe, a desire that had been frustrated in the beginning with my inability to follow my true mother and ended with my unsuccessful begging of Grace to recognize me as her true daughter.

"Look," I tried, for the last time, "the only truth here is love—and the wish to be forgiven," I added, speaking out my guilt that I had never known Jessie and Grace's suffering, though I had loved them enough to want to. My Black self turned around.

"Oh, but you have been, Honey, Ah knows you've

suffered," she said. She came over and gave me a long look as if unsure about going on. "Yo' daddy, he weren't no sweet-assed man, Honey, I knows that fo' sho'. So, Ah forgives you. Let's go get somma that dessert you made."

We took each other's arms and went to munch on a piece of the yellow cake I had made just like Grace used to with lots of eggs and butter. I had cut it into slices so I could pour over them the crisp chocolate sauce of my birth mother's recipe, thin enough to soak up into the whole slice if you don't eat it right away.

"This is GOOD! Lamb, how'd you make it?" my friend asked, brown sauce dripping from her red tipped fingers.

"Well, it's very important not to let the chocolate heat too much so you put it to melt with a tiny bit of warm water in a double boiler…"

"IN A WHAT?" Unable to wipe her fingers clean because of the long nails, my Black self began to lick them with great and noisy relish. I continued with a relish of my own.

"You have to take a pan and get the water hot but not simmering and put another smaller pan in it where the chocolate and warm water go. And then you stir it with a wooden spoon and don't go away for a minute because you have to add the sugar. An' remember, no glunky stuff like corn starch or milk, even cream…well maybe a smidgen…"

"Oh my GOD, Honni, ain't you one 'cyclopedia of talk! I jes' aksed you somethin' little and look what I got down on the end of my line!"

"I love to cook. I got that from my two nannies."

"Now isn't that just so! Tell me 'bout it. No wait don't. We gonna be here all night."

The strangest thing had happened. My two racial parts had not only separated into many selves, but now they had begun to flow so easily from one to the other, it was as if they had synthesized into one person right before my eyes. I could have closed up the study of my racial split and gone home, but I knew I wanted to try for a closure that would make a permanent change in me.

Using Didi's theory that most people develop their splits at the ages of two and three, I realized that my separation into a Black self-image and a White one had happened because of my desperate need for safety at a very young age. I had felt secure with the servants and their friends in our kitchen, so I had copied and identified with them while in their presence. To reassure myself that I would be accepted and valued by Jesse, Grace, and Joe, I had taught myself to filter out of my behavior any touch of Whiteness when with them.

When near the members of my White family, to please *them*, I had suppressed all Blackness, which meant, among other things, that I had learned to control my kitchen habits of cavorting around and loud talking, delighting in noisy eating or licking my fingers, singing to myself or humming, and laughing with my whole body doubled over. Most importantly, I learned to switch my language, the dialect of the kitchen not allowed in the White part of the house.

My terror of being killed as a child meant that I had felt my survival depended on being accepted by whichever group I was around. I recognized how desperate I had been—not just as a child, but during my whole life—to avoid making mistakes when I was around people of different cultures.

Completing the protocol I had learned both in Jungian psychology and in psychosynthesis, I asked how this insight could affect my life now. It meant, I told myself, that I no longer had to be so careful to fit in with people from different cultures. My survival was not dependent on it. My minority and majority parts could relax and enjoy their differences rather than be afraid of each other.

I received my certificate from Scott Thompson at Psychosynthesis Manhattan several years later, learning more tools for healing; among them was the joy of gaining insight from guided meditation and role playing different parts as a way to experience forgiveness. I thought back to the work I had done in synthesizing my White and Black natures and realized that my own story had been an excellent case upon which to begin studying psychosynthesis' understanding of personality and its parts.

Chapter 28 – Analyzing my Mother and Dance as Healer

A literary agent who had read some chapters of my book tried to help guide me toward publication. She sympathized with me.

"I was raised by a Black nanny, too, whom I loved. I see that you want to honor yours for her support and courage. But you must answer this question for me and for your readers: What was your mother's diagnosis?

Seeing me speechless, she added, "I mean, I need, and the reader needs, to have a way of understanding your mother's condition."

I mumbled something.

"Let's look at it this way," she persisted. "When did you realize that your mother was different from other children's mothers?" I had no answer because I had *never* recognized it. In grade school, I hadn't thought my mother was different from other mothers because she seemed to be normal, though a bit impatient, and I had forgotten my early life. Even as an adult of forty remembering the abuse—or at sixty and finished with my six years of therapy—I tried to understand her in normal terms. I rationalized that my mother had been angry, sexually frustrated, and in depression because of her bitter disappointment that the fetus inside her had not turned out to be her long-awaited *son*. These things were true, but they didn't take into account the criminal nature of her behavior.

Apparently, even as an adult, I was finding it more palatable to harbor some sense that if I had been different, my mother would have been all right. That was easier than accepting her difference "from other mothers" or, translated, how *scary* she had been. In addition, because of the dire threats I had received as a child not to talk about my mother's behavior, I had felt unconsciously that my *sharing* about it was the crime, not what she had done.

A few weeks after this conversation, I contacted the hospital where my mother had been a patient just before she started hurting me. Three months later a heavy box arrived filled with a four-inch thick pile of closely typed 8.5" x 11" sheets. These contained medical records about the sick woman's condition during her various visits to the hospital and letters between the therapist and my father. I found detailed conversations between my mother and her doctor during her month-long stay just before my second birthday. The words of a disturbed thirty-seven-year-old woman looked up at me from darkly typed pages.

> *I went to the closet where Harry hid his gun. It wasn't there. I had spent a lot of time figuring out where I should place the rifle against his head to do the most good. I had planned to kill him before I killed the girls so he wouldn't stop me.*

Her doctor had added his comments:

> *Mr. Davidson had taken the gun to his office because of Margaret's suicide threats.*

To my astonishment, the therapist hadn't seemed concerned about my mother's detailed plans to murder her family. Nor did he seem to pay attention to her worries, as she looked back from the safe vantage point of the hospital and recognized the intensity that had accompanied her search for the gun.

> *It frightens me to look back on how strongly I felt about what I wanted to do.*

In a summary consistent with ideas in psychiatry at that time, the late 1930s, my mother's psychotherapist wrote a tepid summary.

> *I consider Mrs. Davidson's remarks to be flights of fancy.*

On a Monday, her last day after a month at the hospital just before she was to return home, my mother pleaded with the doctor by letter, a copy of which was tucked in among the reports. She wrote how let down she felt by my father's decision not to visit her on the weekend before as they had planned.

> *He had promised to come because I had told him that there were some very personal things I needed to discuss with him before coming home. We were going to have a nice dinner at the town's Inn before going to bed.*

I had been told by my oldest sister Louise that my mother had complained to her about my father being an *in-and-out-kind of guy* during his love making. This remark, combined with what I'd learned about my mother's strong sex drive from my memories, as well as from the medical record's reference to her sexually-active teenage years, confirmed what I had always thought. My mother was frustrated with a husband who didn't respond to her well-developed sensuality. I suspect that she had wanted to discuss with my father her sexual frustration. Having been raised by her Puritan parents to think that sexual feelings were wrong, it is probable that my mother needed the supportive atmosphere of the hospital, with its relaxed, rural ambiance and distance from the duties and stresses of home, in order to gain the courage to demand from her husband what she felt she needed in their relationship.

> *I feel so confused about how disappointed I am now that I haven't had my chance to explain things to Harry. I am beginning to feel anxious about going home again. The thought of more painful and disappointing Saturdays scares me. Please help me with my decision.*

At the end of her letter, in which she referred to her difficulty with telling those at home that she needed to stay at the hospital longer, my mother wrote that she felt *unstable.*

Strangely, this same word was used by the doctor himself in a letter to my father, when he advised him to keep my mother's stress to the minimum. This was a naïve request for a husband and tired servants who had all been overworked from the chore of moving into a new house, in addition to their regular jobs, but *unstable* was the only diagnosis that I could find in response to the agent's question.

It is obvious that my mother was asking her doctor to help her be selfish and take the extra time she felt she needed at the institution. Her therapist could have eased his patient's guilt at the thought of not going back to perform her motherly responsibilities by sharing a letter my father had written him, in which he had said that the household was doing perfectly well without his wife.

There may have been financial concerns preventing a last

minute change of plans. The private hospital was expensive, and financial papers I found among the medical records showed my father had already asked for leniency in paying the bills. But, *at the least*, the doctor should have communicated to him the possibility of danger to his children if his wife were to come home. If he had done so, my father might have insisted she stay at the hospital longer and sought financial adjustments. Even just the slightest improvement for me would have been the preparation in my father's mind for the news Jessie brought to him that his wife was beating me.

Once my parent was home and began her aberrant behavior, the chance for honesty in the ongoing outpatient relationship with her therapist became impossible. In the correspondence I found between my mother and her doctor, immediately following her second attack on me, my mother composed her letter in a cheerful and resigned manner, making no mention of what she had done.

As she committed more acts of violence, she found simple ways to hide what she was doing—as if she were a clever teenager lying to her parents—in order to save herself from long-term hospitalization, as well as a loss of her place in the family and the chance that she would be ostracized in her social circle if the truth came out. My oldest sister Louise told me that lying was an art for my mother, as I myself had observed by her continual reference to my falls as "accidents."

Over time, she developed a less deceitful and, therefore, less lonely method of handling her misbehavior. She simply forgot the violence she had committed. Though I imagine that this denial had the benefit of making her feel better about herself and less worried about what she might or might not say, I realize that it caused her distress, confusion, and hurt as she watched her youngest child run away from her touch with no way to understand why.

I sat back on my pillows, physically sick, nauseated, and faint from reading the reports and thinking about them. It took me a month to recover, but during this process, I found the answer to my publishing problem.

My story fulfilled another demand of the memoir market: my book could be considered *unique* because of my abnormal situation. How many people had been almost killed by their mothers eight times before the age of five—one of the incidents causing brain damage—and had survived, with help from servants and sisters, to be sure? How many people had remembered such terrible events at the age of forty as clearly as if they had happened yesterday, had gone through a period of darkness, and then regained sanity at a higher level of consciousness and awareness than at any time before? How many people had been forced as adults to separate from their parents because of similar memories? Dave Pelzer's story of abuse came close to mine, and readers hadn't seemed to tire of *his* story, their interest extending to his second and third books.

I wrote all of this to the literary agent, thanking her for the suggestion she had given me to try and get a diagnosis for my mother, which, in turn, had encouraged me to ask for the medical records.

I heard nothing back from her.

One day by chance I met an actress from New York City on vacation in our rural town. The fifty-year-old redhead and I sat near each other on a stone slab porch under shady trees behind the town's new and upscale café, where we had both come to indulge ourselves with its freshly baked almond Danish—reminding me of Holland—and coffee. She seemed to have time and be interested, so I told her my story, both of life and the publishing industry.

"My dear," she said. "Your story is perfectly horrible. I can see why you want to tell it and get it out of you. But my idea from the publishing industry is that in order for a memoir to sell, it has to have a universal theme, something that everyone can identify with."

"Oh, I see," I said. "You're right. My life is too unusual—too grotesque, really—for a reader to be able to associate with it."

"Well, sort of, but I wouldn't have put it quite that way." We promised to keep in touch, because she said she wanted to know what happened.

That night, my husband retrieved my inch-thick manuscript, half of it still in handwritten form, from the waste basket in what I called my "writing room."

"I think you should keep this in case you change your mind," my beloved said.

I returned to dance, and I was grateful for it. I found in the comforting yet terrible hours of silent movement within the stable setting of Contemplative Dance—as taught in a full year's program by the wise and insightful team of Alton Wasson and Daphne Lowell—dramatic and satisfying ways to unload the delayed reactions of horror and terror that recognizing the extent of my mother's sickness had unleashed.

The following year I repeated the release of expressing my stories bit by bit through the intriguing internationally active group program called *InterPlay*. Though dance is not in the name of this practice, I found within the course my first chance to create the deep and dramatic choreography I had been interrupted from developing in The Netherlands. Now, however, with the encouragement of our excellent leaders, I learned to combine movement with words, realizing that dance, which had been a vehicle for my stopped tongue—a legacy of my father's threat not to talk—could be enhanced verbally.

Through this year-long monthly weekend program, my

vocal chords opened up so much that I became able to share my story, not just as I always had—with a therapist, husband, good friend, or professionally with a literary agent—but now with peers in a group I had come to trust. I realized that I wanted to tell others about my life, regardless of who cared to read or buy my book, just because I wanted to. I owed it to myself for my years of suppressed speech. I would self-publish!

In this positive mood, I looked back at my mother's records with a calmer eye. I wanted to try and understand her better. I found an old picture of a lovely thirteen-year-old girl in sepia color, her body fully developed but slender, sitting sideways and sending out a flashing smile to the photographer, her soft hair sliding down to relaxed shoulders. This was my mother when still in the family circle, before being sent off to boarding school in shame after being caught for her sexual activity with boys at the boarding school where her parents worked.

The medical records mentioned that my mother had been severely punished for this transgression. Though there was no reference in the records to physical beatings, judging from the ferocity with which my mother hit me, as well as the number of incidents, and using the *psychological golden rule* that we do unto others what has been done to us—unless we have had enough training towards goodness through therapy, religion, or the good and strong example of others—my judgment was that my mother had been severely beaten and often.

Each of her seven older brothers and sisters had been assigned at different times to "watch her" after she had been caught playing sexually as a very young child, and it may well be that the most vicious attacks had come from those immature siblings who had been given the unpleasant chore of monitoring their embarrassing youngest sister. This disapproval of her entire family, if not perhaps ostracism by the whole school community, explains the terror my mother felt later, when I knew her, about what other people thought of her.

Another supposition I made at this time about the full-blooded and sensual woman who bore me, was that she probably had been harshly punished, as I was, for touching herself as a youngster. If I am right, the incident had stayed inside her subconscious all through her life, the terror connected to it removing from her the tool with which to relieve her aching body in the midst of a continually unsatisfactory spousal relationship. Why else would she ask her small daughter to help her masturbate while sitting on the living room couch and pretending to read to me?

Her sexual frustration had been a strain for the lively and sensual body she had enjoyed before her seventeen years of marriage, but at the lusty age of thirty-seven, it became another catalyst for the rage that set out to kill me for being a bothersome third child—and a disappointing girl-child at that—when the resolution for her unhappiness lay elsewhere. My mother seemed to me a perfect example of the statement German psychoanalyst Wilhelm Reich wrote on page xviii of his introduction to *The Invasion of Compulsory Sex-Morality:* the "… contention that no cure of a neurosis was possible without the establishment of a satisfactory genital love life …"

I began to believe that the last weekend of her stay at the hospital before coming home and starting the abuse had been a desperate moment for her, expressing the panic she felt in her need to confide, trust, and beg understanding of her husband as her sexual partner before she returned home. My father's betrayal of her trust, by not responding to the honesty with which she had declared the importance of the visit, triggered, I believed, her childhood fury at never having been listened to or understood by her family in connection to her sexual drive.

My mother confided to me, as an adult in my thirties, that she suffered from a lack of self-discipline. I believe that the harsh reaction and mortifying punishments by her family, imposed when she was still young and imprinting her soul with shame, precluded any chance for her to be guided into a workable and autonomous sense of self-discipline.

Among the things not thrown away at my mother's death, was a box of beautiful poems, written ten years before I was born, all set into the discipline of iambic pentameter and praised by the teacher whom she had sought out in our town. Never having gone to college, she had tried to educate herself in the field of literature, but once she had been rejected by several New York City magazines and become involved with child bearing, she had forgotten this part of herself.

Perhaps because of looking over my mother's beautiful poetry—on whose publication she had given up too soon—I decided to make one last try for my own manuscript within the publishing world. I attended a writer's conference in New York City, where Lisa Dale Norton, the well-known author, teacher, and editor was giving a workshop on memoir. So inspired by her class I spoke to her afterwards.

"If I sent you one chapter, do you think you could answer the question whether my work is publishable in the traditional sense of the word?" She agreed.

A few months later she replied that if the main subject or theme of my book was child abuse, then the answer would be "No." However, Lisa wrote, she had seen five other themes in my work, and if I wrapped my story around one of them—which would mean a total rewrite—then it would be possible. One of these themes was *growing up feeling Black*.

That was it! I said to myself. Enough of my attempt to understand my birth mother and find reasons for the savagery she had exposed me to! The point of *my* life was that I had been rescued and saved by the people I had loved so much that I had come to believe I was one of them!

This theme was close to what had originally inspired me to put my stories into a book five years before. My decision had come during a woodland walk in early spring when I become lost. I had stood on a bridge not knowing which way to turn, but as I looked through the dusk I felt only a mild concern, glimpsing suddenly that I knew the right way after all.

Suddenly I heard Jessie's voice: "Promise me, Anne, that you will write this book. I want it to be known, not for me but for my people. I want it to be known how hard we tried, and that it took courage, and, yes, heroism, to try to make a difference for you."

"Oh, I do promise you, Jessie, I will. I promise I will."

I resumed work on my manuscript as soon as I returned from my weekend in the woods.

As I looked back on that day, I realized, for the first time, that Jessie must have gone on hearing about my sister and me within the tightknit Black community in our town. Grace told me just before she passed away that Jessie had *not* gone to the south after being fired, as my parents had told my sister and me, but had stayed on in my hometown and been there in her nineties when I returned to America, living for five more years.

I grieved that I'd missed the chance to thank and praise Jessie for her heroism and concern for me, but my sorrow made me redouble the commitment I had made to record what Black people had done to help me, only now I was going to add that I had felt I was one of them.

Chapter 29 – Understanding Those I Loved

In spite of the serenity I achieved during my sixties from synthesizing my different racial parts, I still needed more time to validate and fully recognize my inner Black identity. I am ashamed to admit the extent to which the brain washing I had received in my childhood home and from the White public culture of that time influenced my delay in appreciating this part of me.

I am speaking of the disgraceful social attitude that those who do menial jobs, who are different in culture from the Anglo Saxon majority, who are poor, who are less educated, even those who live more earthy or sensual and emotional lives, are lesser. As a youngster, I saw that the brown people were servants in my house, and I didn't know that they were being paid. I saw them subservient to my parents, so I doubly took in the lesson that they were somehow lesser than my parents.

This was confusing for me, for it meant that all the things I treasured in life—love and touching, kindness and being listened to, enjoyment of play, and moving with rhythmic abandon, as well as the delights of food and laughing with gusto—were lesser.

It has taken a lifetime for me to develop the strength and sense of independence to say, "WAIT! What the White culture said wasn't true! The Black women I knew were better than the White ones! The culture that knows how to mix work and play is better than the one that demands people work themselves to death! Expression of feeling is better than suppression, and passion can be beautiful.

"Black people have given us jazz music, a form beloved by many Whites, as well as, together with Jewish composers, America's internationally famous art form called the Musical! To say nothing of the dances Whites have gobbled up during the twentieth century, most of them based on the syncopation of African rhythms!"

Still, I have wondered how it can have taken me so long to recognize the strength of my love for the Black people who cared for me, and to acknowledge their part in the formation of my personality, values, preferences, and soul.

Born into an unstable household run by a mentally sick mother and punitive father, each of whom had been crippled by neglect and a strict Puritanical upbringing, I believe I would never have had the many engaging and satisfying years I've experienced, without the Black people I knew early on. I might not have won my fight against mental illness if I had not had the joy of dancing to African drums, the music of Motown and other Soul songs that had lifted me out of depression.

I have been forced to conclude that a lingering resentment toward my early caregivers for not being able to help me more than they did has impeded my way towards full recognition of Jessie, Grace, and Joe's importance to me.

I became furious as a young child when I realized that Jessie's promise to me of my father's protection had been false. Grace betrayed me by her passivity and lack of communication, both before and after she left. After having been a supportive force for two years, Joe punished me harshly to protect my mother and his secret. Then he left me without a follow-up card or word of any kind!

I have tried to understand those who meant so much to me, meditating and drawing on other spiritual practices in order to achieve the peace I have needed during my growing awareness of how important my Black family was to me, as a child, and then during my whole life.

I increased my courage to think independently while role playing the practice of being a leader in an eight-week, intensive Internet course called *Feminine Power,* given by a group of therapists living in California. Using their techniques, I talked to my betrayed and bitter inner child. First listening to her fury, I explained that Jessie had been powerless, living in a society that wouldn't have listened to her reports about my father's inadequacy to protect me. Once fired, there was no way she could have come back to look in on me, though I expected her to because I had already witnessed the spunk she was capable of.

The fact that our Black cook dared, in 1940, to go downtown on the bus to my father's prominent law office in order to get justice for me stayed with me underneath my conscious mind all of my life. I see now that Jessie's moral strength was like a flag deep in my memory, emerging from my subconscious and waving at me when I felt scared and challenged. Right now, I say to myself, if Jessie dared to make that scary trip downtown to speak with my father, I can manage the courage to publish an account of the stories I was threatened with death many times as a child not to divulge

Jessie's sense of justice and her willingness to act on it has worked its power in me as a passionate political activist. It has been a moving experience working in the rural sections of Florida, the state where I now reside, registering many voters who had thought they were no longer on the rolls. I enjoyed taking two eighty-year-old Black women, beautifully dressed and elegant as they stood waiting for me on Election Day, to the polls. Fantasizing that I had come to the South, the way I had wanted to as a child, and found Jessie and Grace in their old age,

I listened to my passengers' banter and gentle teasing of each other while we traveled old sandy roads to the polling station. I said to myself, "I am fulfilling what I was always meant to do and giving back to those who helped me."

As I have recognized these truths about Jessie's influence on me, I have felt more real, more grounded, and less shakable. In humility, I claim Jessie's moral certainty and iron strength as a part of my adopted heritage.

The therapist who helped me at the time of Grace's death, Shamai Currim, reminded me that Joe was not only someone Grace loved—he was also her ticket out of domestic servitude. Her workload doubled after our cook, Jessie, left. She was awake by five-thirty and down in the kitchen an hour later with her uniform freshly ironed, if not also freshly washed, ready for a day of cooking, cleaning (our house had ten rooms, two long halls, three bathrooms, and a cellar that included a large playroom and laundry), babysitting, washing, and ironing. I am sure that her head did not rest on the pillow until eleven o'clock at night.

These reasons to understand and forgive Grace for leaving me are nothing compared to my gratitude for what she gave me during the nearly five years she managed to stay, as a loyal caretaker, in our dysfunctional household. My soul would not have survived without her. Grace gave me the support and the knowledge of what it was to be loved—an experience that bolstered me later, when I found myself able to trust those who helped me at Austen Riggs Center.

Recently, I have remembered more of Grace's spiritual teachings and wisdom, which I have included in this memoir. For these, for the years of tender care I received from her, and for her heroic behavior in December of 1941 when she sacrificed her own safety to protect me from my mother's knife, I am now able to feel genuine forgiveness for her abrupt departure from my life, ten years after I voiced those words "I forgive you" to her. Grace's perseverance, loyalty, and generosity of spirit are the qualities that I would like to emulate and keep as my heritage from her.

As for Joe, though I understand why he felt that he had to punish me harshly after I had caught him with my mother, and, as a child, I forgave him, I know now that his overpowering and mean treatment of me contributed to my feeling that girls were too vulnerable for me to remain thinking I was one.

Yet it has been imperative for me to forgive him because I have recognized that I passionately loved him. I not only survived my childhood because of his physical rescues, I went on to live the richness of my professional life—in dance and in my friendship with Felix—because of our playful and engaging times dancing together. I learned from him lessons that counteracted those taught by my birth family: pleasurable sensations in the body are good, and it is okay to express anger and fury at someone if they have hurt you. I wouldn't have met and loved the passionate men I married, if I hadn't known and loved Joe. In my marital choices, I have been attracted to partners who fight hard for what they want, just as in childhood I loved Joe because he taught me how to stand tough for my survival. Fierceness of spirit, both in play and in work, is what I wish most to adopt as my gift from him.

However, I feel a need to go even further in summing up my life with my two families. I wonder if I have been harboring an old fear of my birth family's outrage, as I now dare to declare this truth: after the Black people left our household, I can liken my parents' behavior to that of half-hearted foster parents, fulfilling their obligation to raise the child under their care and pay her costs, but neither giving nor receiving love well. I felt like a brown orphan left behind in a White people's house, singed with an undercurrent of racial prejudice because of my love and preference for those who had left.

A fellow writer has said, "Your search all your life hasn't been for Black people; your search hasn't been racial; it has been for those who were able to love." Yet when I joined an African American social group recently in my new southern town, my skin rejoiced as if liberated and allowed to breathe, sensing that the brown people around me with their smiles and relaxed manner were mirror images of me and that I had finally found the tribe I had been looking for all my life.

What does that kind of love mean, then?

To me, it means to be accepted for who and what I am. That is what I felt at that club. Of course, I'd had to earn my dues, having been given a microphone at the first meeting to introduce myself as the newest member, the implication being that I needed some explanation for why I'd come. Speaking with a stronger and more relaxed voice than I'd expected, I told them the truth:

"I was raised by African-Americans when my mother was very sick, and I have felt Black underneath all my life. Sadly, I lost the woman who cared for me in my childhood but found her when I was sixty, and was able to take care of her in her last years. I've written a book to honor her."

Then is tolerance and acceptance what love means to a child? What did love from Jessie, Grace, and Joe mean to me as a youngster? This is my song for the family that loved me:

The Black family made a fuss over me, gave me time, played games, made me feel happy and special, praised me, encouraged me, and complimented me, made me feel wanted, led me to believe that life was mine to have and to hold and to love forever. I learned from them that food was to be enjoyed with every taste and with gusto, the preparation of it to be talked about and learned about, that it was important to know how tastes for different foods were right for different times. They taught me how to keep myself clean and hang my clothes up, leaving my room nice for the next day. If I was down, they cuddled me so that I could be up again. My brown family loved life and gave me back the hugs of joy I offered to them.

I was encouraged to trust time—to think of the bed and sleep as something to treasure, and to trust—that rest would be only temporary instead of fearing it as the thief of my frenetic but exciting life, and that living would return in the morning. Grace and Jessie gave me my basic trust in life and my first lesson in God's purpose for us: we are put here to enjoy life and do our best, as well as to give back to others the good things we have received.

Most of all, I was taught that there is a future, a land out there that waits for children to enter it with patient eagerness. Grace was the one whom my eyes sought—as a child returning from nursery school, wild with fierce joy, as if I could have articulated it by saying, "This, today, is the future you promised, Grace! This is the reality you taught me to expect—the heaven you spoke of—life with other children and other adults, heavenly beings who mean what they say and are *good!*"

It is truly astounding to think how two Black women could have come into the household of descendants from the race that had enslaved their ancestors, and given so much love and care to their employers' children.

I believe the answer can be found in the ancient African proverb, "It takes a village to raise a child."

Jesse and Grace could have placed strict boundaries around their jobs, letting my sisters and me flounder inside the bewildering house of our psychotic mother. Instead, they reached out to us, putting into practice their spiritual and cultural beliefs of connection to, and responsibility for, one another's children. The Black women who took care of us must have said to themselves, "These are not Whitey's children, these are

God's children, and it is our God-given duty to treat them as if they were our own."

Epilogue

I recognize that many people have had the formative experience of being raised as young children by people of a different culture from their own parents. My sister Susan is one of these. The difference between my experience and hers is that she successfully transitioned from her first caretakers to our birth parents, so that, as an adult, she unconsciously began to attribute qualities of Jessie—her substitute mother—back onto our birth mother, qualities that our parent never had.

I never made that transfer. Instead, I blocked all memory of my caregivers' love and protection—as well as my parents' abuse—out of my mind. This meant that when I returned to pick up my forgotten pieces, I saw clearly the gifts of those who had taken care of me, which would have gone unrecognized if I had followed the normal route of assimilation.

There is a loss in the seamlessness that many, including my sister, experience. They can forget the people who actually gave them the richest care. Those who nurtured them early on do not get the credit except indirectly, as in the example of a White professor, raised by Blacks, who developed a life-long passion and scholarly devotion to African culture—or as in my own unconscious search for the Katherine Dunham style of dance. It is possible that the professor did not recognize, as I didn't—until my experience in Europe freed me to do so—the deep reason we had been driven to follow these paths.

Our society has been able to develop similar blindfolds. We have valued African Americans enough to hire them as caregivers for our children, yet many of us have not recognized them as equals on a social level. Why is this? In preferring to have others care for our children, did we treat them badly out of shame to admit that their wisdom and down-to-earth methods with children were better than ours?

From the wise old Black man in the wonderful children's story, *Song of the South*—and in the adult's version *Driving Miss Daisy*—to the strong, caring nanny in *Gone with the Wind*, our stories show how much we have learned and benefited from African American nurturing. Yet, as a society, we have not registered our appreciation of African Americans for what they have given to the children in their charge. Like the British colonists in India, Anglo-Americans have shown insufficient respect for the ethnic groups that have given us so many of the gifts we enjoy. A duality of thinking allows us to love and use other cultures, yet persist in posturing that our way is better.

Felix, my teacher in The Netherlands, had his answer, which he gave me in an unusual moment of anger and resentment at the White community.

"It's been a rip-off. They took our stuff, copied it, and called it theirs," by which he meant that in this way Whites didn't have to acknowledge that Blacks had been the source. The world gives thanks for jazz and the American musical which Black music—along with Jewish songs, lyrics, and soul—made possible. It is time that we Americans, as conscious adults, honor those in our society who have enriched our lives.

Who can wander the streets of New York City and not love the world created by its ethnic groups, most evident in the variety of food and restaurants available, as well as in the sounds of different languages? What would America be like if we had known only the culture of England and of other countries belonging to the Caucasian race? We would have our laws and skilled training with words, but would we know the rich variety in customs and art as well as experience the grounded wisdom of other ethnic cultures?

We are all immigrants, and we need to recognize the equality of worth that is demanded by that truth, but, in addition, we should remember that Blacks are unique because *unlike any other ethnic group,* they did not choose to come to America.

This country has made progress toward recognizing the gifts as well as suffering of African Americans by designating a month to honor them and their history. Just as the British in India came to accept the fact that, in the leadership of Gandhi, brilliance had sprung from the very people they had been denigrating, our nation now honors the great Black civil rights leader, Martin Luther King, with a national holiday.

But how is it that we can allow the sons of the fathers and mothers who gifted us in so many ways to languish in prison? The lack of education and jobs, our drug war, and substance abuse have put more than one in ten African Americans in jail, many of them not for the use of drugs but for dealing in the drugs that White people pay lucrative sums to use.

I believe we are not making enough effort to understand the particular plight and needs of those descended from the Africans whom we enslaved and who have not been able to flourish in our society. I know that to be forced against your will breaks you and coats your insides with bitterness.

My memoir has shown the effect of the past on an adult's current life. The message that has been handed down by Blacks to their children, whether said out loud or received once their history has been revealed to them is the following: "We were stolen, and don't ever forget that bitter truth."

When the American government extended an apology to the African American community for the unforgivable crimes committed by slavery's practices and its aftermath, the question of reparations came up. It was suggested that instead of individual payments, funds be set aside for education. I would add that, in addition to money for training in the skills needed for today's modern job market, funds should be made available to prisoners and troubled students for counseling, and I do not mean talk therapy alone. I mean all forms of psychological practices, such as what I have benefited from, which enabled me to transcend what was done to me, aggression relief being one of the most important.

How can a young person who has heard about his people being lynched—after all it happened only fifty-five years ago in northern Florida—or has, himself, been a victim of racial profiling, remain in balance? Many do, but others either succumb to the disintegration of personality as I did or, more dangerous, take aggressive actions against others The use of a room in prison in which to rage and beat the walls as well as the chance to enjoy dramatic expression, both of these therapies under professional guidance and counseling, could alleviate the emotional pressure of many who suffer from societal as well as personal abuse.

Many Blacks have been able to transcend the legacy of slavery and the cruelties that followed. Many have survived and thrived, their inner strength shining out like a beacon for others. Perhaps the greatest gift I received as a child from Jessie, Grace, and Joe was this message: It is possible to go on living—in joy, in forgiveness, in understanding, and in love—despite horrendous abuse in the past.

Appendix

Resources Mentioned in the Text

Institutions, Organizations, Practices, and Individuals Fostering Mental, Emotional, and Spiritual Growth

Institutions, Organizations, and Practices

Association for the Advancement of Psychosynthesis (AAP.) www.aap-psychosynthesis.org.

Austen Riggs Center. Phone: (800) 51-RIGGS. www.austenriggs.org.

Craig Hamilton. Evolutionary spiritual teacher. www.integralenlightenment.com.

Contemplative Dance. Phone: (413) 268-3294. www.contemplativedance.org.

Feminine Power. www.femininepower.com.

InterPlay. www.interplay.org.

Synthesis Center. Phone: (413) 256-0772. www.synthesiscenter.org.

Therapists

Keith Alstedter, Psy.D. Phone: (877) 333-7766, (805) 682-2476. www.deersong.com.

J.D. Gold, Ph.D., clinical psychologist. Phone: (352) 502-3525. www.goldpsychology.vpweb.com.

Renee Rocklin, LCSW. Phone: (203) 239-7775.

Scott Thompson M.Div., M.S., LMHC, psychosynthesis counselor in Manhattan. Phone: (917) 279-9960.

Individuals and Practices Fostering Physical Care and Support

Individuals

Debra Gibson, ND, naturopathic physician. Phone: (203) 431-4443. www.debragibsonnd.com.

Phyllis Liu, OD, FCOVD, behavioral optometrist specializing in visual therapy. Phone: (203) 387-0038.
Email: drliuod@cs.com.

Sherry Stemper, ND, naturopathic physician with training in counseling specialization. Phone: (203) 579-4261; www.sherrystemper.com.

Practices

Eyelights. www.eyelights.com.
Intensity, for pelvic floor health. www.pourmoi.com.

Organizations and Individuals offering Writers' Support

Janell Walden Agyeman, literary agent/publishing consultant.
Phone: (678) 515-7907. Email: jwagyeman@att.net.

Florida Writers Association. www.floridawriters.net.

International Women Writers Guild, IWWG. Phone: (917) 720-6959. http://www.iwwg.org.

Richard McClintock, computer expert, M. C. Systems.
Phone: (203) 263-4743. Email: r.d.mcclintock@gmail.com.

Virginia Monseau, PhD, editor, proofreader, writer.
Email: profed98@gmail.com. www.profed.elance.com.

Lisa Dale Norton, author, editor, and manuscript development expert. www.lisadalenorton.com.

Mary Lois Sanders, author, editor, and publishing consultant.
http://courtjesterpublications.net;
http://MaryLoisSandersauthor.net.

Bibliography

Non-fiction

Assagioli, Roberto. *Psychosynthesis, A Collection of Basic Writings*. Amherst, Massachusetts: The Synthesis Center, Inc., [in cooperation with The Berkshire Center for Psychosynthesis], 2000.

Barbach, Lonnie, ed. *Pleasures, Women Write Erotica*. New York: Harper and Row, 1985.

Bernstein, Leonard. *Findings, Fifty Years of Meditations on Music*. New York: Simon & Schuster, 1982.

Bronowski, Jacob. *The Ascent of Man*. Boston/Toronto: Little, Brown and Company, 1973.

Brown, Molly Young. *Unfolding Self, The Practice of Psychosynthesis*. New York: Allworth Press, 2004.

Busch, F.N., and Larry S. Sandberg. *Psychotherapy and Medication: The Challenge of Integration*. New York, London: Analytic Press, 2007.

Constitution of the United States, with the Declaration of Independence and the Articles of Confederation, The. Includes the twenty-seven Constitutional Amendments—Bill of Rights, Civil War and Voting Rights, as well as those concerning the structure of government—and an Introduction by R.B. Bernstein. New York: Fall River Press, 2002.

Deikman, Arthur. *Personal Freedom, On Finding Your Way to the Real World*. New York: Grossman Publishers, a division of The Viking Press, 1976.

de Mille, Agnes. *Speak to Me, Dance with Me.* New York: Popular Library, 1973.

de Tocqueville, Alexis. *Democracy in America,* Vol. 1. Ed. Bradley Phillips. New York: Vintage Books, copyright by Alfred A. Knopf, Inc., 1945.

__*Democracy in America,* Vol. 2. New York: Vintage Books, copyright by Alfred A. Knopf, Inc. and Random House, 1945.

Dyson, Freeman. *Disturbing the Universe.* London: Harper and Row Ltd., 1979.

Erikson, Erik. *Childhood and Society.* New York: W. W. Norton & Company, 1950.

__*Gandhi's Truth, on the Origins of Militant Nonviolence.* New York: W. W. Norton & Company, 1969.

Field, Joanna. *A Life of One's Own.* London: Chatto & Windus, 1936.

Firman, John, and Ann Gila. *The Primal Wound.* Albany, New York: State University of New York Press, 1997.

Frankl, Viktor E. *Man's Search for Meaning.* New York: Washington Square Press, 1984.

Galbraith, John Kenneth. *The Affluent Society.* London: Hamish Hamilton, 1958.

Joyce, Mary. *First Steps in Teaching Creative Dance to Children, Third edition.* Mountain View, California: Mayfield Publishing Company, 1994.

Kempf, Edward J., M.D. "Abraham Lincoln's Organic and Emotional Neurosis." American Medical Association Archives of Neurology and Psychiatry, Vol.67, April 1952.

Lamb, Wally, and the Women of York Correctional Institution. *Couldn't Keep It to Myself.* New York: Regan Books, 2003.

Lerner, Betsy. *The Forest for the Trees.* New York: Riverhead Books, 2000.

Norton, Lisa Dale. *Shimmering Images, A Handy Little Guide to Writing Memoir.* New York: St. Martin's Press, 2008.

Pallaro, Patrizia, ed. *Authentic Movement, Essays by Mary Starks Whitehouse, Janet Adler, and Joan Chodorow.* London: Jessica Kingsley Publishers, 1999.

__*Authentic Movement: Moving the Body, Moving the Self, Being Moved, A Collection of Essays,* Vol. 2. London: Jessica Kingsley Publishers, 2007.

Pelzer, Dave. *A Child Called It.* Deerfield Beach, Florida: Health Communications, Inc., 1995.

__*The Lost Boy.* Deerfield Beach, Florida: Health Communications, Inc., 1997.

__*A Man Called Dave.* New York: Plume Printing, 2000.

Proust, Marcel. *Remembrance of Things Past,* Vol. 1: *Swann's Way.* Paris: Self-published 1913. New York: Penguin, 1957.

Prudden, Bonnie. *Pain Erasure.* Copyright by Bonnie Prudden 1980, 2nd ed. New York: Ballantine Books, 1982.

Reich, Howard. *Prisoner of Her Past: A Son's Memoir.* Chicago: Northwestern University Press, 2011.

Reich, Wilhelm. *The Function of the Orgasm.* New translation from the German, including "General Survey" by Wilhelm Reich, written for the first translation in 1940. New York: Simon and Schuster, 1973.

___*The Invasion of Compulsory Sex-morality,* with preface by Wilhelm Reich, written for the first English translation, 1951. New York: The Noonday Press, 1971.

Roberts, Monty. *The Man Who Listens to Horses, The Story of a Real-Life Horse Whisperer.* New York: Ballantine Books, 2009.

Russell, Joan. *Creative Dance in the Primary School.* London: MacDonald and Evans, 1965.

Sagan, Carl. *The Dragons of Eden, Speculations on the Evolution of Human Intelligence.* New York: Random House, 1977.

Sahari, Nadia. *Breakaway, How I Survived Abuse.* San Antonio, Texas: Pink Butterfly Press, 2009.

Schaub, Bonney Gulino and Richard Schaub. *Dante's Path, a Practical Approach to Achieving Inner Wisdom.* New York: Gotham Books, 2003.

Schlesinger, Arthur M., Jr. *The Cycles of American History.* Boston: Houghton Mifflin, 1986.

Shostak, Marjorie. *Nisa, The Life and Words of a !Kunga Woman.* New York: Vintage Books, 1983.

Siegel, Marcia. *Please Run on the Playground.* Hartford, Connecticut: Connecticut Commission on the Arts, 1975.

Singh, Rajinder. *Inner and Outer Peace Through Meditation.* London: Element, Harper Collins, 2003.

Stauffer, Edith R. *Unconditional Love and Forgiveness.* Diamond Springs, California: Triangle Publishers, 1987.

Stone, Merlin. *When God was a Woman.* New York: Doubleday, 1976, Barnes and Noble, Inc., 1993.

Winton-Henry, Cynthia, with Phil Porter. *What the Body Wants, from the Creators of InterPlay*. Kelowna, British Columbia, Canada: Wood Lakes Books, 2004.

Wosien, Maria-Gabriele. *Sacred Dance, Encounter with the Gods*. New York: Avon Books, 1974.

Historical Fiction

Schwartz, Cora. *Gypsy Tears, Loving a Holocaust Survivor*. Brookline, New Hampshire: Hobblebush Books, 2007.

Fiction

Anton, Maggie. *Rashi's Daughters, Book I: Joheved*. New York: Penguin, 2005.

Brown, Dan. *The Da Vinci Code*. New York: Doubleday, 2003.

Diamant, Anita. *The Red Tent*. New York: Picador USA, 1997.

Evans, Nicholas. *The Horse Whisperer*. New York: Bantam Doubleday Dell, 1995.

Heaney, Seamus, translator. *Beowulf*, bilingual edition. New York: Farrar, Straus and Giroux, 2000.

Jong, Erica. *Fanny*. London: Granada Publishing, 1980.

Llanos-Figueroa, Dahlma. *Daughters of the Stone*. New York: Thomas Dunne Books, 2000.

Metalious, Grace. *Peyton Place,* with an historical Introduction by Ardis Cameron. Boston: Northeastern Univ. Press, 1999.

Payne, David. *Confessions of a Taoist on Wall Street*. New York: Ballantine Books, 1985.

Stockett, Kathryn. *The Help*. New York: Penguin, 2010.

Made in the USA
Charleston, SC
24 January 2014